KU-166-465

COLLINS JUNIOR DICTIONARY

Written by Evelyn Goldsmith

HarperCollins Children's Books
A Division of HarperCollins Publishers Ltd,
77-85 Fulham Palace Road, Hammersmith, London W6 8JB

First published in 1992 in the United Kingdom
Revised edition first published in 1994

ISBN: 0 00 196476 3

A CIP record for this book is available from the British Library

Printed and bound in Great Britain by
HarperCollins Book Manufacturing Ltd, Glasgow

COLLINS JUNIOR DICTIONARY

Collins
A Division of HarperCollins*Publishers*

HARPERCOLLINS JUNIOR DICTIONARY

Evelyn Goldsmith

Introduction

This dictionary is for young readers of eight and upwards. The meanings of well over 5,000 words have been carefully explained, using full sentences. This not only makes the definition clearer: it also shows how the word itself is used in context. For instance, the entry for **absurd** reads 'Something that is absurd seems silly because it is quite different from what you would expect'. If extra help seems to be needed where words are more difficult to explain, another sentence is given as an example.

The words to be defined were selected as a result of a recent and extensive research programme which studied the conversation of young children and analysed their favourite books and television programmes. It also took into account books in regular use at school. The dictionary therefore includes not only familiar words, but also those that the children might be expected to meet during the course of reading and learning.

Parts of speech are given, together with the plurals of nouns, the comparative and superlative forms of adjectives, and three or four forms of each verb: the third person form of the present tense (the -s form); the present participle (the -ing form); the past tense (the -ed form); and, where it is different, the past participle.

The clear typography with two-colour entries combine to give a lively, friendly feel to the whole dictionary. We hope that it will give many hours of enjoyment, as well as providing a valuable source of reference.

How to use this dictionary

You can use this dictionary for lots of things:

* You can find out what a word means.
* You can see that sometimes a word has more than one meaning.
* If you are not quite sure how to spell a word, the dictionary can help.
* It can show you how to use a word properly.
* You can find out whether a word is a noun, a verb, an adjective, a preposition or an adverb. (If you are not sure what these are, look them up: they are explained in the dictionary too!)
* You can find out the plurals of nouns, other forms of adjectives, and the way verbs work. For example:

  1 Look up **child**. It has '(children)' after it.
  This means that you say one child, but two children.

  2 Look up **good**. It has '(better, best)' after it. You know what good means: you say things are good if you like them. If you like them more, they are better. And the ones you like most of all are best.

  3 Look at **run**. It has '(runs, running, ran, run)' after it. These are the forms of 'run' that you use at different times. For example: Tom always runs to school . . . I'm running as fast as I can . . . We ran to meet Dad . . . I have just run all the way home.

Dictionaries are arranged in the same order as the alphabet: a, b, c, and so on, right through to z. So if you want to look up, for example, **butterfly**, you must go past all the words beginning with a, and look at words beginning with b. There are lots of b words. How can you find **butterfly** without looking at every one? Look at the second letter of **butterfly**. It is a u. You know that u is near the end of the alphabet, so bu must be near the end of the b words. Now you can see there are lots of words beginning with bu. Where can **butterfly** be? Look at the third letter of **butterfly**. It is a t. Keep looking until you come to words beginning with but. Now **butterfly** really cannot be far away. There it is, just after **buttercup.**

As you get used to looking up words in the dictionary, you will find you can do it much more quickly!

A

abandon (abandons, abandoning, abandoned) *verb*
1. If you abandon something, you leave it and don't look after it any more: *They found a tiny cub that had been abandoned by its mother.*
2. If you abandon a piece of work, you stop doing it before it is finished.
ability (abilities) *noun*
If you have the ability to do something, you can do it.
able (abler, ablest) *adjective*
1. If you are able to do something, you can do it.
2. Someone who is able is very good at doing something.
>**ably** *adverb*
aboard *preposition*
If you are aboard a ship or plane, you are on it or in it.
about *adverb*
You say about in front of a number to show it is not exact: *I'll be home at about five o'clock.*
about *preposition*
If you talk or write about something, you say things that are to do with that subject: *He is going to talk about boats.*
above *preposition*
If something is above something else, it is over it, or higher up.
abroad *adverb*
When you go abroad, you go to a different country.
absent *adjective*
If someone is absent, they are not here.
absolutely *adverb*
You can use absolutely to make what you are saying sound stronger: *You must stay absolutely still - don't even breathe.*
absorb (absorbs, absorbing, absorbed) *verb*
1. If you are absorbed in something, you are giving it your full attention.
2. If something absorbs a liquid or a gas, it soaks it up or takes it in.
absurd *adjective*
Something that is absurd seems silly, because it is quite different from what you would expect: *It's absurd to wear your new jumper in this heat.*
>**absurdly** *adverb*
abuse *noun*
Abuse means being cruel to someone.
accelerate (accelerates, accelerating, accelerated) *verb*
1. When someone accelerates, they go faster.
2. If something accelerates an action or process, it makes it happen faster.
accept (accepts, accepting, accepted) *verb*
1. If you accept something that you have been offered, you say yes to it.
2. If you are accepted by an organization like a school or club, you are allowed to belong to it.
accident (accidents) *noun*
1. An accident is something nasty that happens by chance: *He broke his leg in a climbing accident.*
2. If something happens by accident, it has not been planned: *They were pleased when they met by accident in the supermarket.*
account (accounts) *noun*
1. An account is something written or spoken that tells you what has happened.
2. If you have an account with a bank or building society, you leave money with them and draw it out when you need it.
account (accounts, accounting, accounted) *verb*
If you account for something, you explain how it happened: *How do you account for this broken window?*
accurate *adjective*
1. An accurate measurement is exactly right.
2. An accurate description of something gives a true idea of what it is like.
>**accurately** *adverb*
ache (aches) *noun*
An ache is a dull, lasting pain.

achieve (achieves, achieving, achieved) *verb*
If you achieve something you want, you get it by hard work.
acid (acids) *noun*
An acid is a sour-tasting liquid. Some acids can burn through solid materials and can badly burn your skin.
acid rain *noun*
Acid rain is rain that is very dirty because it is mixed with tiny specks of acid and other dirty things in the air. It can damage or destroy trees and plants.
acorn (acorns) *noun*
An acorn is a nut which grows on an oak tree.
acrobat (acrobats) *noun*
An acrobat is someone who does difficult and exciting tricks like balancing on a high wire, or jumping on and off a galloping horse.
across *preposition*
If you go across something, you go from one side to the other: *She jumped in a boat and rowed across the river.*
act (acts) *noun*
1. An act is something you do: *Rescuing the man from the sea was a brave act.*
2. Stage plays are divided into parts called acts.
act (acts, acting, acted) *verb*
1. When you act, you do something: *He had to act quickly to put the fire out.*
2. If you act in a play or film, you have a part in it.
action (actions) *noun*
An action is a movement of part of your body.
active *adjective*
Someone who is active moves about a lot, or is very busy.
>actively *adverb*
activity (activities) *noun*
Activity is when there are a lot of things happening.
actor (actors) *noun*
An actor is a man whose job is to act in plays or films.
actress (actresses) *noun*
An actress is a woman whose job is to act in plays or films.
actually *adverb*
If you say something actually happened, you mean it is true.
adapt (adapts, adapting, adapted) *verb*
If you adapt to something new, you change in some way that helps you: *My grandfather has just retired, and he's finding it hard to adapt.*
adaptable *adjective*
Someone who is adaptable can change their ways to deal with new situations.
add (adds, adding, added) *verb*
1. If you add something, you put it with whatever you have already: *Put flour in the bowl and add an egg.*
2. If you add numbers of things together, you find out how many you have: *I have two marbles in the bag. If I add the two on the floor, that makes four altogether.*
addition *noun*
Addition is adding numbers together.
address (addresses) *noun*
Your address is the name or number of your house, and the street and town where you live.
adhesive (adhesives) *noun*
An adhesive is something, like glue, that sticks things together.
adjective (adjectives) *noun*
An adjective is a word that describes someone or something. 'Beautiful', 'green' and 'thin' are all adjectives.
adjust (adjusts, adjusting, adjusted) *verb*
1. If you adjust to a new situation, you get used to it by changing in some way.
2. If you adjust something, you change it to put it right: *The television picture's a bit bright. Can you adjust it?*
admiration *noun*
If you feel admiration for someone, you like and respect them.
admire (admires, admiring, admired) *verb*
1. When you admire someone, you think very highly of them.

2 When you admire something, you enjoy looking at it: *They stopped the car to admire the view.*
admit (admits, admitting, admitted) *verb*
1. If you admit something, you agree that it is true.
2 If people are admitted to a place, they are allowed to go in.
adopt (adopts, adopting, adopted) *verb*
If a person adopts someone else's child, they make it their own child by law.
adore (adores, adoring, adored) *verb*
If you adore someone, you love them very much.
adult (adults) *noun*
An adult is a grown-up person or animal.
advance (advances, advancing, advanced) *verb*
If someone advances, they move forward: *The army advanced nine miles in one day.*
>**in advance** *phrase*
If you do something in advance, you do it before the time: *They wanted to be sure of seeing the play, so they booked seats well in advance.*
advantage (advantages) *noun*
An advantage is something that puts you in a better position than other people: *His long legs give him an advantage in all the races.*
adventure (adventures) *noun*
If you are having an adventure, you are doing something exciting and perhaps even dangerous.
adverb (adverbs) *noun*
An adverb is a word that answers questions like how? when? where? why? and how much? For example, 'quietly' is an adverb. In the sentence 'The girl came quietly into the room', the word 'quietly' tells you how the girl came in.
adverse *adjective*
Adverse conditions are the opposite of the ones you want: *Sports day had to be abandoned because of adverse weather conditions.*
>**adversely** *adverb*
advertisement (advertisements) *noun*
An advertisement is a notice in a paper or on television, telling people about a job or something for sale.
advice *noun*
If you give someone advice, you say what you think they should do.
advise (advises, advising, advised) *verb*
When you advise someone, you tell them what you think they should do.
aerial *adjective*
Aerial photographs are ones that have been taken from the air.
aerial (aerials) *noun*
An aerial receives or sends radio or television signals.
aeroplane (aeroplanes) *noun*
An aeroplane is a flying vehicle. It has wings and one or more engines.
aerosol (aerosols) *noun*
An aerosol is a small can which sends out a fine spray when you press the button on top.
affect (affects, affecting, affected) *verb*
When something affects someone or something else, it makes them change in some way.
affection *noun*
Affection is a feeling of caring for someone.
afford (affords, affording, afforded) *verb*
If you can afford something, you have enough money to buy it or to do it.
afraid *adjective*
Someone who is afraid thinks something nasty might happen.
after *adverb*
The day after is the very next day.
after *preposition*
If something happens after something else, it happens at a later time: *We'll watch television after supper.*
afternoon (afternoons) *noun*
The afternoon is part of the day. It starts at 12 o'clock or lunchtime, and ends at about six o'clock.
again *adverb*
If you do something again, you do it once more.

against *preposition*
1. If you lean against something, you stand close to it and touch it: *She felt tired and leaned against the tree.*
2. If you play against someone, you are not on their side.
age (ages) *noun*
1. Your age is the number of years you have lived.
2. An age is a special period in history, like the Stone Age.
ago *adverb*
If something happened four days ago, it is four days since it happened.
agree (agrees, agreeing, agreed) *verb*
1. If you agree with someone about something, you think the same as they do about it.
2. If you agree to do something, you say you will do it.
agreement *noun*
Agreement means deciding on something that you all agree with.
ahead *adverb*
1. Something that is ahead is in front of you.
2. If a vehicle is moving ahead, it is going forwards.
3. If someone is ahead in a competition, they are winning.
aim (aims, aiming, aimed) *verb*
1. If you aim at something, you point a weapon at it.
2. If you aim to do something, you plan to do it.
air *noun*
1. Air is the mixture of gases that we breathe.
2. If you go by air, you fly in an aircraft.
air (airs, airing, aired) *verb*
When you air clothes, you put them somewhere warm to make sure they are dry.
aircraft *noun*
An aircraft is any vehicle which flies. Helicopters, gliders and aeroplanes are all aircraft.
aircrew *noun*
The aircrew on a plane are the pilot and other people who fly it and look after the passengers.
air force (air forces) *noun*
An air force is one of the forces that a country uses for fighting. Air forces use aircraft to fight in the air and to attack from the air.
airmail *noun*
Airmail is the system of sending letters, parcels and other things by air.
airport (airports) *noun*
An airport is a place where aircraft land and take off.
ajar *adjective*
If a door is ajar, it is slightly open.
alarm (alarms) *noun*
1. Alarm is a feeling of fear: *He looked at the bear in alarm.*
2. An alarm is something like a bell or flashing light that warns you of something.
alarm (alarms, alarming, alarmed) *verb*
If something alarms you, it makes you afraid.
album (albums) *noun*
1. An album is a special book with blank pages that you can fill with things like stamps or photographs.
2. One or more long-playing records sold in one package can be called an album.
alight *adjective*
If something is alight, it is burning.
alike *adjective*
If two or more things are alike, they are the same in some way.
alive *adjective*
If a person or animal is alive, they are living now.
alley (alleys) *noun*
An alley is a narrow passage or street with buildings or walls on both sides.
alligator (alligators) *noun*
An alligator is a reptile. It is of the same family as a crocodile, but smaller. An American alligator is about three metres long. The female lays from 20 to 70 eggs in a large nest made of mud.
allow (allows, allowing, allowed) *verb*

If someone allows you to do something, they let you do it.
almost *adverb*
Almost means very nearly, but not quite: *He tripped and almost fell.*
alone *adjective*
1. If you are alone, there is nobody with you.
2. If two people are alone, there is nobody else with them.
along *preposition*
If you go along something, like a path or a street, you move towards one end of it.
alongside *preposition*
If something is alongside something else, the two things are next to each other.
aloud *adverb*
If you read something aloud, you read so that people can hear you.
alphabet (alphabets) *noun*
An alphabet is all the letters used to write words in a language. The letters of an alphabet are written in a special order.
already *adverb*
If you have done something already, you did it earlier: *I've already done the washing-up.*
also *adverb*
You say also when you want to add something else: *She was good at cricket, and also football.*
alter (alters, altering, altered) *verb*
When you alter something, you change it in some way.
alternate (alternates, alternating, alternated) *verb*
When two things alternate, they regularly happen after each other: *He alternates between being nice and completely ignoring me.*
altogether *adverb*
1. If you say there are a number of things altogether, you mean you are counting all of them: *I've picked four apples and two pears, so that's six fruits altogether.*
2. You can use altogether to mean completely: *The train got slower and slower, then stopped altogether.*
aluminium *noun*
Aluminium is a light, silver-coloured metal. It is used for making things like saucepans and parts of vehicles.
always *adverb*
1. If you always do something, you do it every time: *He always puts his things away when he has finished with them.*
2. If something has always been so, it has been that way for as long as anybody can remember: *They have always been good friends.*
3. If you say you will do something always, you mean you will keep on doing it: *I'll always love you.*
amazement *noun*
You feel amazement when something surprises you so much you can hardly believe it.
amazing *adjective*
If you say something is amazing, you mean it is very surprising or wonderful.
>**amazingly** *adverb*
ambition (ambitions) *noun*
1. If you have an ambition to do something, you very much want to do it.
2. If someone has ambition, they want to be successful and powerful.
ambulance (ambulances) *noun*
An ambulance is a vehicle that is used to take people to hospital.
amount (amounts) *noun*
An amount is how much you have or need of something: *When my brother comes, we eat twice the usual amount.*
amount (amounts, amounting, amounted) *verb*
If you ask what something amounts to, you want to know what the separate parts add up to.
amphibian (amphibians) *noun*
An amphibian is an animal, such as a frog, that is able to live on land and in water.
amuse (amuses, amusing, amused) *verb*
If you amuse somebody, you make them smile or stop them feeling bored.
anchor (anchors) *noun*
An anchor is a heavy metal hook on a long chain. It is dropped over the side of a boat to stop it moving.

ancient *adjective*
1. If something is ancient, it is very old.
2. Ancient history is about things that happened a very long time ago.

anger *noun*
Anger is the strong feeling you have about something which is unfair or cruel.

angle (angles) *noun*
An angle is the shape that is made when two lines or surfaces join. The shape of an angle is measured in degrees. A square has four angles, one at each corner, and each one measures 90 degrees.

>at an angle *phrase*
1. If something is at an angle, it is not standing straight.
2. If you throw a ball and it hits something at an angle, it will not come straight back to you.

angry (angrier, angriest) *adjective*
If you feel angry, you are very cross.

>angrily *adverb*

animal (animals) *noun*
All living things except plants are animals. People, dogs, birds, fish, reptiles and insects are all animals.

ankle (ankles) *noun*
Your ankle is the joint between your foot and your leg.

announce (announces, announcing, announced) *verb*
1. If someone announces something important, they tell people about it publicly: *My sister's engagement was announced last week.*
2. If you announce something, you say it in an important voice.
3. If things are announced at an airport or railway station, people hear them over a loudspeaker system.

annoy (annoys, annoying, annoyed) *verb*
If you annoy someone, you make them cross.

annual *adjective*
Something that is annual happens once a year, like a birthday or school sports day.

>annually *adverb*

annual (annuals) *noun*
1. An annual is a book that comes out once a year.
2. A plant that only lives one year is called an annual.

anorak (anoraks) *noun*
An anorak is a warm waterproof jacket that usually has a hood.

answer (answers) *noun*
If someone asks you something, whatever you say next is your answer.

answer (answers, answering, answered) *verb*
1. If you answer the telephone, you pick it up when it rings.
2. If you answer an advertisement, you say you are interested in whatever was advertised.

ant (ants) *noun*
Ants are small insects which live in large groups called colonies. There are more than 5000 different kinds of ant in the world, and most of them build nests in the ground.

antelope (antelopes) *noun*
Antelopes are animals that look like deer, but their horns are not branch-shaped. There are many different kinds of antelope, and most of them live in Africa.

antenna (antennae/antennas) *noun*
The antennae of something like a butterfly or a lobster are the two long, thin parts on its head that it uses to feel with.

antique (antiques) *noun*
An antique is an old object, such as a clock or a vase, which is valuable because it is beautiful or rare.

antiseptic (antiseptics) *noun*
An antiseptic is a substance that prevents infection by killing germs.

anxious *adjective*
Someone who is anxious is nervous or worried about something.

>anxiously *adverb*

apart *adverb*
1. If something is apart from something else, there is a space between them: *He stood with his feet apart.*

2. If you take something apart, the pieces are separated from each other.

ape (apes) *noun*
Apes are like monkeys but are larger and have no tails. Chimpanzees, gorillas, gibbons and orang-utans are all apes.

apologize/apologise (apologizes, apologizing, apologized) *verb*
When you apologize to someone, you say you are sorry you have hurt them or caused them trouble.

apology (apologies) *noun*
An apology is something you say or write to someone to tell them you are sorry you have hurt them or caused them trouble.

apparatus *noun*
Apparatus is the equipment that is needed for a particular purpose.

apparently *adverb*
You say apparently when you are telling someone what you have heard, but you are not sure it is true: *Apparently the head teacher is leaving next year.*

appear (appears, appearing, appeared) *verb*
1. When something appears, it moves into a place where you can see it.
2. When something new appears, it begins to exist: *People did not appear until long after the dinosaurs had become extinct.*
3. When someone appears in a play or show, they take part in it.

appearance (appearances) *noun*
1. Someone's appearance in a particular place is their sudden arrival there.
2. Your appearance is the way you look to other people.

appetite (appetites) *noun*
If you have an appetite, you are looking forward to eating something.

applause *noun*
Applause is a way of showing how much you liked something by clapping your hands.

apple (apples) *noun*
An apple is a round, crisp fruit which grows on a tree.

apply (applies, applying, applied) *verb*
If you apply for something, like a job, you ask for it in writing.

appreciate (appreciates, appreciating, appreciated) *verb*
If you appreciate something, such as kindness, you feel grateful for it.

approach (approaches, approaching, approached) *verb*
When someone approaches you, they get nearer to you.

approve (approves, approving, approved) *verb*
1. If you approve of something that is happening, you are pleased about it.
2. If you approve of someone, you like and admire them.

apricot (apricots) *noun*
An apricot is a small, round, yellow-orange fruit with a large stone in the centre. Apricots grow on trees in parts of Asia, Europe and the United States.

April *noun*
April is the fourth month of the year. It has 30 days.

apron (aprons) *noun*
An apron is a piece of material that hangs down the front of you to keep your clothes clean when you are doing something like cooking.

aquarium (aquaria/aquariums) *noun*
An aquarium is a glass tank filled with water. You can keep fish and other underwater animals in it.

arch (arches) *noun*
An arch is usually made from brick, stone or iron, in the shape of a curve. It is used to cross openings such as doorways, or to link pillars on bridges.

archer (archers) *noun*
An archer is a person who shoots with a bow and arrow.

area (areas) *noun*
1. The area of something flat is its size.
2. You use the word area to talk about things in or around a place: *There are lots of shops in this area.*

argue (argues, arguing, argued) *verb*
If you argue with someone, you show that you do not agree with them, and give your reasons.

argument (arguments) *noun*
An argument is a talk between two or more people who do not agree with one another. In some arguments, people shout angrily.
arithmetic *noun*
Arithmetic is about adding, subtracting, multiplying and dividing numbers.
arm (arms) *noun*
Your arm is the part of your body between the shoulder and the hand.
arm (arms, arming, armed) *verb*
If you arm someone, you give them a weapon.
armchair (armchairs) *noun*
An armchair is a comfortable chair which has a support on each side for your arms.
armour *noun*
1. Armour is special clothing, usually made of metal, that soldiers used to wear in battle.
2. The armour of something, like a tank, is the thick hard outer covering that protects it against attack.
army (armies) *noun*
An army is a large organized group of people who are armed and trained to fight on land in case of war.
around *adverb*
1. You can say around when you mean in all directions: *She owns the land for miles around.*
2. Around can mean close by: *Until my father arrived, we could do nothing but wait around.*
around *preposition*
1. You say around when things are in various places: *There are lots of cupboards around the house.*
2. Around can also mean going from place to place: *We spent our holiday cycling around Scotland.*
3. You can use around when something is on all sides of something else: *The earth's atmosphere is the air around it.*
arrange (arranges, arranging, arranged) *verb*
1. If you arrange something like a party or holiday, you make plans for it.
2. If you arrange things like books or flowers, you group them in a special way.
arrangement (arrangements) *noun*
1. Arrangements are plans that you make so that something can happen.
2. If you make an arrangement with someone, you agree to a particular plan.
3. An arrangement can be a group of things, like flowers or furniture, that are put together in a special way to make them look attractive.
arrest (arrests, arresting, arrested) *verb*
If the police arrest someone, they catch them and take them to the police station.
arrive (arrives, arriving, arrived) *verb*
1. When you arrive at a place, you reach it at the end of your journey.
2. When something like a letter or newspaper arrives, it is delivered to you.
arrow (arrows) *noun*
1. An arrow is a long, thin weapon which is shot from a bow. It has a point at one end and usually feathers at the other.
2. An arrow can also be a sign which shows people which way to go.
art *noun*
Art is something, like painting or sculpture, which is beautiful or has a special meaning.
artery (arteries) *noun*
An artery is a tube in the body of a person or animal which carries blood from the heart to the rest of the body.
article (articles) *noun*
1. An article is a piece of writing on a particular subject in a magazine or newspaper.
2. An article can also be a particular object: *What is this strange article?*
artificial *adjective*
Artificial objects or materials are made by people. They do not occur naturally.
>artificially *adverb*
artist (artists) *noun*
An artist is a person who does things like painting, drawing or sculpture.
ash (ashes) *noun*

1. Ash is the dust that is left over from a fire.
2. An ash is a tree. It can grow to about 35 metres.
ashamed *adjective*
Someone who is ashamed feels sorry because of something they have done.
ask (asks, asking, asked) *verb*
1. If you ask someone something, you are trying to find something out.
2. If you ask someone for something, you want them to give it to you.
asleep *adjective*
If you are asleep, your eyes are closed and your whole body is resting.
ass (asses) *noun*
An ass is like a horse but smaller and with longer ears. A donkey is a kind of ass.
assemble (assembles, assembling, assembled) *verb*
1. When people assemble, they come together in a group, usually for a particular purpose.
2. If you assemble something, you fit the parts of it together.
assistant (assistants) *noun*
1. A person's assistant is someone whose job is to help them.
2. An assistant is a person who works in a shop selling things to customers.
astonish (astonishes, astonishing, astonished) *verb*
If something or someone astonishes you, they surprise you very much.
astronaut (astronauts) *noun*
An astronaut is someone who is trained to fly in a spaceship.
astronomer (astronomers) *noun*
An astronomer is a scientist who studies the stars, planets and other natural objects in space.
atlas (atlases) *noun*
An atlas is a book of maps.
atmosphere (atmospheres) *noun*
A planet's atmosphere is the layer of air or other gas around it. When people talk about the atmosphere, they mean the air around the earth.
atom (atoms) *noun*
An atom is a very, very tiny part of something. You can only see an atom through a microscope.
attach (attaches, attaching, attached) *verb* When you attach something to an object, you join or fasten it to the object.
attached *adjective*
If you are attached to someone or something, you are very fond of them.
attack (attacks) *noun*
1. When a person or an army attacks other people, it is called an attack.
2. If you have an attack of an illness, you suffer from it for a short time.
attack (attacks, attacking, attacked) *verb*
1. If a person attacks somebody, they try to hurt them.
2. If a group of people such as an army attacks, they begin to use weapons to hurt people or destroy buildings.
3. If players attack in a game of something, like football, they try to score goals.
attempt (attempts, attempting, attempted) *verb*
If you attempt something difficult, you try to do it.
attend (attends, attending, attended) *verb*
1. If someone attends something like a meeting or a ceremony, they are present at it.
2. If you attend something like a school, you go to it regularly.
attendant (attendants) *noun*
An attendant is a person whose job is to serve people in a place such as a museum or garage.
attention *noun*
1. If something attracts your attention, you notice it suddenly.
2. If you pay attention to someone, you listen carefully to what they are saying.
attic (attics) *noun*
An attic is a room at the top of a house, just under the roof.

attract (attracts, attracting, attracted) *verb*
1. If something attracts people or animals, something about it causes them to come to it: *Moths are attracted to light.*
2. If something attracts your attention, it makes you notice it.
3. If something like a magnet attracts an object, it makes it move towards it.
attractive *adjective*
1. If something is attractive, it is nice to look at.
2. If you are attractive, people want to be near you.
>**attractively** *adverb*
audience (audiences) *noun*
An audience is a group of people watching or listening to something like a play, film, talk or piece of music.
August *noun*
August is the eighth month of the year. It has 31 days.
aunt (aunts) *noun*
Your aunt is the sister of one of your parents, or the wife of your uncle.
author (authors) *noun*
1. The author of a piece of writing is the person who wrote it.
2. An author is a person whose job is to write books.
authority (authorities) *noun*
1. Authority is a quality or strength that someone has that makes people take notice of what they say.
2. An authority on a particular subject is someone who knows a lot about it.
3. The authorities are people, like the government, who have a lot of power.
autograph (autographs) *noun*
An autograph is the signature of someone famous.
automatic *adjective*
1. An automatic machine is one that can do things on its own.
2. If something you say or do is automatic, you don't have to think about it, usually because you have done it many times before.
3. If something like a punishment is automatic, it always happens as a result of something else.
>**automatically** *adverb*
autumn (autumns) *noun*
Autumn is the season between summer and winter. The weather becomes cooler and many trees begin to lose their leaves.
avalanche (avalanches) *noun*
An avalanche is a large mass of snow and ice that falls down a mountain.
avenue (avenues) *noun*
An avenue is a wide road with trees on either side.
avoid (avoids, avoiding, avoided) *verb*
1. If you avoid doing something, you try hard not to do it.
2. If you avoid someone or something, you keep away from them.
awake *adjective*
If you are awake, you are not sleeping.
award (awards) *noun*
1. An award is a prize that you are given for doing something well.
2. An award is also a sum of money that you may be given for special training or study.
aware *adjective*
If you are aware of something, you know about it.
away *adverb*
1. If you move away from somewhere, you move so that you are further from that place: *He turned and walked away.*
2. If you put something away, you put it in a safe place.
3. If you are away, you are not in the place mentioned: *Is Katherine at school today? – No, she's away.*
awkward *adjective*
1. If you say someone can be awkward to deal with, you mean they might not be very helpful.
2. If people are awkward, they are clumsy and do not move gracefully.
>**awkwardly** *adverb*
axe (axes) *noun*
An axe is a tool with a long handle and a heavy sharp blade at one end. It is used for chopping wood.

B

baby (babies) *noun*
A baby is a very young child.
back *adverb*
1. If you step or fall back, you move away from the way you are facing.
2. If you go back to a place, you go somewhere you have just been, or have been before: *He went back to the kitchen... At the end of the summer they went back home.*
back (backs) *noun*
1. Your back is the part of your body which is behind you, from your neck to the top of your legs.
2. The back of an animal is the part on top, between its neck and the beginning of its tail.
3. The back of a house is the part that faces away from the street.
>**back to front** *phrase*
If you have something on back to front, you are wearing it the wrong way round.
background (backgrounds) *noun*
The background of a picture is the part that seems to be furthest from you.
backwards *adverb*
1. If you move backwards, you move with your back facing in the direction you are going.
2. If you do something backwards, you do it in the opposite of the usual way: *Let's try running this tape backwards.*
bacon *noun*
Bacon is meat which comes from the back or sides of a pig and has been salted and sometimes smoked.
bacteria *noun*
Bacteria are very tiny creatures, which you cannot see without using a microscope. Some kinds of bacteria cause diseases.
bad (worse, worst) *adjective*
1. You say bad when you are talking about somebody who is naughty or wicked.
2. Bad food is not fresh.
3. If something is bad, it could hurt you in some way: *Sailors don't like bad weather.*
4. Bad work is work that has not been well done.
>**badly** *adverb*
badge (badges) *noun*
A badge is a sign. People sometimes wear badges to let you know they belong to a school or a club. Cars have badges to let you know what make they are.
badger (badgers) *noun*
A badger is a strongly built animal with short legs and neck. It has long grey fur and a striped head, and eats mainly rodents.
badminton *noun*
Badminton is a game in which players use rackets to hit a small feathered object called a shuttlecock across a net.
bag (bags) *noun*
A bag is for carrying or holding things. Bags are soft and usually made of paper, cloth or plastic.
bagpipes *noun*
Bagpipes are a musical instrument, played by blowing air into a bag and squeezing it out through pipes.
bait *noun*
Bait is food that you use to trap animals.
bake (bakes, baking, baked) *verb*
When you bake food, you cook it in an oven.
baker (bakers) *noun*
A baker makes and sells bread, cakes and pies. The place where a baker works is called a bakery.
balance (balances, balancing, balanced) *verb*
When you balance, you keep steady: *She tried to balance on one leg.*
balance (balances) *noun*
Balance is the steadiness that someone or something has: *She found it hard to keep her balance.*
balcony (balconies) *noun*
A balcony is a platform fixed to the outside of a building with a railing or wall around it.
bald (balder, baldest) *adjective*
People who are bald have no hair on the top of their head.

ball (balls) *noun*
Anything round can be called a ball. You need a ball for lots of games, like tennis and football.
ballet (ballets) *noun*
A ballet is a sort of play without words. The story is told with dancing and music.
balloon (balloons) *noun*
A balloon is a small rubber bag. If you blow hard into it, it gets bigger and makes a very light toy or decoration.
ballpoint (ballpoints) *noun*
A ballpoint is a kind of pen. When you write, the ink comes out round a tiny ball.
bamboo *noun*
Bamboo is a kind of grass which often grows much higher than a person. It has strong, hollow stems, which are useful for garden canes or for making furniture.
ban (ban, banning, banned) *verb*
If someone is banned from doing something, they are told officially that they must not do it.
banana (bananas) *noun*
A banana is a fruit which grows on trees in hot countries. Bananas hang from the tree in bunches of about a hundred.
band (bands) *noun*
1. A band is a small number of people, like a gang of robbers or a group of musicians.
2. A band can also be a strip of material such as iron, cloth or rubber.
bandage (bandages) *noun*
A bandage is a strip of cloth used to cover a wound.
bandage (bandages, bandaging, bandaged) *verb*
To bandage someone, you wind a strip of clean cloth round a part that is injured.
bandit (bandits) *noun*
A bandit is a robber who steals from travellers.
bang (bangs) *noun*
A bang is a sudden, short, loud noise.
bang (bangs, banging, banged) *verb*
If something bangs, or if you bang it, it makes a loud noise.
banister (banisters) *noun*
A banister is one of the posts that hold up a handrail on stairs.
bank (banks) *noun*
1. A bank is a building which has strong rooms for keeping people's money safe.
2. The bank of a river is the ground either side of the water.
3. Any steeply sloping piece of ground can be called a bank.
banner (banners) *noun*
A banner is a piece of cloth stretched between two poles. Banners have designs or words on them, and they are carried by people in processions.
bar (bars) *noun*
1. A bar is a long piece of something hard, like metal or wood.
2. A bar can also be a counter where people can buy drink.
barbecue (barbecues) *noun*
1. A barbecue is a grill on which food is cooked over hot charcoal, usually out of doors.
2. A barbecue is also a party where the guests eat food cooked on a barbecue.
bar code (bar codes) *noun*
A bar code is a pattern of numbers and lines printed on something that is for sale, so that the price can be read by a machine.
bare (barer, barest) *adjective*
1. If part of your body is bare, it is not covered by clothes.
2. If a room is bare, there is no furniture in it.
bargain (bargains) *noun*
A bargain is something which is sold at a low price, and which you think is good value.
bark (barks) *noun*
1. A bark is a loud noise that dogs make.
2. Bark is the outside covering of a tree.
bark (barks, barking, barked) *verb*
When a dog barks, it makes a sudden rough, loud noise.
barn (barns) *noun*
A barn is a large building where a farmer stores hay and other crops.
barrel (barrels) *noun*
1. A barrel is a wooden, metal or plastic

container for holding liquids. Barrels are wider in the middle than at the top and bottom.
2. The barrel of a gun is the long metal part.
barrier (barriers) *noun*
A barrier is something, like a fence or wall, that stops people or things getting from one area to another.
base (bases) *noun*
The base is the bottom of something.
basement (basements) *noun*
The basement of a building is a floor below ground level.
basic *adjective*
1. Basic is used to describe things, like food and equipment, that people need in their ordinary lives.
2. Basic also means the simplest and most important things that you need to know about a subject.
>**basically** *adverb*
basket (baskets) *noun*
A basket is used for holding or carrying things. Baskets are usually made from strips of thin wood or cane.
bat (bats) *noun*
1. In some games, like table tennis or baseball, you need a bat to hit the ball.
2. A bat is also a small animal like a mouse with leathery wings. Bats fly at night, and sleep hanging upside down.
bat (bats, batting, batted) *verb*
If you are batting, you are having a turn at hitting the ball with a bat in cricket, baseball or rounders.
bath (baths) *noun*
A bath is a container for water. It is big enough to sit or lie in, so that you can wash yourself all over.
bathroom (bathrooms) *noun*
The bathroom is the room where the bath or shower is.
battery (batteries) *noun*
A battery is a thing which gives you electric power. You use tiny batteries for things like watches, and large batteries for cars and other vehicles.
battle (battles) *noun*
A battle is a fight between enemy forces, on land, at sea or in the air.
bay (bays) *noun*
1. A bay is a deep curve in a coastline.
2. A bay is also a small evergreen tree.
beach (beaches) *noun*
The beach is the ground, covered with sand or pebbles, that is next to the sea.
beak (beaks) *noun*
A beak is the hard outside part of a bird's mouth that it uses for picking up food.
beam (beams) *noun*
1. A beam is a long, thick bar of wood, metal or concrete, especially one that is used to support the roof of a building.
2. A beam of light is a line of light that shines from an object such as a torch or the sun.
beam (beams, beaming, beamed) *verb*
If you beam, you give a big smile because you are pleased about something.
bean (beans) *noun*
A bean is a vegetable. Its outer covering is called a pod, and inside it has several large seeds. The seeds are also called beans.
bear (bears) *noun*
A bear is a large, heavy animal measuring up to three metres. Bears usually make their homes in caves. Most bears can climb, and all of them swim well.
beard (beards) *noun*
A beard is hair which grows on the lower part of a man's face.
beat (beats, beating, beat, beaten) *verb*
1. If you beat someone in a race or competition, you do better than they do.
2. If someone beats another person or an animal, they hit them hard, sometimes with something like a stick.
3. When a bird or insect beats its wings, it moves them up and down.
4. Your heart beats with a regular sound all the time.
beat *noun*
The beat of a piece of music is the main rhythm that it has.

beautiful *adjective*
1. You say something is beautiful if it gives you great pleasure to look at it or listen to it.
2. You say someone is beautiful if you think they are lovely to look at.
>**beautifully** *adverb*

beaver (beavers) *noun*
A beaver is a strong animal, nearly a metre long. It has a flat scaly tail and webbed back feet. A beaver's home is called a lodge, and is built from sticks plastered with mud.

beckon (beckons, beckoning, beckoned) *verb*
If you beckon to someone, you signal to them to come to you, by moving your hand or finger repeatedly in a curving movement towards your body.

become (becomes, becoming, became, become) *verb*
To become means to start being different in some way: *The smell became stronger.*

bed (beds) *noun*
1. A bed is a piece of furniture to lie down on when you rest or sleep.
2. The bed of the sea or of a river is the bottom of it.

bedroom (bedrooms) *noun*
The bedroom is the room where you sleep.

bedtime *noun*
Your bedtime is the time when you usually go to bed.

bee (bees) *noun*
A bee is a flying insect. Some people keep bees for the honey and wax that they make.

beech (beeches) *noun*
A beech is a tree. It can grow as high as 40 metres.

beef *noun*
Beef is the meat from a bull or cow.

beehive (beehives) *noun*
A beehive is a house for bees, made so that the beekeeper can collect the honey.

beetle (beetles) *noun*
A beetle is an insect with four wings. The front two act as hard covers to the body when the beetle is not flying.

beetroot *noun*
Beetroot is a dark red root vegetable.

begin (begins, beginning, began, begun) *verb*
1. When you begin, you start to do something.
2. When something begins, it starts at that time: *School begins on Thursday.*

beginner (beginners) *noun*
A beginner is someone who has just started to learn something.

beginning (beginnings) *noun*
The beginning of something is the first part of it.

behave (behaves, behaving, behaved) *verb*
1. If someone is behaving badly, they are not being good.
2. If someone tells you to behave yourself, they want you to be good.

behaviour *noun*
A person's behaviour is the way they act with other people.

behind *adverb*
If you stay behind, you stay after other people have gone.

behind *preposition*
1. Behind means on the other side of something: *She was behind the counter.*
2. If you are behind someone, you are at the back of them.

believe (believes, believing, believed) *verb*
If you believe someone or something, you think what is being said is true.

bell (bells) *noun*
A bell is a piece of metal shaped like a cup, which rings when something hits it.

belong (belongs, belonging, belonged) *verb*
1. If something belongs to you, it is your own.
2. If you belong to something, like a club, you are a member of it.
3. If something belongs to something else, it is part of it, or fits it: *I think this piece belongs to that jigsaw.*

below *preposition*
If something is below something else, it is under it or lower down.

belt (belts) *noun*
A belt is a strip of material, such as leather or plastic, that you put round your waist.

bench (benches) *noun*
1. A bench is a long seat, usually made of wood.
2. In a workshop or laboratory, a bench is a table where people work.

bend (bends, bending, bent) *verb*
When something bends, it becomes curved or crooked.

beneath *preposition*
If something is beneath something else, it is underneath it or lower down.

berry (berries) *noun*
A berry is a small, round, soft fruit that grows on a bush or a tree. Some berries are good to eat, but others are poisonous.

beside *preposition*
If something is beside something else, it is at the side of it or next to it.

best *adjective*
1. Best means of the highest standard or quality: *That's the best programme I've seen.*
2. Best can also mean the most skilful or intelligent: *Julia's the best swimmer in our class.*
3. People say it would be best to do a particular thing when they are giving advice: *It's best to wear something warm.*

best *noun*
Someone's best is the highest standard they can reach.

better *adjective*
1. Something that is better than something else is of a higher standard or quality: *Your bicycle is better than mine.*
2. Someone who is better at something is more successful or skilful: *I wish I could find a better dentist.*
3. Better can mean more pleasant or enjoyable: *I had a better day at school today.*
4. Better can also mean more sensible: *It would be better to go the other way home.*
5. If you are feeling better after an illness, you are not feeling so ill.
6. When you are better after an illness, you are completely recovered.

beware *verb*
You tell people to beware if there is danger of some kind: *Beware of the bull.*

bicycle (bicycles) *noun*
A bicycle is a vehicle with two wheels. You sit on it and turn pedals with your feet to make it go. A bicycle is often called a bike for short.

big (bigger, biggest) *adjective*
Something or somebody big is large in size.

bike (bikes) *noun*
See **bicycle.**

bin (bins) *noun*
A bin is a container, usually with a lid. It can be for rubbish, or for storing things in.

binary system *noun*
The binary system is a way of counting and calculating using only two numbers, 0 and 1.

bind (binds, binding, bound) *verb*
1. If you bind something, you tie something, like string or cloth, tightly round it so that it is held in place.
2. When a book is bound, the pages are joined together and the cover is put on.

biology *noun*
Biology is the study of living things, such as plants and animals.

birch (birches) *noun*
A birch is a tall tree that has thin, peeling bark.

bird (birds) *noun*
A bird is an animal with feathers. It has two legs and two wings. Most birds can fly. The young are hatched from eggs.

birth (births) *noun*
The birth of a baby is when it comes out of its mother's body.

birthday (birthdays) *noun*
Your birthday is a special date that is remembered every year, because it was the day you were born.

biscuit (biscuits) *noun*
A biscuit is a small, flat, crisp kind of cake.

bit (bits) *noun*
1. A bit of something is a small piece of it: *You've got a bit of biscuit on your face.*
2. A bit is a piece of metal that goes in a horse's mouth when you put the reins on.
3. A bit is also the tiniest piece of information that can be stored by a computer. It is either 0 or 1.

bite (bites, biting, bit, bitten) *verb*
If you bite something, you cut it with your teeth.

bitter (bitterest) *adjective*
1. A bitter wind or bitter weather is very cold and unpleasant.
2. Someone who is bitter feels very angry and disappointed.
>**bitterly** *adverb*

black (blacker, blackest) *adjective*
If the colour of something is black, it is as dark as it can possibly be.

blackberry (blackberries) *noun*
A blackberry is a small, soft, dark purple fruit that grows wild on brambles in hedgerows.

blackbird (blackbirds) *noun*
A blackbird is about 25 centimetres long. The male has black feathers and a yellow beak. The female has brown feathers. The song of a blackbird is lovely to listen to.

blackcurrant (blackcurrants) *noun*
Blackcurrants are very small, dark purple fruits. They grow in bunches on bushes.

blade (blades) *noun*
1. The blade of something which cuts, like a knife, is the thin flat piece with a sharp edge.
2. A single piece of grass is called a blade.

blame (blames, blaming, blamed) *verb*
If somebody blames a person for something bad that happened, they think or say that person made it happen.

blank (blanker, blankest) *adjective*
1. A blank piece of paper has no writing or other marks on it.
2. If you look blank, your face shows no interest or understanding.
>**blankly** *adverb*

blank *noun*
If your mind is a blank, you cannot think of anything.

blanket (blankets) *noun*
A blanket is a large, warm cloth, often used to cover people in bed.

blastoff *noun*
Blastoff is the moment when a rocket or spaceship leaves the ground to begin its journey into space.

blaze (blazes) *noun*
A blaze is a strong, bright fire.

bleed (bleeds, bleeding, bled) *verb*
If a part of your body bleeds, blood comes out of it.

blend (blends, blending, blended) *verb*
1. When you blend two or more things together, they become a very smooth mixture: *Blend the butter and sugar together.*
2. When things like colours or sounds blend, they come together in a pleasing way.

blind *adjective*
Someone who is blind cannot see because of something wrong with their eyes.

blind (blinds) *noun*
A blind is rolled material that you pull down to cover a window.

blind (blinds, blinding, blinded) *verb*
If something, like light, blinds you, you cannot see for a short period of time.

blindfold (blindfolds) *noun*
A blindfold is a strip of cloth that can be tied round someone's head so that it covers their eyes and they cannot see.

blink (blinks, blinking, blinked) *verb*
When you blink, you shut your eyes and then you open them again very quickly.

blister (blisters) *noun*
A blister is a painful swelling that contains a clear liquid. Blisters can be caused by burning or by something rubbing constantly against the skin.

blizzard (blizzards) *noun*
A blizzard is a very bad snowstorm with strong winds.

block (blocks) *noun*
1. A block of flats or offices is a large, tall building.
2. A block in a town or city is an area of land with buildings on it and streets on all sides.
3. A block of something, like stone or wood, is a large, rectangular piece of it.

block (blocks, blocking, blocked) *verb*

1. If something blocks a road, it goes across it and stops traffic getting through.
2. If something blocks your view, it stops you seeing something because it is in the way.
3. If someone blocks your path, they stop you from going somewhere by standing in the way.
blockage (blockages) *noun*
A blockage in something, like a pipe or tunnel, is something that stops things moving along it.
blood *noun*
Blood is the red liquid that your heart pumps round inside your body.
blossom *noun*
Blossom is the flowers that appear on a tree before the fruit.
blot (blots) *noun*
A blot is a drop of liquid, especially ink, that is spilled on to a surface.
blouse (blouses) *noun*
A blouse is a kind of shirt worn by a girl or woman.
blow (blows) *noun*
1. A blow is a hard hit with a fist or weapon.
2. A blow can also be something you hear about that makes you unhappy or disappointed.
blow (blows, blowing, blew, blown) *verb*
1. When a wind blows, the air moves.
2. If you blow, you send out a stream of air from your mouth.
3. When you blow your nose, you force air out through your nose to clear it.
4. If something blows up, it is destroyed by an explosion.
5. If you blow up a balloon or tyre, you fill it with air.
6. If someone blows up a photograph, they print a larger copy of it.
blue (bluer, bluest) *adjective*
Something that is blue is the colour of the sky on a sunny day.
bluebell (bluebells) *noun*
A bluebell is a flower than often grows wild in woods in Europe. It is 20-50 centimetres tall, with blue flowers like bells hanging from the stems.
blunt (blunter, bluntest) *adjective*
1. If a knife is blunt, it does not cut properly.
2. A long, thin object that is blunt has a rounded, rather than pointed end: *My pencil's blunt.*
3. When someone is being blunt, they are speaking without trying to be polite.
>**bluntly** *adverb*
blurred *adjective*
When something is blurred, it has no distinct outline and you cannot see it clearly.
blush (blushes, blushing, blushed) *verb*
When you blush, you become red in the face, usually because you are embarrassed.
board (boards) *noun*
A board is a flat, thin, rectangular piece of something like wood or cardboard. There are many different kinds of board that are used, for example in schools, or for cooking, building, or games.
board (boards, boarding, boarded) *verb*
If you board a ship, train or aircraft, you get on it to go somewhere.
boast (boasts, boasting, boasted) *verb*
If you boast, you talk too proudly about something you have done or something you own.
boat (boats) *noun*
A boat is a small vessel for travelling on water. It can hold only a few people.
body (bodies) *noun*
1. A person's or animal's body is every part of them: *He lay on the bed, his whole body limp with tiredness.*
2. You can say body when you mean just the main part of a person, not counting head, arms and legs.
boil (boils) *noun*
A boil is a painful, red swelling on the skin.
boil (boils, boiling, boiled) *verb*
When liquid boils, it gets very hot. It starts bubbling and steam rises from it.

bolt (bolts) *noun*
1. A bolt is a long, round metal object that looks like a screw with a flat end. It screws into a nut to fasten things together.
2. A bolt on a door is a metal bar that you can slide across to keep the door shut.

bolt (bolts, bolting, bolted) *verb*
1. When you bolt a door or window, you slide the bolt across to fasten it.
2. When a person or animal bolts, they suddenly start to run very fast, usually because they are frightened.

bomb (bombs) *noun*
A bomb is a weapon which explodes and damages or destroys a large area.

bone (bones) *noun*
A person's or animal's bones are the hard parts inside their body which make up the skeleton.

bonfire (bonfires) *noun*
A bonfire is a fire that is lit outdoors, usually to burn garden rubbish.

bonus (bonuses) *noun*
1. A bonus is an amount of money that someone gets as well as their ordinary pay, usually as a reward.
2. A bonus can also be something good that you did not expect, in addition to something else.

bony (bonier, boniest) *adjective*
A person or animal that is bony is very thin, with very little flesh covering their bones.

book (books) *noun*
A book is pieces of paper fixed together on one edge, inside a cover, with a story or ideas written inside.

boot (boots) *noun*
1. A boot is a shoe that covers the whole foot and part of the leg.
2. The boot of a car is the space for luggage.

border (borders) *noun*
1. The border between two countries or other areas is the dividing line between them.
2. A border is a strip or band along the edge of something, usually as a decoration.
3. A border is also a strip of ground with plants in it, usually along the edge of a lawn.

bore (bores, boring, bored) *verb*
1. If you bore a hole in something, you make a hole with a tool like a drill.
2. If somebody bores you, you do not find them interesting and you begin to feel tired and impatient.

bored *adjective*
When you are bored, you feel tired and impatient because you have lost interest in something or because you have nothing to do.

boring *adjective*
1. Something boring is so dull that it makes people feel tired and impatient.
2. You say something is boring if it does not look interesting: *My room's really boring. I must put some posters up.*

born *adjective*
When a baby is born, it comes out of its mother's body and begins its life as a separate person.

borrow (borrows, borrowing, borrowed) *verb*
When you borrow something, someone lets you have it for a while but they expect you to give it back later.

boss (bosses) *noun*
Someone's boss is the head of the place where they work.

botany *noun*
Botany is the study of plants.

bother (bothers, bothering, bothered) *verb*
1. If you do not bother to do something, you do not do it because you think it is unnecessary or too much trouble.
2. If you say that something does not bother you, you mean you do not mind it.

bottle (bottles) *noun*
A bottle is a container for keeping liquids in. Bottles are usually made of glass or plastic.

bottom (bottoms) *noun*
1. The bottom of something is the lowest part of it.
2. Your bottom is the part of your body that you sit on.

boulder (boulders) *noun*
A boulder is a big, rounded rock.

bounce (bounces, bouncing, bounced) *verb*
When something bounces, it springs back in the opposite direction as soon as it hits something hard, like the ground or a wall.
bound (bounds, bounding, bounded) *verb*
To bound means to run or move suddenly and quickly, with large leaps and jumps.
>bound to happen *phrase*
If you say something is bound to happen, you mean it is sure to happen.
bow (bows) *noun*
1. A bow is a kind of knot with two loops used to tie laces and ribbons.
2. A bow is also a weapon used for shooting arrows.
3. The bow of a stringed musical instrument is a long piece of wood with horsehair stretched along it.
bow (bows, bowing, bowed) *verb*
When you bow, you stand in front of someone and bend your body forward.
bowl (bowls) *noun*
A bowl is a container with an open top. Bowls are usually round and not very deep.
box (boxes) *noun*
A box is a container with straight sides, made from something stiff, like cardboard, wood or plastic.
box (boxes, boxing, boxed) *verb*
When you box, you fight someone using the rules of the sport of boxing.
boy (boys) *noun*
A boy is a male child.
bracelet (bracelets) *noun*
A bracelet is a band or chain, usually made of metal, which is worn round the wrist or arm as an ornament.
bracing *adjective*
If you say a place or its climate is bracing, you mean it makes you feel energetic.
brain (brains) *noun*
Your brain is the organ inside your head that you use for thinking and feeling.
brake (brakes) *noun*
The brake is the part of a vehicle or machine that slows it down or stops it.
brake (brakes, braking, braked) *verb*
When a driver brakes, they make their vehicle slow down or stop by using the brakes.
bramble (brambles) *noun*
A bramble is a wild trailing bush with thorns. Its fruits are called blackberries.
branch (branches) *noun*
1. A branch is part of a tree that grows out from the trunk.
2. A branch of an organization is one of its shops or offices which serve customers in a particular town.
brandish (brandishes, brandishing, brandished) *verb*
If you brandish something like a weapon, you wave it in the air to scare people.
brass *noun*
1. Brass is a yellow-coloured metal made from copper and zinc. It is used for making things like ornaments and some musical instruments.
2. The brass in an orchestra is made up of instruments like the trumpet, tuba and trombone.
brave (braver, bravest) *adjective*
If you are brave, you show that you can do something even if it is frightening.
>bravely *adverb*
bray (brays, braying, brayed) *verb*
When a donkey brays, it makes a loud, harsh sound.
bread *noun*
Bread is a very common food, made with flour and baked in an oven.
breadth *noun*
The breadth of something is the distance that it measures from one side to the other.
break (breaks) *noun*
A break is a short period of time when you stop what you are doing to have a rest.
break (breaks, breaking, broke, broken) *verb*
1. If you break something, it splits into pieces or stops working.
2. If you break a promise, you act differently from the way you said you would.
breakdown (breakdowns) *noun*
If you have a breakdown in your car, it stops working in the middle of a journey.
breakfast *noun*
Breakfast is the first meal of the day.

breath *noun*
Your breath is the air that you take into and let out of your lungs.
breathe (breathes, breathing, breathed) *verb*
When you breathe, you take air into your lungs through your nose or mouth, and then let it out again.
breathless *adjective*
If you are breathless, you find it hard to breathe properly, for example if you are ill, or have been running.
>**breathlessly** *adverb*
breed (breeds) *noun*
A breed of an animal is a particular kind. For example, a labrador is a breed of dog.
breeze (breezes) *noun*
A breeze is a gentle wind.
brew (brews, brewing, brewed) *verb*
1. When you let tea or coffee brew, you leave it in the pot for a few minutes before pouring.
2. When you brew a hot drink, you make it by pouring hot water onto something like tea or coffee.
3. When people brew beer, they make it.
brick (bricks) *noun*
A brick is a block used for building. It is made of baked clay, and is usually red or yellow.
bride (brides) *noun*
A bride is a woman on or near her wedding day.
bridegroom (bridegrooms) *noun*
A bridegroom is a man on or near his wedding day.
bridesmaid (bridesmaids) *noun*
A bridesmaid is a woman or girl who helps a bride on her wedding day.
bridge (bridges) *noun*
A bridge is something built over things like rivers, railways or roads, so that people or vehicles can get across.
brief (briefer, briefest) *adjective*
1. Something that is brief lasts for only a short time.
2. A piece of writing or speech that is brief does not have too many words or details.
>**briefly** *adverb*
briefcase (briefcases) *noun*
A briefcase is a firm, rectangular case which has a small handle at the top. You use a briefcase to carry things like papers and books.
bright (brighter, brightest) *adjective*
1. Someone who is bright is quick at learning or noticing things.
2. Bright colours are clear and easy to see.
3. A light that is bright is shining strongly.
>**brightly** *adverb*
brilliant *adjective*
1. Someone who is brilliant is extremely clever or skilful.
2. A brilliant colour is extremely bright.
3. Brilliant light shines very brightly.
>**brilliantly** *adverb*
brim (brims) *noun*
1. The brim of a hat is the lower part of it that sticks outwards from the head.
2. If you fill a cup to the brim, you fill it right up to the top.
bring (brings, bringing, brought) *verb*
1. If you bring someone on a visit, they come with you.
2. If you bring something, you have it with you when you arrive.
3. If you bring something to an end, you stop it.
brink *noun*
If you are on the brink of something important or exciting, it is just about to happen.
brisk (brisker, briskest) *adjective*
Someone who is brisk behaves in a busy, confident way that shows that they want to get things done quickly.
>**briskly** *adverb*
bristle (bristles) *noun*
1. Bristles are thick, strong animal hairs that are sometimes used to make brushes.
2. The bristles of a brush are the thick hairs or thin pieces of plastic which are fixed to the main part of it.
bristle (bristles, bristling, bristled) *verb*
If the hair on an animal's or person's body bristles, it rises away from their skin. This

can happen if for example they are feeling cold, frightened or angry.
brittle (brittler, brittlest) *adjective*
If something is brittle, it is hard but easily broken.
broad (broader, broadest) *adjective*
Something, such as a road or river, that is broad is very wide.
broadcast (broadcasts, broadcasting, broadcast) *verb*
When a programme is broadcast, it is sent out by radio waves so that it can be heard on the radio or seen on television.
broadcast (broadcasts) *noun*
A broadcast is a programme that is heard on the radio or seen on television.
brooch (brooches) *noun*
A brooch is a small piece of jewellery, which is worn pinned to a dress, blouse or coat.
broom (brooms) *noun*
A broom is a kind of brush with a long handle. You can use a broom to sweep the floor or other places where you walk.
broomstick (broomsticks) *noun*
A broomstick is the long handle of a broom which has a bundle of twigs at the end. In stories, witches fly on broomsticks.
brother (brothers) *noun*
Someone's brother is a boy or man who has the same parents as they have.
brown (browner, brownest) *adjective*
Something that is brown is the colour of earth or of wood.
bruise (bruises) *noun*
A bruise is an injury usually made when part of the body is hit by something. The skin is not broken but a purple mark appears.
brush (brushes) *noun*
A brush is a lot of bristles fixed into wood, metal or plastic. There are different brushes for jobs like painting, or cleaning your teeth.
brush (brushes, brushing, brushed) *verb*
If you brush against something, you touch it lightly as you are passing.
bubble (bubbles) *noun*
A bubble is a hollow, very light ball of soap or liquid.
bubble (bubbles, bubbling, bubbled) *verb*
When a liquid bubbles, it makes a lot of bubbles because it is boiling or fizzy.
bucket (buckets) *noun*
A bucket is a container with an open top and a handle. Buckets are often used for carrying water.
buckle (buckles) *noun*
A buckle is a fastening which is fixed to one end of a belt or strap.
bud (buds) *noun*
A bud is a small lump on a plant, which will open into a leaf or flower.
Buddhist (Buddhists) *noun*
A Buddhist is someone who follows the teachings of Buddha.
budget (budgets) *noun*
A budget is a plan which shows how much money there is and how it is to be spent.
budget (budgets, budgeting, budgeted) *verb*
When you budget for something, you work out how much money you can spend.
buffalo (buffaloes) *noun*
A buffalo is an animal found in Asia, Africa and America. It is like a large cow with long, curved horns. Buffaloes live mostly in the wild, but they are sometimes used to pull carts, or give milk.
bugle (bugles) *noun*
A bugle is a brass musical instrument like a small trumpet.
build (builds, building, built) *verb*
If you build something, you make it by joining things together.
building (buildings) *noun*
A building is something, like a house or a factory, that has walls and a roof.
bulb (bulbs) *noun*
1. A bulb is the part of an electric lamp that is made of glass and gives out light.
2. A bulb is also a root shaped like an onion. Many spring flowers, such as daffodils and tulips, grow from bulbs.
bulge (bulges, bulging, bulged) *verb*
If something bulges, it sticks out in a lump: *His pockets bulged with conkers.*
bulge (bulges) *noun*
A bulge is a lump on a surface that is usually flat.

bull (bulls) *noun*
A bull is a male animal of the cattle family. Male elephants and whales are also called bulls.
bulldozer (bulldozers) *noun*
A bulldozer is a large powerful tractor with a steel blade on the front. It is used for moving large amounts of earth or stone.
bullet (bullets) *noun*
A bullet is a small piece of metal with a rounded end that is fired from a gun.
bully (bullies) *noun*
A bully is someone who uses their strength or power to hurt or frighten other people.
bump (bumps, bumping, bumped) *verb*
If you bump into something, you hit it while you are moving.
bump (bumps) *noun*
1. A bump is an accident in which a moving object hits something.
2. If you hear a bump, it sounds like something falling to the ground.
3. A bump is a small swelling that comes up when something has hit you.
4. A bump is also a raised uneven part on a surface such as a road.
bun (buns) *noun*
A bun is a small cake similar to a soft bread roll, but made with sugar and dried fruit.
bunch (bunches) *noun*
1. A bunch of flowers is a number of flowers on their stems which have been picked and put together.
2. A bunch of fruit is a group growing together on one stem. Grapes and bananas grow in bunches.
bundle (bundles) *noun*
A bundle is a number of small things that have been tied together so that they can be carried or stored.
bungalow (bungalows) *noun*
A bungalow is a house with all its rooms on one floor.
bunk (bunks) *noun*
A bunk is a bed that is fixed to the wall.
bunk beds *noun*
Bunk beds are two single beds fixed one above the other.
burglar (burglars) *noun*
A burglar is someone who breaks into buildings and steals or damages things.
burly (burlier, burliest) *adjective*
A burly man has a broad body and strong muscles.
burn (burns, burning, burned/burnt) *verb*
1. If something is burning, it is being spoiled or destroyed by fire.
2. People often burn fuel, such as coal, to keep warm.
burn (burns) *noun*
A burn is an injury caused by heat or fire.
burrow (burrows) *noun*
A burrow is a hole in the ground or a tunnel dug by a small animal such as a rabbit, to live in or to take shelter.
burst (bursts, bursting, burst) *verb*
When something, like a balloon or a tyre, bursts, it splits open suddenly.
burst (bursts) *noun*
A burst of speed is when something or someone suddenly moves much faster for a short time.
bury (buries, burying, buried) *verb*
1. When you bury something, you put it in a hole in the ground and cover it up.
2. When you bury your face in something, you hide or partly hide your face in it.
bus (buses) *noun*
A bus is a large vehicle which travels on the road, stopping at bus stops. People pay to go on buses.
bush (bushes) *noun*
1. A bush is a large, woody plant with lots of branches. It is smaller than a tree.
2. The bush is the wild area of Australia, New Zealand and Africa.
business (businesses) *noun*
1. Business is work that is to do with making, buying and selling things or services.
2. A business is a group of people who work together to make and sell goods or provide a service.
bus stop (bus stops) *noun*
A bus stop is a place where people can get on or off buses.

busy (busier, busiest) *adjective*
1. When you are busy, you are working hard on something or giving it your full attention.
2. A place that is busy is full of people doing things or moving about.
>**busily** *adverb*

butcher (butchers) *noun*
A butcher is a shopkeeper who cuts up meat and sells it.

butter *noun*
Butter is a solid, yellowish fat which is made from fresh cream. You can spread it on bread or use it for cooking.

buttercup (buttercups) *noun*
A buttercup is a small, bright yellow, wild flower.

butterfly (butterflies) *noun*
A butterfly is an insect with four large wings. Butterflies' babies are caterpillars, which hatch from eggs. When the caterpillar is ready, it spins a cocoon round itself and later comes out as a butterfly.

button (buttons) *noun*
1. A button is a small, round fastening sewn on to clothes, such as shirts.
2. A button is also a small part of something electrical that you press to make it work.

buy (buys, buying, bought) *verb*
When you buy something, you get it by paying money for it.

byte (bytes) *noun*
A byte is a piece of information that can be stored by a computer. It is made up of several bits.

C

cab (cabs) *noun*
1. The cab is the place where the driver sits in a bus, truck or train.
2. A cab is a taxi.

cabbage (cabbages) *noun*
A cabbage is a vegetable that looks like a large ball of leaves. The leaves can be green, white or purple.

cabin (cabins) *noun*
1. A cabin is a room in a ship, boat or aeroplane for passengers or crew.
2. A cabin is also a small house, usually made of wood, in a wild place such as a forest.

cactus (cactuses/cacti) *noun*
A cactus is a thick, fleshy plant. It is covered with spikes and has no leaves. Cactuses grow in hot, dry places like deserts.

café (cafés) *noun*
A café is a place where there are tables and chairs and you can buy drinks and snacks.

cage (cages) *noun*
A cage is a box or room made with bars. Pets like birds, hamsters and gerbils are usually kept in cages, and some of the animals in zoos also live in cages.

cake (cakes) *noun*
A cake is a sweet food made with flour, sugar, fat and eggs, and baked in an oven.

calculation (calculations) *noun*
A calculation is something you think about and work out, or one that you do on a machine such as a calculator.

calculator (calculators) *noun*
A calculator is something which gives you the answer to sums if you press the right buttons.

calendar (calendars) *noun*
A calendar is a chart which divides the year into months, weeks and days.

calf (calves) *noun*
1. Calves are young cattle. Young elephants, giraffes, buffaloes, whales and seals are also called calves.
2. Your calf is the thick part at the back of your leg between your knee and your ankle.

call (calls, calling, called) *verb*
1. If you call someone something, you give them a name.
2. If an animal or a thing is called something, that is the right name to use for it.
3. If you call someone, you shout for them or telephone them.
4. If you call on somebody, you go to see them for a little while.

calm (calmer, calmest) *adjective*
1. If you are calm, you do not seem worried or excited.
2. If a lake or the sea is calm, it is smooth and still because there is no wind.
>**calmly** *adverb*
camel (camels) *noun*
A camel is a large animal which carries people and things in the desert. There are two kinds of camel. The Arabian camel has one hump on its back, and the Bactrian camel has two.
camera (cameras) *noun*
A camera is a piece of equipment you use to take photographs.
camp (camps) *noun*
A camp is a place where people live in tents or stay in tents on holiday.
can (could) *verb*
1. You say you can do something if you are able to do it.
2. If you ask if you can do something, you want to know if you are allowed to do it.
can (cans, canning, canned) *verb*
If someone cans food or drink, they put it into a metal container and seal it so that it will remain fresh for a long time.
can (cans) *noun*
A can is a metal container for something like food, drink or paint. Cans are often sealed to keep things fresh.
canal (canals) *noun*
A canal is a long, narrow stretch of water that has been made for boats to travel along.
cancel (cancels, cancelling, cancelled) *verb*
1. If you cancel something that has been arranged, you stop it from happening.
2. If you cancel something like a seat at the theatre, you say you no longer want it.
candle (candles) *noun*
A candle is a stick made of wax. It has a piece of string called a wick right through the middle. You light the wick and it burns slowly to give light.
cane (canes) *noun*
1. Cane is the long, hollow stems of a plant such as bamboo.
2. Cane can also be strips of the stems of plants that are used for weaving things such as baskets.
3. A cane is a tall, narrow stick, which is used for supporting plants in gardens.
cannon (cannons) *noun*
A cannon is a large gun, usually on wheels, which was used in the past to fire heavy, metal balls at the enemy in battle.
canoe (canoes) *noun*
A canoe is a small, light boat, usually pointed at both ends.
canvas (canvases) *noun*
1. Canvas is strong, heavy cloth, usually made of cotton or linen. It is used for making things like tents, sails and bags.
2. A canvas is a piece of canvas stretched on a frame. It is used for painting on.
canyon (canyons) *noun*
A canyon is a narrow valley with very steep sides, often with a river at the bottom.
cap (caps) *noun*
1. A cap is a soft, flat hat with a peak at the front.
2. A cap is also a small, flat lid on a bottle or container.
capacity (capacities) *noun*
1. The capacity of something is the largest amount that it can hold, produce or carry.
2. A person's capacity is the ability that they have to do a particular thing.
capital (capitals) *noun*
1. The capital is the main city in a country: *Paris is the capital of France.*
2. A capital is a big letter of the alphabet. People's names start with a capital letter.
captain (captains) *noun*
1. A captain is the person in charge of a ship.
2. The pilot in charge of an air liner is also called the captain.
3. A captain in a sport like cricket, football or hockey is the person who leads the team.

captor (captors) *noun*
A captor is someone who has captured a person or animal.
capture (captures, capturing, captured) *verb*
If you capture somebody, you take them prisoner.
car (cars) *noun*
A car is a road vehicle powered by an engine. It needs a driver and usually has room for three or four passengers and some luggage.
caravan (caravans) *noun*
A caravan is a vehicle with beds and a place to cook, so that people can spend holidays or live in it. Some caravans can be pulled along the road by a car.
card (cards) *noun*
1. Card is strong, stiff paper.
2. Playing cards are small pieces of card with numbers or pictures on them. They are used for card games.
3. A greetings card usually has a picture on the front and words inside, and is sent to people on special days such as birthdays.
cardboard *noun*
Cardboard is thick, stiff board made of paper. It is used to make things like boxes.
cardigan (cardigans) *noun*
A cardigan is a knitted jacket. You fasten it at the front with buttons or a zip.
care (cares, caring, cared) *verb*
1. If you care about something, you think it is important.
2. If you care for somebody, you like them very much.
>**take care** *phrase*
If you take care of something, like an animal, you look after it well so that it stays healthy and happy.
career (careers) *noun*
Someone's career is the kind of work they do, in which they hope to be able to move to higher positions: *John wants a career in teaching.*
careful *adjective*
If someone is careful, they behave sensibly and think about what they are doing.
>**carefully** *adverb*
careless *adjective*
If you are careless, you don't pay enough attention to what you are doing, so that you are clumsy, you lose things, or accidents happen.
>**carelessly** *adverb*
caretaker (caretakers) *noun*
A caretaker is a person who looks after a large building, such as a school.
carnival (carnivals) *noun*
A carnival is a special sort of party in the streets that anyone can go to. There is usually music and dancing, and people dress up and decorate cars and trucks.
carpenter (carpenters) *noun*
A carpenter is a person who works with wood, usually for furniture, buildings or ships.
carpet (carpets) *noun*
A carpet is a thick covering, usually made of something like wool. People put carpets on floors and stairs to make them quiet and comfortable to walk on.
carriage (carriages) *noun*
1. A carriage is one of the vehicles that are joined together to make up a passenger train.
2. A carriage is also an old-fashioned vehicle with four wheels, pulled by one or more horses.
carrot (carrots) *noun*
A carrot is a long thin orange-coloured vegetable that grows under the ground.
carry (carries, carrying, carried) *verb*
1. When you carry something, you hold it off the ground and take it with you.
2. If a sound carries, it can be heard a long way off.
cart (carts) *noun*
A cart is a heavy, wooden vehicle pulled by horses or cattle on farms.
carton (cartons) *noun*
1. A carton is a strong cardboard box for packing things in.
2. A carton is also a container made of cardboard or plastic, for holding food or drink.

cartoon (cartoons) *noun*
1. A cartoon is a funny drawing in a magazine or newspaper.
2. A cartoon film is a film where the characters are drawn, instead of being real people.
cartwheel (cartwheels) *noun*
A cartwheel is a fast, acrobatic movement in which someone throws themselves sideways onto one hand, then puts the other hand down, and then ends up back on their feet.
carve (carves, carving, carved) *verb*
1. If you carve an object, you make it by cutting it out of something like stone or wood.
2. If someone carves a piece of meat, they cut slices from it.
case (cases) *noun*
1. A case is a box for keeping or carrying things in.
2. In museums and shops, a case is a container for displaying things.
cash *noun*
Cash is money in coins and bank notes.
cassette (cassettes) *noun*
A cassette is a small plastic container with magnetic tape inside it, which you can use to record sounds and listen to them on a special machine called a cassette recorder. You can record pictures as well as sounds on a video cassette.
cast (casts, casting, cast) *verb*
1. If something casts a shadow on to a place, it makes a shadow fall there.
2. If someone, like a witch, casts a spell on someone or something, they do magic that affects that person or thing.
cast (casts) *noun*
1. The cast of a play or film is all the people who act in it.
2. A cast is an object that has been made by pouring something like liquid plaster or metal into a container, so that, when it hardens, it has the same shape as the container.
castle (castles) *noun*
A castle is a large building with very strong walls. Castles were built hundreds of years ago to keep the people living inside safe from attack.
cat (cats) *noun*
A cat is a furry mammal. Small cats are often kept as pets. There are also larger, wild cats, such as lions and tigers.
catalogue (catalogues) *noun*
A catalogue is a book in which things that are for sale are listed, along with their prices.
catch (catches, catching, caught) *verb*
1. If you catch something like a ball, you take hold of it when it is moving.
2. If you catch a bus or train, you get on it to go somewhere.
3. If you catch something like measles, you get that illness.
catch (catches) *noun*
A catch is a fastener on a lid or door.
caterpillar (caterpillars) *noun*
A caterpillar is a small animal like a worm with legs, that will turn into a butterfly or moth.
cattle *noun*
Bulls and cows on a farm are called cattle.
cauldron (cauldrons) *noun*
A cauldron is a large, round, metal pot, used for boiling liquids or cooking food over a fire.
cauliflower (cauliflowers) *noun*
A cauliflower is a vegetable. It has a large white centre and green leaves round the outside.
cause (causes, causing, caused) *verb*
To cause something means to make it happen.
>**in a good cause** *phrase*
If something is in a good cause, it is worth doing because it will help other people.
cautious *adjective*
Someone who is cautious acts very carefully to avoid possible danger.
>**cautiously** *adverb*
cave (caves) *noun*
A cave is a large hole in the side of a hill or cliff, or under the ground.
cavern (caverns) *noun*
A cavern is a large, deep cave.

cavity (cavities) *noun*
A cavity is a small hole or gap in something solid.
ceiling (ceilings) *noun*
The ceiling is the inside roof of a room.
celebrate (celebrates, celebrating, celebrated) *verb*
If you celebrate something, you do something enjoyable, like having a party, to show that it is a special occasion.
celery *noun*
Celery is a vegetable with several white stems and pale green leaves. The stems are crisp, and you can eat them raw or cooked.
cell (cells) *noun*
1. A cell is the smallest part of an animal or plant that is able to exist by itself.
2. A cell is also a small room where a prisoner, or a monk or nun, lives.
3. A cell can be something that uses energy from things like heat or light to make electricity.
cellar (cellars) *noun*
A cellar is a room under a house. Cellars are often used for storing things in.
Celsius *adjective*
You use Celsius to measure the temperature of something. In the Celsius scale, 0 degrees is the freezing point of water and 100 degrees is its boiling point, so if you say it is 10 degrees Celsius, you mean it is 10 degrees above freezing point.
cement *noun*
Cement is a grey powder made from limestone and clay. When it is mixed with sand and water, it makes mortar for sticking bricks together.
cemetery (cemeteries) *noun*
A cemetery is a place where dead people are buried.
centigrade *adjective*
Centigrade means the same as Celsius.
centimetre (centimetres) *noun*
A centimetre is a measure of length. It is the same as 10 millimetres.
centipede (centipedes) *noun*
A centipede is a small animal. It looks like a tiny worm, but it has lots of legs.
central *adjective*
Something that is central is positioned in the middle of an object or an area.
>**centrally** *adverb*
central heating *noun*
Central heating is a system of heating a building. Air or water is heated in one main tank and travels round the building through pipes and radiators.
centre (centres) *noun*
1. The centre of anything is the middle of it.
2. A centre is a building where people can go for particular purposes, for example sports.
century (centuries) *noun*
1. A century is a period of 100 years.
2. If someone says the 20th century, they mean some time between 1900 and 1999.
cereal (cereals) *noun*
1. Cereal is a plant which has seeds called grain that can be used for food.
2. Cereal is also a food made from grain, that is often eaten for breakfast.
ceremony (ceremonies) *noun*
A ceremony is a set of actions and words that are performed or spoken at a special occasion such as a wedding.
certain *adjective*
If you are certain of something, you are sure it is true.
>**certainly** *adverb*
certificate (certificates) *noun*
A certificate is a special piece of paper which says that something important, like a birth or a marriage, took place.
chain (chains) *noun*
A chain is made from rings of metal joined together in a line.
chair (chairs) *noun*
A chair is a seat with a back, for one person.
chalk *noun*
Chalk is a soft, white rock. It can be made into sticks for writing on blackboards.
champion (champions) *noun*
A champion is a person who has beaten everyone else in a contest.

chance (chances) *noun*
1. If someone says there is a chance that something will happen, they mean it might happen.
2. If you are given a chance to do something, you are allowed to do it if you want to.
>**by chance** *phrase*
If something happens by chance, it has not been planned.
change (changes) *noun*
1. If there is a change in something, it becomes different in some way.
2. If you say something is a change, you mean that it is different, often in a pleasant or interesting way.
3. Change is the money you are given when you pay too much for something because you do not have the right amount.
change (changes, changing, changed) *verb*
1. When something changes, it becomes different.
2. When you change your clothes, you put on different ones.
3. When you change trains, you get off one and on to another.
channel (channels) *noun*
1. A channel is a passage for water or other liquid.
2. Television companies use different channels to broadcast programmes.
chaos *noun*
Chaos is a state of complete confusion, where nothing is organized.
character (characters) *noun*
1. The character of a person or a place is all the qualities they have that make them the way they are.
2. The characters of a book, film or play are the people it is about.
charge (charges, charging, charged) *verb*
1. If someone charges you an amount of money, they are asking you to pay that amount for something you have bought or received.
2. If something or someone charges towards you, they move quickly towards you, usually to attack you.
>**in charge** *phrase*
If you are in charge of something, you are the person looking after it.
charity (charities) *noun*
A charity is an organization which raises money for a particular cause, such as people in need.
charm (charms) *noun*
1. You say people or places have charm if they are attractive and pleasant.
2. A charm is a small ornament that is fixed to a bracelet or necklace.
3. A charm is also a thing, or something someone does or says, that is supposed to bring good luck.
chart (charts) *noun*
1. A chart is a sheet of paper showing things like dates or numbers clearly.
2. A chart can also be a map of the sea or of the stars.
chase (chases, chasing, chased) *verb*
If you chase a person or animal, you run after them to try to catch them.
chat (chats) *noun*
A chat is a friendly talk about things that are not very important.
cheap (cheaper, cheapest) *adjective*
Something which is cheap costs very little money, or less than you might expect.
>**cheaply** *adverb*
cheat (cheats, cheating, cheated) *verb*
When someone cheats, they lie or behave dishonestly to get what they want.
check (checks) *noun*
A check is a pattern of squares.
check (checks, checking, checked) *verb*
If you check something, you make sure it is correct or safe.
checkout (checkouts) *noun*
A checkout is the place in a supermarket where you pay.
cheek (cheeks) *noun*
Your cheeks are the soft parts of your face on each side of your nose and mouth.
cheer (cheers, cheering, cheered) *verb*
1. When you cheer, you shout loudly to show you are pleased about something or to encourage people, for example a

football team.
2. When you cheer up, you stop feeling low and become more cheerful.
cheerful *adjective*
Someone who is cheerful shows they are feeling happy.
>**cheerfully** *adverb*
cheese (cheeses) *noun*
Cheese is a food made from milk. It can be hard or soft. Some cheeses have a strong flavour.
cheetah (cheetahs) *noun*
A cheetah is a large wild animal of the cat family. Cheetahs can run very fast, reaching over 100 kilometres an hour.
chemist (chemists) *noun*
1. A chemist is a person who makes up medicine.
2. The chemist is a shop where you can buy medicine and things like soap and toothpaste.
chemistry *noun*
Chemistry is the scientific study of how substances are made up and how they change when you combine them with other substances.
cheque (cheques) *noun*
A cheque is a printed piece of paper that people can use to pay for things.
cherry (cherries) *noun*
A cherry is a small, round fruit with a hard seed called a stone in the middle. Cherries can be red, yellow or black.
chess *noun*
Chess is a game for two people, played on a board marked out in squares.
chest (chests) *noun*
1. Your chest is the top part of the front of your body, between your neck and your waist.
2. A chest is a large, heavy box, usually made of wood.
chestnut (chestnuts) *noun*
1. A chestnut is a shiny, brown nut that grows inside a light green covering.
2. A chestnut is also the large tree on which chestnuts grow.
chew (chews, chewing, chewed) *verb*
When you chew food, you bite it several times to make it easier to swallow.
chick (chicks) *noun*
A chick is a baby bird.
chicken (chickens) *noun*
1. A chicken is a bird which is kept on a farm. Most of the eggs that we eat are laid by chickens.
2. Chicken is the meat of a chicken.
chickenpox *noun*
Chickenpox is a disease caught especially by children. It causes a high temperature and spots that itch.
chief *adjective*
The chief cause or part of something is the most important one.
chief (chiefs) *noun*
1. A chief is a person who has authority over a group or organization.
2. A chief is also the head of a tribe.
>**chiefly** *adverb*
child (children) *noun*
A child is a young boy or girl.
childhood *noun*
A person's childhood is the time of life when they are a child.
chilly (chillier, chilliest) *adjective*
If you feel chilly, you are not quite warm enough to be comfortable.
chime (chimes) *noun*
A chime is the musical sound made by a bell or a clock.
chimney (chimneys) *noun*
A chimney is a pipe which goes up from a fireplace or factory furnace to above the level of the roof. It takes the smoke up into the air.
chimpanzee (chimpanzees) *noun*
A chimpanzee is an ape, smaller than a gorilla. Chimpanzees live in rainforests.
chin (chins) *noun*
Your chin is the part of your face that sticks out below your mouth.
china *noun*
China is a fine clay mixture used to make things like cups, saucers and plates, and also ornaments.

chip (chips) *noun*
1. A chip is a long, thin, fried piece of potato.
2. A silicon chip is a tiny piece of special material that is used in computers.
chip (chips, chipping, chipped) *verb*
When you chip something, you accidentally damage it by breaking a small piece off.
chisel (chisels) *noun*
A chisel is a long, thin tool with a sharp blade used for cutting wood or stone.
chocolate (chocolates) *noun*
1. Chocolate is a brown sweet or drink made from cocoa.
2. A chocolate is a sweet covered with a layer of chocolate.
choice (choices) *noun*
1. A choice is the different things that you can choose from.
2. A choice can also be someone or something that you choose.
choir (choirs) *noun*
A choir is a group of people who sing together, often in a church or at school.
choke (chokes, choking, choked) *verb*
1. If you choke, you cannot breathe properly because there is not enough air getting to your lungs.
2. If things choke a place, they fill it and stop any movement.
choose (chooses, choosing, chose, chosen) *verb*
When you choose something, you pick out the one you want.
chop (chops) *noun*
A chop is a slice of meat on a bone.
chop (chops, chopping, chopped) *verb*
When someone chops something, like wood, they cut it with an axe.
Christian (Christians) *noun*
A Christian is someone who follows the teachings of Jesus Christ.
chuckle (chuckles, chuckling, chuckled) *verb*
When you chuckle, you laugh quietly.
church (churches) *noun*
A church is a building where Christians worship.
chute (chutes) *noun*
A chute is a steep, narrow slope which people or things can slide down.
cinema (cinemas) *noun*
A cinema is a place where people watch films.
circle (circles) *noun*
A circle is a curved line with both ends joined, making the shape of a ring.
circuit (circuits) *noun*
A circuit is the complete path of wires and connections that an electric current flows through.
circus (circuses) *noun*
A circus is a group of people such as clowns, acrobats and jugglers, who travel to different places to give shows.
city (cities) *noun*
A city is a very large, busy town.
claim (claims) *noun*
1. A claim is saying that something is true.
2. A claim is also a demand that people should agree you have a right to something like land or a title.
3. A claim can also be money that someone applies for because they think they have a right to it.
claim (claims, claiming, claimed) *verb*
1. If someone claims something, they say it is true, although they might not be able to prove it.
2. If someone claims something like money or land, they say it is theirs.
3. If you claim money from someone, like the government or an insurance company, you ask for it because you think you have a right to it.
clamber (clambers, clambering, clambered) *verb*
If you clamber somewhere, you climb there with difficulty, using your hands and feet.
clap (claps, clapping, clapped) *verb*
When you clap, you make a noise by hitting your hands together several times.
class (classes) *noun*
1. A class is a group of people who are taught together.
2. A class is also a group of people or things

that are alike in some way.

class (classes, classing, classed) *verb*
If you class something in some way, you say it belongs to that group: *Whales are classed as mammals, not as fish.*

classroom (classrooms) *noun*
A classroom is a room in a school where children have lessons.

claw (claws) *noun*
1. The claws of a bird or animal are the hard curved nails at the end of its feet.
2. The claws on a creature such as a lobster are two hard pointed parts at the end of its front legs.

claw (claws, clawing, clawed) *verb*
1. If an animal claws something, it digs its claws into it.
2. If a person or animal claws at something, they try to get hold of it.

clay *noun*
Clay is a special sort of sticky earth that goes hard when it is dry. It is used for making bricks and pots.

clean (cleaner, cleanest) *adjective*
If something is clean, it is free from dirt.

clear (clearer, clearest) *adjective*
1. If a thing is clear, you can see through it.
2. If something you say is clear, it is easy to understand.
>**clearly** *adverb*

clear (clears, clearing, cleared) *verb*
1. If you clear a pathway, you move things out of the way so that people can get through.
2. If you clear something like a fence, you jump over it without touching it.
3. When you clear your throat, you give a little cough.
4. When you clear up, you put things away tidily.

clench (clenches, clenching, clenched) *verb*
1. When you clench your fist, you curl your fingers up tightly, usually because you are angry.
2. When you clench your teeth, you squeeze them together firmly, usually because you are angry or upset.

clever (cleverer, cleverest) *adjective*
1. Someone who is clever is able to learn and understand things easily.
2. You say someone is clever if they are very good at doing something.
>**cleverly** *adverb*

cliff (cliffs) *noun*
A cliff is a hill with very steep sides that go almost straight down. You often find cliffs near the sea.

climate (climates) *noun*
The climate of a place is the sort of weather it usually has.

climb (climbs, climbing, climbed) *verb*
When you climb something, like a mountain or a tree, you move towards the top of it. Climbing is usually quite hard work.

cling (clings, clinging, clung) *verb*
If you cling to someone or something, you hold on to them tightly with your arms.

clinic (clinics) *noun*
A clinic is where people go to see doctors or to get help and advice about their health.

clip (clips) *noun*
A clip is something small and springy which holds things in place.

clip (clips, clipping, clipped) *verb*
If you clip something, like a hedge, you cut small pieces off it.

cloak (cloaks) *noun*
A cloak is a loose coat that fastens at the neck and does not have any sleeves.

clock (clocks) *noun*
A clock is an instrument that measures time, and shows you what the time is. Clocks with numbers instead of hands are called digital clocks.

clockwork *noun*
Clockwork is the machinery in some kinds of toys or models that makes them move when they are wound up with a key.

close (closer, closest) *adjective*
If something is close, it is very near.
>**closely** *adverb*

close (closes, closing, closed) *verb*
1. When you close something, like a door, you move it so that it fills a gap.
2. When something like a shop or library closes, you can't go in until it opens again.

cloth (cloths) *noun*
1. Cloth is material made from something like cotton or nylon.
2. A cloth is a piece of cloth that you use for a particular purpose, such as covering a table.
clothes *noun*
Clothes are the things people wear, such as shirts, trousers and dresses.
cloud (clouds) *noun*
1. A cloud is a patch of white or grey mist that floats in the sky.
2. You can use cloud to describe a lot of smoke, steam or dust.
clover *noun*
Clover is a small wild plant with pink or white flowers and leaves which grow in threes.
clown (clowns) *noun*
A clown is someone in a circus who dresses in strange clothes, has a brightly painted face, and does funny things to make people laugh.
club (clubs) *noun*
A club is a group of people who are interested in the same thing, such as chess or riding.
clue (clues) *noun*
1. A clue is something that helps you solve a problem.
2. A clue is also something that helps a detective find out who did something.
clump (clumps) *noun*
A clump is a small group of people, plants or other things, standing or growing together.
clumsy (clumsier, clumsiest) *adjective*
Someone who is clumsy moves or handles things awkwardly, so that things get broken or knocked over.
>**clumsily** *adverb*
cluster (clusters) *noun*
A cluster is a number of things close together in a small group.
cluster (clusters, clustering, clustered) *verb*
If things cluster together, they gather in a small group, especially round a central point.
clutch (clutches, clutching, clutched) *verb*
If you clutch something, you hold it tightly with your hand.
clutter *noun*
Clutter is a lot of things lying about untidily, especially things that are not useful.
coach (coaches) *noun*
1. A coach is a large vehicle which carries people on journeys by road.
2. A coach drawn by horses is a closed-in vehicle that used to carry passengers. Coaches are still used at special times.
coach (coaches, coaching, coached) *verb*
If someone coaches you, they train you for a sport or give you extra lessons.
coal *noun*
Coal is a kind of hard, black rock which is dug out of the ground and burned to give heat.
coarse (coarser, coarsest) *adjective*
1. Anything that is coarse looks and feels rough.
2. A person who is coarse talks and acts in a rude way.
>**coarsely** *adverb*
coast (coasts) *noun*
The coast is the place where the land meets the sea.
coat (coats) *noun*
1. A coat is a piece of clothing with long sleeves, that you wear over other clothes when you go out.
2. An animal's coat is its fur or hair.
3. A thin layer of paint is called a coat: *Put another coat of paint on the door.*
coax (coaxes, coaxing, coaxed) *verb*
If you coax someone to do something, you try to persuade them to do it by asking them gently.
cobweb (cobwebs) *noun*
A cobweb is a net made by a spider to trap insects.
cock (cocks) *noun*
A cock is any male bird.
cocoa *noun*
1. Cocoa is a brown powder made from the seeds of the cacao tree.
2. Cocoa is also a hot drink made from cocoa powder and milk or water.

coconut (coconuts) *noun*
A coconut is a fruit which has a hard, hairy shell. Inside there is a milky juice and white flesh that you can eat. Coconuts grow on palm trees in tropical countries.

cocoon (cocoons) *noun*
A cocoon is a covering of silky threads that the larvae of some insects make for themselves before they grow into adults.

cod *noun*
A cod is a large sea fish which is caught for food.

code (codes) *noun*
1. A code is a set of ideas about the proper way to behave.
2. A code is a system of changing letters in a message for other letters or symbols, so that only people who know the code can read it.
3. A dialling code is a telephone number that you dial before someone's personal number, to connect you with the right area.

coffee *noun*
1. Coffee is a coarse powder made by grinding roasted coffee beans.
2. Coffee is also a hot drink made by pouring water on to ground coffee.

cog (cogs) *noun*
1. A cog is a wheel with teeth round the edge, which is used in a machine to turn something else.
2. The teeth round the edge of a cog are also called cogs.

coil (coils) *noun*
A coil is a series of loops into which something like rope or wire has been wound.

coin (coins) *noun*
A coin is a small piece of metal used as money.

cold (colder, coldest) *adjective*
1. If the weather is cold, the temperature outside is low.
2. Cold food is food that is meant to be eaten cold, such as salad.
3. People who are cold do not show much affection.
>**coldly** *adverb*

cold (colds) *noun*
A cold is a common illness. If you have a cold, you sneeze and your nose feels blocked.

collapse (collapses, collapsing, collapsed) *verb*
1. If someone or something collapses, they suddenly fall down.
2. If an object is meant to collapse, it is made so that it can be folded smaller or flatter when it is not being used.

collar (collars) *noun*
1. The collar of a shirt or jacket is the part that fits round your neck.
2. A collar for a dog or cat is a band or chain that is put round its neck.

collect (collects, collecting, collected) *verb*
1. If you collect a number of things, you bring them together: *She collected sticks for firewood.*
2. If someone collects something from somewhere, they go and fetch it.

college (colleges) *noun*
A college is where people go to study something, usually after they have left school.

collision (collisions) *noun*
A collision between two things is when a moving object hits something else.

colon (colons) *noun*
A colon is a punctuation mark (:) which you can use in several ways, such as in front of an example or in front of a list of things.

colossal *adjective*
Something that is colossal is very large.

colour (colours) *noun*
The colour of something is the way it looks in daylight: *The colour of grass is green.*

column (columns) *noun*
1. A column is a tall post shaped like a solid cylinder. Columns are usually made of stone and have decorated tops. They can be part of a building, or stand on their own.
2. A column is also a vertical strip of print in a newspaper or magazine.

comb (combs) *noun*
A comb is a flat piece of plastic or metal with narrow teeth all along one edge.

comb (combs, combing, combed) *verb*
When you comb your hair, you tidy it using a comb.

combine harvester (combine harvesters) *noun*
A combine harvester is a large farm machine. As it is driven through a cornfield, it cuts, sorts and cleans the grain.
comedy (comedies) *noun*
A comedy is a play or film that makes people laugh and has a happy ending.
comet (comets) *noun*
A comet is an object with a long bright trail behind it, which travels around the sun.
comfort (comforts, comforting, comforted) *verb*
If you comfort someone, you make them feel less worried or unhappy.
comfortable *adjective*
Furniture that is comfortable is nice to use. If clothes, such as shoes or trousers, are comfortable, they fit well.
>**comfortably** *adverb*
comic (comics) *noun*
A comic is a magazine that tells stories in pictures.
comma (commas) *noun*
A comma is a punctuation mark (,) which is used to separate parts of a sentence or items on a list.
command (commands, commanding, commanded) *verb*
If you command someone to do something, you order them to do it.
commercial *adjective*
Commercial means to do with business.
commercial (commercials) *noun*
A commercial is an advertisement that is broadcast on television or radio.
common (commoner, commonest) *adjective*
If something is common, you often see it or it often happens.
>**commonly** *adverb*
>**in common** *phrase*
If people or things have something in common, it means that they are alike in some way: *Alligators and robins have something in common - their babies hatch from eggs.*
common sense *noun*
If you only need common sense to do something, you do not need any special knowledge.
commotion *noun*
A commotion is a lot of noise, confusion and excitement.
communicate (communicates, communicating, communicated) *verb*
If you communicate with someone, you use signals such as speech, radio signals or body movements, to give them information.
compact disc (compact discs) *noun*
A compact disc is a round, flat silver coloured object on which a sound, especially music, is recorded. You play a compact disc on a compact disc player in which there is a laser.
company (companies) *noun*
A company is a group of people who work together making or selling things.
>**keep someone company** *phrase*
If you keep someone company, you stay with them because they do not want to be on their own.
compare (compares, comparing, compared) *verb*
When you compare two or more things, you look at them to see in what ways they are the same or different.
compass (compasses) *noun*
1. A compass is an instrument with a needle that always points to north.
2. A compass is also an instrument for drawing circles.
competition (competitions) *noun*
A competition is something that is organized to find out who is best at doing something.
complain (complains, complaining, complained) *verb*
If you complain, you tell someone about something affecting you that you do not like.
complete *adjective*
1. If something is complete, it has been finished.
2. If you talk about a complete thing, you mean all of it: *I need a complete new outfit for school next year.*
>**completely** *adverb*
complication (complications) *noun*

A complication is a problem that makes something harder to deal with.

compose (composes, composing, composed) *verb*
1. If you compose something, like a poem or a piece of music, you write it.
2. If you compose yourself, you make an effort to stop being angry or excited.

computer (computers) *noun*
A computer is a machine that stores information and works things out according to instructions in a program.

conceal (conceals, concealing, concealed) *verb*
If you conceal something, you hide it carefully.

concentrate (concentrates, concentrating, concentrated) *verb*
If you concentrate on something, you give all your attention to it.

concert (concerts) *noun*
A concert is a performance by musicians, usually in a big hall.

conclusion (conclusions) *noun*
1. A conclusion is something you decide is true because of other things you know.
2. The conclusion of something is its ending.

concrete *noun*
Concrete is a building material made of cement, sand, small stones and water, which goes very hard when it is set.

condition (conditions) *noun*
1. The condition of something is the state that it is in.
2. A condition is a rule you must agree to before you are allowed to do something: *You can go out on one condition: you must be home by five.*

conduct *noun*
Your conduct is the way you behave.

cone (cones) *noun*
A cone is a solid shape that is rounded at the bottom and pointed at the top.

confess (confesses, confessing, confessed) *verb*
If you confess something, you admit you have done something you feel ashamed of or embarrassed about.

confident *adjective*
1. If you are confident about something, you are sure it will happen in the way you want it to.
2. People who are confident feel able to deal with things and do not worry too much about them.

>**confidently** *adverb*

confuse (confuses, confusing, confused) *verb*
1. If something confuses someone, they are not sure what they are supposed to do: *The new road layout confused everyone.*
2. If you confuse two things, you mix them up by mistake: *I always confuse cheetahs with leopards because they both have spots.*

confusion *noun*
1. Confusion is when it is not clear what is happening.
2. There is also confusion when nothing is organized and there are a lot of different things happening at the same time.

congratulate (congratulates, congratulating, congratulated) *verb*
If you congratulate someone, you tell them you are pleased that something special and nice has happened to them.

conjuror (conjurors) *noun*
A conjuror is a person who entertains people by doing tricks in which things appear and disappear as if by magic.

connect (connects, connecting, connected) *verb*
If you connect two things, you join them together.

conquer (conquers, conquering, conquered) *verb*
1. If one country or group of people conquers another, they take control of them or their land by defeating them in war.
2. If you conquer something difficult or dangerous, you get control of it through great effort and determination: *She conquered her fear of the water and began to swim.*

conqueror (conquerors) *noun*
A conqueror is someone who conquers a country or group of people.

conscious *adjective*
1. If you are conscious of something, you notice what is happening.
2. Someone who is conscious is awake.
consider (considers, considering, considered) *verb*
1. If you consider a person or thing to be something, this is what you think they are.
2. If you consider something, you think about it carefully.
consist (consists, consisting, consisted) *verb*
Something that consists of particular things is made up of them.
consolation (consolations) *noun*
A consolation is something that makes someone feel happier when they are disappointed or upset.
consonant (consonants) *noun*
A consonant is any letter of the alphabet except a, e, i, o and u.
construct (constructs, constructing, constructed) *verb*
If you construct something, you build it or make it.
consult (consults, consulting, consulted) *verb*
If you consult someone, you ask them for their advice.
consume (consumes, consuming, consumed) *verb*
1. If you consume something, you eat it or drink it.
2. To consume an amount of something, like energy or time, means to use it up.
contain (contains, containing, contained) *verb*
1. If something like a box or a room contains a particular thing, it has that thing inside it.
2. If something like food or medicine contains a particular thing, it has that thing in it: *This tablet contains aspirin.*
container (containers) *noun*
A container is something you put things in.
contempt *noun*
If you have contempt for something or someone, you don't like them and think they are not important.
content *adjective*
If you are content with something, you are quite happy with it.
contents *noun*
1. The contents of something like a bottle or a room are everything that is in it.
2. The contents of something like a letter are everything that it says.
3. The list of contents in a book or magazine is the list at the beginning which gives you the title of every section or article, and the page that it starts on.
contest (contests) *noun*
A contest is a competition or game in which people try to do better than others so that they will win a prize.
continent (continents) *noun*
A continent is a very large area of land, usually made up of several countries. Africa is a continent.
continue (continues, continuing, continued) *verb*
If you continue to do something, you go on doing it.
contract (contracts) *noun*
A contract is a written agreement between two people or organizations.
contradict (contradicts, contradicting, contradicted) *verb*
If you contradict someone, you say the opposite of what they have just said.
control *noun*
1. Control is being able to make something behave exactly as you want it to.
2. Control is also being able to stop yourself behaving in an excited way.
control (controls, controlling, controlled) *verb*
If a person controls something, like a machine or a car, they make it do what it is supposed to do.
convenient *adjective*
1. Something that is convenient fits in well with someone's plan.
2. Convenient can also describe something that is useful because it saves you time and trouble.

>**conveniently** *adverb*
conversation (conversations) *noun*
If you have a conversation with someone, you talk to each other.
convince (convinces, convincing, convinced) *verb*
If someone or something convinces you, they make you believe that something is true.
cook (cooks) *noun*
A cook is a person who cooks and prepares food.
cook (cooks, cooking, cooked) *verb*
When you cook food, you prepare it for eating by heating it in a particular way, for example by frying, boiling or baking it.
cooker (cookers) *noun*
A cooker is used to heat food. The inside is called the oven and is used for roasting and baking. The top of the cooker is called the hob and is used for boiling and frying.
cool (cooler, coolest) *adjective*
1. If something is cool, its temperature is low but it is not cold.
2. Someone who behaves in a cool way is calm and does not show any excitement or anger.
>**coolly** *adverb*
cool (cools, cooling, cooled) *verb*
If you leave something hot to cool, you wait for it to get cooler.
cope (copes, coping, coped) *verb*
If you cope with a task or problem, you deal with it successfully.
copier (copiers) *noun*
A copier is a machine that makes copies of writing or pictures on paper.
copper *noun*
Copper is a reddish-brown metal.
copy (copies) *noun*
1. A copy is something that is made to look like something else.
2. A copy is also one book or magazine, when there are many others exactly like it.
copy (copies, copying, copied) *verb*
1. If you copy something that someone has written, you write it down exactly as it was written before.
2. To copy something also means to make a copy of it by using a machine.
3. If you copy someone, you try to be like them in some way.
cord (cords) *noun*
Cord is thick, strong string.
cork (corks) *noun*
1. Cork is the light bark of the cork oak tree.
2. A cork is a piece of cork or plastic used to block the open end of a bottle.
corn *noun*
Corn is a cereal crop, such as wheat or sweetcorn, which is grown so that the seeds can be used as food. The seeds are called grain.
corner (corners) *noun*
1. The corner of something is the place where two edges or sides join.
2. The corner of a street is the place where two roads meet.
correct *adjective*
1. Something that is correct does not have any mistakes in it.
2. If what you say is correct, it is true.
>**correctly** *adverb*
corridor (corridors) *noun*
A corridor is a long passage in a building or train.
cost (costs) *noun*
The cost of something is the amount of money needed to pay for it.
cost (costs, costing, cost) *verb*
If something costs an amount of money, you can buy it for that amount.
costume (costumes) *noun*
A costume is a special set of clothes worn by an actor or someone at a fancy-dress party.
cosy (cosier, cosiest) *adjective*
A house or room that is cosy is comfortable and warm, and not too big.
>**cosily** *adverb*
cot (cots) *noun*
A cot is a bed with high sides for a baby or a young child.
cottage (cottages) *noun*
A cottage is a small house, usually in the country.

cotton *noun*
1. Cotton is a tall plant that is grown in hot countries. It has soft fine hairs, called fibres, round its seeds.
2. Cotton is also a cloth woven from the soft fibres of the cotton plant.
3. Cotton fibres can be used to make a thread for sewing, which is also called cotton.
cotton wool *noun*
Cotton wool is soft, fluffy cotton, used for putting liquids or creams on to your skin.
cough (coughs) *noun*
A cough is a noise made by someone forcing air out of their throat.
count (counts, counting, counted) *verb*
1. When you count, you say all the numbers one after the other.
2. If you count a number of people or things, you add them up to see how many there are.
counter (counters) *noun*
1. A counter is a long, narrow table in a shop, where things are sold.
2. A counter is also a small, round, flat piece of something like plastic that is used in board games.
countless *adjective*
Countless means very many.
country (countries) *noun*
1. A country is a land that has its own government and language.
2. The country is land away from towns, where there are fields, trees and farms.
countryside *noun*
The countryside is land which is away from towns and cities.
couple (couples) *noun*
1. Two people are sometimes called a couple, especially if they are married.
2. A couple of things means a few. You say this when the exact number does not really matter.
coupon (coupons) *noun*
A coupon is a piece of printed paper that allows you to pay less than usual for something.
courage *noun*
Courage is not showing that you are afraid of something.
course (courses) *noun*
A course is a series of lessons on a particular subject.
>of course *phrase*
You use of course to make something you are saying stronger:
Do you still want to go to the fair?
- Of course I do.
court (courts) *noun*
1. A court is an area marked out for playing a game like tennis or badminton.
2. A court is also a place where things to do with the law are decided.
3. The court of a king or queen is the place where they live with their family and the people who advise them.
courtesy *noun*
Courtesy is behaviour that is polite and thoughtful.
courtyard (courtyards) *noun*
A courtyard is a flat, open area of ground with buildings or walls all round it.
cousin (cousins) *noun*
Your cousin is a child of your uncle or aunt.
cover (covers) *noun*
1. The covers on a bed are the blankets or duvet that you have over you to keep you warm.
2. The cover of a book or magazine is the outside of it.
3. Cover is trees, rocks or other places where you shelter from the weather or hide from someone.
cover (covers, covering, covered) *verb*
1. If you cover something, you put something else over it to protect it or to hide it.
2. If something covers something else, it forms a layer all over it.
3. If you cover a particular distance, that is how far you go.
cow (cows) *noun*
A cow is a large farm animal that gives milk.
coward (cowards) *noun*
A coward is someone who is easily

frightened. A coward is not a brave person.

cowboy (cowboys) *noun*
A cowboy is a man whose job is to look after cattle in America.

cowgirl (cowgirls) *noun*
A cowgirl is a woman whose job is to look after cattle in America.

crab (crabs) *noun*
A crab is a sea creature. It has a flat, roundish body covered by a shell, and five pairs of legs with large claws on the front pair.

crack (cracks) *noun*
1. A crack is a very narrow gap between two things.
2. A crack is also a line on something breakable that shows it is slightly damaged.

crack (cracks, cracking, cracked) *verb*
When something cracks, it becomes slightly damaged.

cracker (crackers) *noun*
1. A cracker is a thin, crisp biscuit, often slightly salty.
2. A cracker is also a small firework that makes a noise when you light it.
3. A cracker can be a cardboard tube covered in coloured paper, that people have at parties. It makes a sharp sound when you pull the ends apart.

cramped *adjective*
A cramped room or building is one which is not big enough for the people or things in it.

crane (cranes) *noun*
1. A crane is a machine that moves heavy things by lifting them.
2. A crane is also a large water bird with long legs and a long neck.

crash (crashes) *noun*
1. A crash is a traffic accident.
2. A crash is also a sudden loud noise like something breaking.

crash (crashes, crashing, crashed) *verb*
If something crashes, it hits something and is smashed.

crate (crates) *noun*
1. A crate is a large wooden box made for sending or storing things in.
2. A crate is also a tray divided into sections and used to carry bottles.

crawl (crawls, crawling, crawled) *verb*
When you crawl, you move forward on your hands and knees.

crayon (crayons) *noun*
A crayon is a coloured pencil.

creak (creaks, creaking, creaked) *verb*
If something creaks, it makes an unpleasant sound when you stand on it or when it moves. Floorboards in old houses often creak.

cream *adjective*
Something that is cream in colour is yellowish-white.

cream *noun*
Cream is the pale yellow liquid that you find on top of milk. You can buy cream on its own, to use in cooking or to pour over fruit or puddings.

create (creates, creating, created) *verb*
To create something means to bring it into existence, or to make it happen.

creature (creatures) *noun*
A creature is any living person or animal, such as a bird, fish or insect.

creek (creeks) *noun*
1. A creek is a strip of water where the sea comes a long way into the land.
2. In America, Canada, Australia and New Zealand, a creek is a small stream.

creep (creeps, creeping, crept) *verb*
If you creep somewhere, you move quietly and slowly.

crescent (crescents) *noun*
1. A crescent is a curved shape that is wider in the middle than at the ends, like a new moon.
2. A crescent is also a street, especially one that is curved.

crevice (crevices) *noun*
A crevice is a narrow crack or gap in rock or between large stones.

crew (crews) *noun*
A crew is made up of people who work on a ship, aircraft or spaceship.

cricket (crickets) *noun*
1. Cricket is an outdoor game between two teams of eleven players.
2. A cricket is a small jumping insect that makes a chirping sound by rubbing its wings together.
crime (crimes) *noun*
A crime is something which is against the law.
criminal (criminals) *noun*
A criminal is someone who has done something that is against the law.
crimson *adjective*
Something that is crimson is dark red.
crinkle (crinkles, crinkling, crinkled) *verb*
When something crinkles, it becomes slightly creased.
crisp (crisper, crispest) *adjective*
1. Things like fruit and biscuits that are crisp are fresh and firm, so that, when you bite them, they are crunchy.
2. Crisp behaviour is cool, sharp and unfriendly.
>**crisply** *adverb*
crisp (crisps) *noun*
A crisp is a thinly sliced piece of potato which is fried until it is crunchy.
criticize/criticise (criticizes, criticizing, criticized) *verb*
If you criticize someone, you tell them what you think is wrong with them.
crockery *noun*
Crockery is things like plates, cups and bowls, which are used at mealtimes.
crocodile (crocodiles) *noun*
A crocodile is a large reptile, about five metres long.
crocus (crocuses) *noun*
A crocus is a small plant that flowers in the spring. It can be white, yellow or purple.
crooked *adjective*
Something that is crooked is bent and twisted.
crop (crops) *noun*
A crop is food, such as corn or potatoes, that is grown in fields.
cross (crosser, crossest) *adjective*
Someone who is cross usually frowns and speaks sharply.
>**crossly** *adverb*
cross (crosses) *noun*
A cross is a sign like the letter X.
cross (crosses, crossing, crossed) *verb*
1. If you cross something like a road, you go from one side to the other.
2. If you cross your arms or legs, you put one on top of the other.
crouch (crouches, crouching, crouched) *verb*
If you crouch down, you bend your legs under you so that you are close to the ground.
crow (crows) *noun*
A crow is a large, black bird with a loud, harsh call.
crowd (crowds) *noun*
A crowd is a large number of people together in one place.
crowded *adjective*
A place that is crowded is very full of people.
crown (crowns) *noun*
A crown is a precious ornament that kings and queens sometimes wear on their heads.
cruel (crueller, cruellest) *adjective*
Someone who is cruel hurts people or animals without caring.
>**cruelly** *adverb*
crumb (crumbs) *noun*
A crumb is a very small piece of dry food, such as bread or biscuit.
crumble (crumbles, crumbling, crumbled) *verb*
If you crumble something that is soft or brittle, it breaks into lots of little pieces.
crunch (crunches, crunching, crunched) *verb*
1. If you crunch something hard, such as a sweet, you crush it noisily between your back teeth.
2. If you crunch something like glass or snow under your feet, it makes a crushing or breaking noise.
crush (crushes, crushing, crushed) *verb*
1. If you crush something, you press it very hard and break it or change its shape.

2. If you are crushed against other people or things in a crowd, you are pressed hard against them.
crust (crusts) *noun*
The crust is a hard layer on the outside of something such as bread.
cry (cries) *noun*
A cry is a sudden sound that you make when you are surprised or hurt.
cry (cries, crying, cried) *verb*
When you cry, tears come from your eyes.
crystal (crystals) *noun*
A crystal is a mineral that has formed into a regular shape.
cub (cubs) *noun*
A cub is a young wild animal such as a lion, fox or bear.
cube (cubes) *noun*
A cube is a solid with six square sides.
cuckoo (cuckoos) *noun*
A cuckoo is a grey bird, Cuckoos lay their eggs in other birds' nests.
cucumber (cucumbers) *noun*
A cucumber is a long, thin vegetable with a dark green skin and pale green flesh. It is used for salads and sandwiches.
cuddle (cuddles, cuddling, cuddled) *verb*
When you cuddle someone, you put your arms round them and hold them close.
cuff (cuffs) *noun*
A cuff is the end part of a sleeve.
culprit (culprits) *noun*
A culprit is someone who has done something wrong and has to take the blame for it.
cunning *adjective*
Someone who is cunning plans things to get what they want, often by tricking other people.
>**cunningly** *adverb*
cup (cups) *noun*
1. A cup is a small container, usually with a handle. People drink liquids such as tea and coffee from a cup.
2. A cup is also a prize for the winner of a game or a competition.
cupboard (cupboards) *noun*
A cupboard is a piece of furniture used for storing things like food, or cups and saucers.
cure (cures) *noun*
A cure is something that makes people better when they have been ill or injured.
cure (cures, curing, cured) *verb*
If someone or something cures a person, they make them well again after an illness or injury.
curiosity (curiosities) *noun*
1. Curiosity is wanting to know about things.
2. A curiosity is an interesting and unusual object.
curious *adjective*
1. Someone who is curious is interested in things and wants to find out about them.
2. Something that is curious is unusual and interesting.
>**curiously** *adverb*
curl (curls) *noun*
Curls are pieces of hair shaped in curves and circles.
curl (curls, curling, curled) *verb*
1. When something, like a leaf, curls, its edges roll in towards the middle.
2. If an animal curls up, it makes itself into a rounded shape.
curly (curlier, curliest) *adjective*
Hair that is curly is full of curls.
currant (currants) *noun*
1. A currant is a small, soft fruit, such as a redcurrant or a blackcurrant.
2. Currants are small, dried grapes, often used in fruit cakes.
current (currents) *noun*
1. A current is a steady movement of water or air.
2. A current is also the movement of electricity through a wire.
curry *noun*
Curry is an Indian dish made with hot spices.
cursor (cursors) *noun*
A cursor is a small sign on a computer screen that shows where the next letter or number will appear.
curtain (curtains) *noun*
A curtain is a large piece of material that hangs from the top of a window. You

pull it across the window to cover it.
curve (curves) *noun*
A curve is a smooth, gradually bending line.
curved *adjective*
A curved object has the shape of a curve.
cushion (cushions) *noun*
A cushion is a bag filled with soft material. You use cushions to sit on or lean back on.
custom (customs) *noun*
A custom is something that people usually do: *It's his custom to take the dog for a walk after supper.*
customer (customers) *noun*
A customer is a person who buys something, especially from a shop.
cut (cuts, cutting, cut) *verb*
1. If you cut yourself, you hurt yourself by accident on something sharp. The skin is broken and you bleed.
2. If someone cuts something, they push a knife through it and take a piece out: *She cut the cake and gave him a piece.*
3. If someone cuts something like hair or a hedge, they take pieces off to make it tidy.
cutlery *noun*
Cutlery is the knives, forks and spoons that you eat your food with.
cycle (cycles) *noun*
A cycle is a bicycle.
cycle (cycles, cycling, cycled) *verb*
If you cycle, you ride a bicycle.
cyclist (cyclists) *noun*
A cyclist is someone who rides a bicycle.
cyclone (cyclones) *noun*
A cyclone is a violent storm in which the air goes round and round very fast.
cylinder (cylinders) *noun*
A cylinder is a shape like a tube with flat circular ends and long straight sides.

D

daffodil (daffodils) *noun*
A daffodil is a yellow trumpet-shaped flower that blooms in the spring.
dagger (daggers) *noun*
A dagger is a weapon like a knife. It is sharp on both sides and pointed at the end.
daily *adjective*
A daily newspaper is one that comes out every day.
dairy (dairies) *noun*
A dairy is a shop or company that sells milk and food made from milk, such as butter and cheese.
daisy (daisies) *noun*
A daisy is a small, common, wild flower with white or pink petals and a yellow centre.
dam (dams) *noun*
A dam is a wall built across a river or stream. The dam stops the water flowing and makes a lake.
damage (damages, damaging, damaged) *verb*
If something damages something else, it spoils or breaks it so that it does not work properly or look as good as it did before.
damp (damper, dampest) *adjective*
Something that is damp is slightly wet.
dance (dances, dancing, danced) *verb*
When you dance, you move your whole body in time to music.
dandelion (dandelions) *noun*
A dandelion is a wild plant with bright yellow flowers. Dandelions have seeds that look like a fluffy ball at the top of the stem.
danger (dangers) *noun*
A danger is something that could harm you.
dangerous *adjective*
If something is dangerous, it is likely to harm you.
>**dangerously** *adverb*
dare (dares, daring, dared) *verb*
1. If you dare to do something frightening, you are brave enough to do it.
2. If you dare someone to do something frightening, you encourage them to do it to prove they are brave enough.
dark (darker, darkest) *adjective*
1. When it is dark, there is not enough light to see properly.
2. If you say someone has dark hair, you mean their hair is brown or black.

darken (darkens, darkening, darkened) *verb*
If a place or the sky darkens, it becomes darker because of shadows or clouds or because it is nearly night.
darkness *noun*
Darkness is when there is not enough light to see properly.
dart (darts, darting, darted) *verb*
If a person or animal darts somewhere, they move suddenly and quickly.
dash (dashes, dashing, dashed) *verb*
If you dash somewhere, you run or go there quickly.
data *noun*
Data is information, especially facts and figures that are stored in a computer.
date (dates) *noun*
1. If someone asks you the date, you tell them the day and the month.
2. A date is a small, brown, sticky fruit with a stone inside. Dates grow on palm trees in hot countries.
daughter (daughters) *noun*
A girl is the daughter of her parents.
dawdle (dawdles, dawdling, dawdled) *verb*
If you dawdle, you spend more time than you need to in going somewhere.
dawn *noun*
Dawn is the time of day when it first begins to get light.
day (days) *noun*
1. A day is the time between one midnight and the next. There are 24 hours in one day.
2. If you do something during the day, you do it between getting up and going to bed.
daydream (daydreams) *noun*
A daydream is pleasant thoughts, usually about things that you would like to happen.
daylight *noun*
Daylight is the light that there is during the day before it gets dark.
daytime *noun*
Daytime is the part of the day when it is light.
dazzle (dazzles, dazzling, dazzled) *verb*
If a light dazzles you, you cannot see properly for a short time.
dead *adjective*
1. A person, animal or plant that is dead is no longer living.
2. If part of your body goes dead, you cannot feel it for a short time.
deaf (deafer, deafest) *adjective*
Someone who is deaf cannot hear very well or cannot hear at all.
deafening *adjective*
A noise that is deafening is so loud that you cannot hear anything else at the same time.
>deafeningly *adverb*
deal (deals, dealing, dealt) *verb*
When you deal in a card game, you give cards to the players.
>deal with *phrase*
If you deal with something, such as a problem, you do whatever is needed to get the result you want.
dear (dearer, dearest) *adjective*
1. When you are writing a letter, you begin with 'Dear' and then put the name of the person you are writing to.
2. If something is dear, it costs a lot of money.
death *noun*
Death is the end of the life of a person or animal.
decay (decays, decaying, decayed) *verb*
When something like a plant or piece of meat decays, it becomes rotten.
deceive (deceives, deceiving, deceived) *verb*
If someone deceives you, they make you believe something that is not true.
December *noun*
December is the twelfth month of the year. It has 31 days.
decide (decides, deciding, decided) *verb*
If you decide to do something, you make up your mind to do it.
decimal (decimals) *noun*
A decimal is a kind of fraction that is written as a dot followed by a number or numbers. .5 is a decimal that means a half.
decision (decisions) *noun*
A decision is a choice that you make about what you think should be done.

deck (decks) *noun*
A deck is one of the floors on a ship or a bus.
deckchair (deckchairs) *noun*
A deckchair is a light, folding chair with a wooden frame and a canvas seat.
decode (decodes, decoding, decoded) *verb*
If you decode a message that has been written or spoken in code, you change it into ordinary language.
decorate (decorates, decorating, decorated) *verb*
1. If you decorate something, you make it more attractive by adding some kind of ornament.
2. If someone decorates a room, they paper it or paint it.
decoration *noun*
Decoration is something that is added to make something look more attractive.
deep (deeper, deepest) *adjective*
1. If something is deep, it goes a long way down: *The river is very deep here.*
2. A deep breath fills the whole of your lungs.
3. If you are in a deep sleep, it is difficult to wake you.
>**deeply** *adverb*
deer *noun*
A deer is a large wild animal that eats leaves and grass. Most male deer have branch-shaped horns called antlers.
defeat (defeats, defeating, defeated) *verb*
If you defeat someone, you win something such as a game or battle.
defence *noun*
Defence is something that is done to protect someone or something against attack.
>**come to someone's defence** *phrase*
If you come to someone's defence, you help them by doing something to protect them.
defend (defends, defending, defended) *verb*
If you defend someone or something, you do something to protect them against danger.
defiant *adjective*
If you are defiant, you refuse to obey someone.
>**defiantly** *adverb*
definitely *adverb*
You can say definitely to show that you are certain about something: *This year we're definitely going on holiday*.
delay (delays, delaying, delayed) *verb*
If something delays you, it causes you to slow down or be late.
deliberate *adjective*
If you do something that is deliberate, you do it on purpose.
>**deliberately** *adverb*
delicate *adjective*
1. Something that is delicate is small and graceful.
2. Someone who is delicate becomes ill easily.
3. A delicate flavour or smell is not strong.
>**delicately** *adverb*
delicious *adjective*
Food that is delicious tastes or smells very nice.
delight *noun*
Delight is a feeling of great pleasure.
delight (delights, delighting, delighted) *verb*
If something delights you, it gives you a lot of pleasure.
deliver (delivers, delivering, delivered) *verb*
If you deliver something, you hand it to someone.
demand (demands, demanding, demanded) *verb*
If you demand something, you ask for it.
demonstration (demonstrations) *noun*
1.If someone gives you a demonstration, they show you how to do something.
2. A demonstration is a public meeting or march held by people who are strongly for or against something.
den (dens) *noun*
A den is the home of some wild animals such as lions or foxes.
dense (denser, densest) *adjective*
1. Dense fog or smoke is difficult to see through.
2. Something that is dense has a lot of things or people in a small area: *They found themselves in a dense forest.*

>**densely** *adverb*
dent (dents, denting, dented) *verb*
If somebody dents something smooth, they make a dip in it by hitting it.
dentist (dentists) *noun*
A dentist is someone who looks after people's teeth.
depart (departs, departing, departed) *verb*
When someone or something departs from a place, they leave it.
department (departments) *noun*
A department is one of the sections in a large organization such as a business or a hospital.
departure *noun*
Departure is going away from somewhere.
depend (depends, depending, depended) *verb*
1. If you depend on someone, you need them.
2. If you can depend on someone, you know you can trust them.
deposit (deposits) *noun*
A deposit is money you give in part payment of something when you agree to buy it.
depth *noun*
The depth of something, like a lake or a hole, is the distance from top to bottom.
describe (describes, describing, described) *verb*
If you describe a person or thing, you say what they are like.
desert (deserts) *noun*
A desert is a large area of land where there is very little water or rain, so hardly any plants can grow.
desert (deserts, deserting, deserted) *verb*
If people or animals desert a place, they leave it, so that it becomes empty.
deserted *adjective*
If a place is deserted, there are no people there.
deserve (deserves, deserving, deserved) *verb*
If you deserve something, you earn it by what you have done.
design (designs) *noun*
1. A design is a drawing to show what something should look like.
2. A design can also be a pattern that is used to decorate something.
design (designs, designing, designed) *verb*
If you design something, you plan it and make a drawing so that it can be built or made.
desk (desks) *noun*
A desk is a special table that people use when they are writing or reading. Desks often have drawers in them.
destroy (destroys, destroying, destroyed) *verb*
If someone destroys something, they damage it so much that it cannot be repaired.
detached *adjective*
A detached house is one that is not joined to any other house.
detail (details) *noun*
A detail is a small part or thing that you notice when you look at something carefully, or remember when you think about it.
detective (detectives) *noun*
A detective is someone whose job is to find something out, especially if it is to do with crime.
determined *adjective*
If you are determined to do something, you will not let anything stop you.
deterrent (deterrents) *noun*
A deterrent is something that prevents you from doing something by making you afraid of what will happen to you if you do it.
develop (develops, developing, developed) *verb*
1. When something develops, it changes over a period of time and becomes, for example, stronger or larger.
2. When a problem develops, it comes into existence.
3. If you develop something like a skill, you improve it by working hard at it.
dew *noun*
Dew is small drops of water that form on the ground and other surfaces outdoors during the night.

diagonal *adjective*
Something that is diagonal is slanting.
>diagonally *adverb*
diagram (diagrams) *noun*
A diagram is a drawing that explains something.
dial (dials) *noun*
A dial is a numbered disc on an instrument like a clock or a speedometer.
diamond (diamonds) *noun*
1. A diamond is a very hard precious stone. When it has been cut, it sparkles.
2. A diamond is also a shape with four straight sides, like a square but slightly flattened.
diary (diaries) *noun*
A diary is a book which has a space for each day. You use a diary to make a note of special dates, like your next visit to the dentist, or of things you have been doing during the day.
dice *noun*
A dice is a small cube made of something like wood or plastic. It has spots on each of its six sides.
dictionary (dictionaries) *noun*
A dictionary is a book in which words are listed in alphabetical order. It tells you what the words mean, and helps you to check the spelling.
die (dies, dying, died) *verb*
When a person, animal or plant dies, they stop living.
diesel (diesels) *noun*
A diesel is a vehicle with an engine that burns a special oil instead of petrol.
diet (diets) *noun*
1. A diet is the food that a person or animal eats regularly.
2. A diet is also a special range of food that a doctor tells someone to eat if they have a health or weight problem.
difference (differences) *noun*
The difference between two things is the way in which they are unlike each other.
different *adjective*
Something that is different from something else is not like it in one or more ways.
>differently *adverb*
difficult *adjective*
1. Something that is difficult is not easy to do.
2. If something is difficult to understand, you cannot understand it without thinking very hard about it.
difficulty (difficulties) *noun*
A difficulty is something that is a problem for you.
dig (digs, digging, dug) *verb*
When people dig, they push something like a spade into the ground to make a hole or to move the earth to somewhere else. When animals dig, they use their claws to make a hole.
digest (digests, digesting, digested) *verb*
When you digest food, it passes through your stomach and is broken down so that your body can use it.
digestion *noun*
Your digestion is the system in your body which digests your food.
digital *adjective*
Digital instruments, such as watches, have changing numbers instead of a dial with hands.
dim (dimmer, dimmest) *adjective*
If the light is dim, it is rather dark and it is hard to see things.
>dimly *adverb*
dimension (dimensions) *noun*
The dimensions of something are its measurements.
din *noun*
A din is a very loud and unpleasant noise that lasts for a long time.
dinghy (dinghies) *noun*
A dinghy is a small open boat that you sail or row.
dining room (dining rooms) *noun*
A dining room is the room where people have their meals.
dinner *noun*
Dinner is the main meal of the day.
dinnertime *noun*
Dinnertime is the time when dinner is eaten.
dinosaur (dinosaurs) *noun*

A dinosaur was a large reptile which lived and became extinct in prehistoric times.

dip (dips, dipping, dipped) *verb*
1. If you dip something into a liquid, you put it in and take it out again quickly.
2. If something like a road dips, it goes down suddenly to a lower level.

direct *adjective*
Direct means in a straight line without stopping, for example on a journey: *Is there a direct flight to Mexico City?*
>**directly** *adverb*

direct (directs, directing, directed) *verb*
A person who directs something, like a film or a television programme, is in charge of it.

direction (directions) *noun*
1. A direction is the way that someone or something is moving or pointing.
2. Directions are instructions that tell you what to do.

dirt *noun*
Dirt is dust, mud or stains on a surface or fabric.

dirty (dirtier, dirtiest) *adjective*
Something that is dirty is marked or covered with mud or stains and needs to be cleaned.

disagree (disagrees, disagreeing, disagreed) *verb*
If you disagree with someone, you think that what they are saying is wrong.

disappear (disappears, disappearing, disappeared) *verb*
If someone disappears, they go out of sight.

disappointed *adjective*
If you are disappointed, you are unhappy because what you were hoping for did not happen.

disappointment (disappointments) *noun*
1. Disappointment is being unhappy because what you were hoping for did not happen.
2. A disappointment is something which is not as good as you had hoped.

disaster (disasters) *noun*
1. A disaster is something very bad such as an earthquake or an air crash, especially one in which a lot of people are killed.
2. A disaster can also be anything that you think is extremely bad: *It would be a disaster if our team lost.*

disastrous *adjective*
A disastrous event is one that is extremely bad.
>**disastrously** *adverb*

disc (discs) *noun*
A disc is a flat, round object.

disco (discos) *noun*
A disco is a place where people go to dance to pop records.

discover (discovers, discovering, discovered) *verb*
When you discover something you did not know before, you find out about it.

discovery (discoveries) *noun*
1. When you make a discovery, you find out about something you did not know before.
2. When someone makes a new discovery, they find out something that nobody knew before.

discuss (discusses, discussing, discussed) *verb*
When you discuss something, you talk about it with someone else.

discussion *noun*
Discussion is talking or writing about something from several different points of view.

disease (diseases) *noun*
A disease is an illness in people, animals or plants.

disentangle (disentangles, disentangling, disentangled) *verb*
If you disentangle something, you remove it from where it has become mixed up with other objects.

disguise (disguises, disguising, disguised) *verb*
If you disguise yourself, you change the way you look so that people will not recognize you.

disgust *noun*
Disgust is a feeling of very strong dislike for someone or something, for example because of their appearance or behaviour.

dish (dishes) *noun*
A dish is a shallow container for cooking or serving meals in.
dishonest *adjective*
If someone is dishonest, they are not to be trusted.
>dishonestly *adverb*
dishwasher (dishwashers) *noun*
A dishwasher is a machine that washes and dries things like plates and saucepans.
disk (disks) *noun*
A disk is a small, round, flat, magnetic plate that is used for storing information in a computer.
dislike (dislikes, disliking, disliked) *verb*
If you dislike someone or something, you think they are unpleasant and you do not like them.
dismay *noun*
Dismay is a feeling of fear, worry or sadness, that is caused by something unexpected.
dismiss (dismisses, dismissing, dismissed) *verb*
When someone in authority dismisses you, they send you away.
disobedient *adjective*
If you are disobedient, you deliberately do not do what someone in authority tells you to do.
>disobediently *adverb*
disobey (disobeys, disobeying, disobeyed) *verb*
If someone disobeys, they deliberately do not do what they have been told to do.
display (displays) *noun*
1. A display is an arrangement of things that is designed to attract people's attention.
2. A display is also a public performance to entertain people: *There's a firework display in the park tonight.*
dissolve (dissolves, dissolving, dissolved) *verb*
If something, such as a powder, dissolves in a liquid, it becomes mixed with it.
distance (distances) *noun*
The distance between two things is the amount of space between them.
distant *adjective*
Distant means very far away.
>distantly *adverb*
distinct *adjective*
If something is distinct, you can hear or see it clearly.
>distinctly *adverb*
distress *noun*
Distress is being extremely unhappy or worried.
distribute (distributes, distributing, distributed) *verb*
If you distribute things like leaflets, you hand them out to several people.
district (districts) *noun*
The district is the area round a particular place: *He's the only doctor in this district.*
disturb (disturbs, disturbing, disturbed) *verb*
If you disturb someone, you interrupt them or spoil their peace and quiet.
disturbance (disturbances) *noun*
A disturbance is something that spoils people's peace and quiet.
ditch (ditches) *noun*
A ditch is a long, narrow channel dug at the side of a road or field, to drain water.
dive (dives, diving, dived) *verb*
When swimmers dive, they jump head first into water with their hands above their head.
divide (divides, dividing, divided) *verb*
1. When something is divided, it becomes separated into two or more smaller parts.
2. When you divide a larger number by a smaller number, you work out how many times the smaller number goes into the larger number: *35 divided by 5 is 7.*
division (divisions) *noun*
1. Division is separating something into two or more parts.
2. Division is also part of arithmetic, in which you divide one number by another.
3. A division is one of the groups of teams which make up a sports league. The teams in each division play against each other during the season.
dizzy (dizzier, dizziest) *adjective*
If you feel dizzy, you feel as though you are going to fall over.

doctor (doctors) *noun*
A doctor is a person who helps people when they are ill, by giving them advice or medicine.

document (documents) *noun*
A document is one or more pieces of paper with writing on, which give important information about something.

dodge (dodges, dodging, dodged) *verb*
If you dodge, you move suddenly out of the way.

dog (dogs) *noun*
A dog is an animal that is often kept as a pet, or used to hunt or guard things.

doll (dolls) *noun*
A doll is a child's toy that looks like a baby or a small person.

dollar (dollars) *noun*
A dollar is a unit of money in some countries, such as the USA, Canada and Australia.

dolphin (dolphins) *noun*
A dolphin is a kind of whale measuring about two or three metres. Dolphins are friendly, intelligent animals that live in groups in the Mediterranean Sea and the Atlantic.

dome (domes) *noun*
A dome is a round roof on a building.

domino (dominoes) *noun*
A domino is a small, rectangular block, marked with spots. Dominoes are used for playing games.

donkey (donkeys) *noun*
A donkey is a kind of ass and belongs to the horse family. It is smaller than a horse, with longer ears. The noise it makes is called a bray.

door (doors) *noun*
A door is usually made of wood, glass or metal. It swings or slides to open and close a cupboard, room or building.

dormitory (dormitories) *noun*
A dormitory is a large bedroom where several people sleep.

dose (doses) *noun*
A dose is a measured amount of a medicine that is to be taken at one time.

dot (dots) *noun*
A dot is a very small, round mark.

double *adjective*
1. If something is double the size or amount of something else, it is twice as big.
2. Double is used to describe something that is for use by two people: *There are three double bedrooms.*
3. You say double when there are two of the same kind: *That egg had a double yolk.*

double (doubles, doubling, doubled) *verb*
1. If you double something like a piece of paper, you fold it in half.
2. If something doubles, it becomes twice as big.

doubt (doubts) *noun*
If you have a doubt about something, you are not sure about it.

doubtful *adjective*
1. Something that is doubtful seems unlikely or uncertain.
2. If you are doubtful about something, you feel unsure about it.
>**doubtfully** *adverb*

dough *noun*
Dough is a floury mixture that can be cooked to make things like pastry or bread. It has a soft, rubbery feel.

doughnut (doughnuts) *noun*
A doughnut is a small cake of sweet dough that has been cooked in hot fat. Some doughnuts have jam inside, and some have a hole in the middle.

down *noun*
Down is small, soft feathers that grow on young birds. It is sometimes used to fill pillows or duvets.

downhill *adverb*
If something is moving downhill, it is moving down a slope.

downstairs *adverb*
1. If you go downstairs, you go towards the ground floor.
2. If something or someone is downstairs, they are on a lower floor than you are.

doze (dozes, dozing, dozed) *verb*
When you doze, you sleep lightly for a short period.

dozen (dozens) *noun*
If you have a dozen things, you have 12 of them.

drag (drags, dragging, dragged) *verb*
1. If you drag something along, you pull it along the ground because it is too heavy to carry.
2. If you drag yourself away from something, you force yourself to leave although you do not want to.

dragon (dragons) *noun*
In stories, a dragon is an animal like a big lizard. It has wings and claws and breathes out fire.

drain (drains) *noun*
A drain is a pipe that carries water away.

drain (drains, draining, drained) *verb*
If a liquid drains away, it flows slowly to somewhere else.

drainpipe (drainpipes) *noun*
A drainpipe is a large pipe through which unwanted water flows.

drama (dramas) *noun*
1. A drama is a serious play for the theatre, television or radio.
2. Drama is exciting and interesting things that happen.

dramatic *adjective*
1. Something dramatic is very exciting, interesting and impressive.
2. If something you say or do is dramatic, it is said or done suddenly, and is meant to impress or surprise people.
>**dramatically** *adverb*

draught (draughts) *noun*
A draught is a stream of air coming into a room or vehicle.

draughts *noun*
Draughts is a game for two people, played with 24 round pieces on a special board.

draw (draws, drawing, drew, drawn) *verb*
1. When you draw, you use something like a pencil or crayon to make a picture or a pattern.
2. When you draw the curtains, you pull them across a window.
3. If two people or teams draw in a game, they finish with the same number of points.

drawbridge (drawbridges) *noun*
A drawbridge is a bridge that can be pulled up to stop people getting into a castle.

drawer (drawers) *noun*
A drawer is a box that slides in and out of a piece of furniture.

drawing pin (drawing pins) *noun*
A drawing pin is a short nail with a flat top. You pin papers to a board by pressing it with your thumb.

dread (dreads, dreading, dreaded) *verb*
If you dread something that is going to happen or may happen, you feel worried about it because you think it will be unpleasant.

dreadful *adjective*
Something that is dreadful is very bad or unpleasant.
>**dreadfully** *adverb*

dream (dreams, dreaming, dreamed/dreamt) *verb*
1. When you dream, pictures and sounds happen in your mind while you are asleep.
2. If you dream while you are awake, you think about things you would very much like to happen, but which are quite unlikely.

dress (dresses) *noun*
A dress is a piece of clothing worn by women and girls. It covers their body and the hem reaches to somewhere on their legs.

dress (dresses, dressing, dressed) *verb*
When you dress, you put on your clothes.

dressing gown (dressing gowns) *noun*
A dressing gown is a piece of clothing shaped like a loose-fitting coat, which you wear over your pyjamas or nightdress.

dressing table (dressing tables) *noun*
A dressing table is a small table with drawers and a mirror, which is used in a bedroom.

dribble (dribbles, dribbling, dribbled) *verb*
1. When babies dribble, water trickles from their mouth.
2. When players dribble the ball in a game like football, they kick it several times quickly to keep it moving.

drift (drifts) *noun*
A drift is a mass of snow that has been built up by the movement of the wind.

drift (drifts, drifting, drifted) *verb*
1. When something drifts, it is carried by wind or water.
2. To drift can also mean to move somewhere slowly and without any purpose.
3. If snow drifts, it builds up into piles.
drill (drills) *noun*
A drill is a tool or machine for making holes.
drink (drinks) *noun*
A drink is a liquid which is all right to swallow.
drink (drinks, drinking, drank, drunk) *verb*
When you drink, you take liquid into your mouth and swallow it.
drip (drips, dripping, dripped) *verb*
When something drips, drops of liquid fall from it one after the other.
drive (drives, driving, drove, driven) *verb*
If someone drives a vehicle, they make it move, and steer it where they want it to go.
driver (drivers) *noun*
A driver is a person who drives a car, bus, taxi or train.
drop (drops) *noun*
A drop is a small amount of liquid shaped like a little ball.
drop (drops, dropping, dropped) *verb*
1. If you drop something, you let it fall, usually by accident.
2. If the temperature drops, you feel colder.
drought (droughts) *noun*
A drought is a long period of time when no rain falls.
drown (drowns, drowning, drowned) *verb*
If someone drowns, they die because they have gone under water and cannot breathe.
drug (drugs) *noun*
A drug is a substance that is used to treat or prevent disease. There are many different kinds of drugs.
drum (drums) *noun*
A drum is a musical instrument shaped like a cylinder. It has skin stretched tightly over the end, and you beat it with sticks or your hand.
dry (drier, driest) *adjective*
Something that is dry has no moisture in it.
duchess (duchesses) *noun*
A duchess is the wife of a duke, or a woman who has the same rank as a duke.
duck (ducks) *noun*
A duck is a common water bird with short legs and webbed feet.
due *adjective*
If something is due at a particular time, it is expected to happen or arrive at that time.
duke (dukes) *noun*
A duke is a man who has a rank just below that of a prince.
dull (duller, dullest) *adjective*
1. Something that is dull is not very interesting.
2. Dull weather is rather cloudy.
3. Dull sounds are not very clear or loud.
4. A dull pain is not very sharp.
5. Light or a colour that is dull is rather dark.
>**dully** *adverb*
dumb *adjective*
1. Someone who is dumb is completely unable to speak.
2. If you are dumb, you are unable to speak for a short while because for example you are angry or shocked.
>**dumbly** *adverb*
dungeon (dungeons) *noun*
A dungeon is a dark underground prison in a castle.
dusk *noun*
Dusk is the part of the day when it is just beginning to get dark.
dust *noun*
1. Dust is very small, dry pieces of earth or sand that fly up from roads when traffic goes by.
2. Dust is also fine powdered dirt that you find inside, on floors and furniture.
dustbin (dustbins) *noun*
A dustbin is a metal or plastic container with a lid, which people keep outside their houses to put rubbish in.
duster (dusters) *noun*
A duster is a soft cloth for removing dust from furniture and ornaments.

dusty (dustier, dustiest) *adjective*
1. Something like a road that is dusty is full of little bits of dry earth, usually because there has been no rain for a long time.
2. Things in a building that are dusty are covered in dust.
duvet (duvets) *noun*
A duvet is a bed cover filled with feathers or other lightweight material.
dwarf (dwarfs) *noun*
In fairy stories, a dwarf is a creature who is like a small, ugly man and often has magic powers.
dye (dyes, dyeing, dyed) *verb*
If you dye something, such as hair or cloth, you change its colour by soaking it in a special liquid.

E

eager *adjective*
If you are eager to do something, you want to do it very much.
>**eagerly** *adverb*
eagle (eagles) *noun*
An eagle is a very large, strong bird with a sharp, curved beak and claws. It kills small animals for food.
ear (ears) *noun*
1. Your ears are the part of your body that you use for hearing.
2. The ears of a cereal plant, such as barley or wheat, are the parts at the top of the stem. They contain the seeds or grain that are used for food.
early (earlier, earliest) *adjective*
If you are early, you get there before the time arranged.
early *adverb*
1. Early means near the beginning of a day: *I got up early and had my breakfast.*
2. Early can also mean near the beginning of a period of time such as a week or a year: *We bought that early last week.*
earn (earns, earning, earned) *verb*
If you earn something, such as money, you get it by working for it.
earring (earrings) *noun*
An earring is a piece of jewellery that is fixed to the ear for decoration.
earth (earths) *noun*
1. The earth is the planet we live on.
2. Earth is the soil that plants grow in.
3. An earth is a hole in the ground where an animal such as a fox lives.
earthquake (earthquakes) *noun*
An earthquake is a shaking of the ground caused by movement of the earth's crust.
earwig (earwigs) *noun*
An earwig is a small, thin, brown insect with a pair of pincers at the back end of its body.
easel (easels) *noun*
An easel is a stand used to hold a blackboard or a picture that an artist is painting.
east *noun*
East is one of the four main points of the compass: *She looked towards the east to watch the sun rise.*
easy (easier, easiest) *adjective*
Something that is easy can be done without difficulty.
>**easily** *adverb*
eat (eats, eating, ate, eaten) *verb*
1. When you eat, you put food in your mouth, chew it and swallow it.
2. To eat also means to have a meal.
eatable *adjective*
Something that is eatable is good enough for a person to eat and enjoy.
echo (echoes) *noun*
An echo is a sound that bounces back from something, like the walls of a cave or building.
eclipse (eclipses) *noun*
An eclipse of the sun is a time when the moon comes between the earth and the sun, so that for a little while you cannot see part or all of the sun.
edge (edges) *noun*
1. An edge is the end of a flat object, such as a table or a book.

2. The edge of a large area is the place where it stops and another area begins: *They played at the water's edge.*

education *noun*

1. Education is the system of teaching people, usually at a school or college.

2. Education can also mean the gradual way in which a person gains knowledge and understanding through learning.

eel (eels) *noun*

An eel is a long, thin fish that looks like a snake. Young eels are called elvers.

effect (effects) *noun*

1. An effect is something that is changed because of something else: *I'm still suffering from the effects of my cold.*

2. The effects in a film or a play are things like sounds, lighting or scenery.

efficient *adjective*

Someone or something that is efficient does a job well without wasting time or energy.

>**efficiently** *adverb*

effort (efforts) *noun*

An effort is an attempt to do something by using a lot of energy.

>**make an effort** *phrase*

If you make an effort, you try very hard to do something.

egg (eggs) *noun*

1. An egg is a cell produced in the body of a woman or a female animal, which can develop into a baby if it is fertilized.

2. An egg is also an oval object laid by female birds and some other creatures. A young bird or animal develops inside the egg until it is ready to come out.

3. An egg can also be a hen's egg, which people cook and eat.

elastic *noun*

Elastic is a rubber material that stretches when you pull it and springs back to its normal size when you let it go.

elbow (elbows) *noun*

Your elbow is the joint in the middle of your arm where it bends.

electric *adjective*

A machine or other object that is electric works by using electricity.

electrician (electricians) *noun*

An electrician is a person whose job is to put in and repair electrical equipment.

electricity *noun*

Electricity is a form of energy that is used for heating and lighting. It also provides power for equipment such as fridges and irons.

electronic *adjective*

An electronic machine or other object is one, like a computer or a television, that works by using silicon chips or valves.

>**electronically** *adverb*

elephant (elephants) *noun*

An elephant is a very large animal with a long nose called a trunk. An adult elephant has tusks at each side of its mouth. Elephants live in groups called herds in India and Africa. Baby elephants are called calves.

elf (elves) *noun*

In fairy stories, an elf is a tiny boy who can do magic things.

elm (elms) *noun*

An elm is a tall tree that loses its leaves in winter.

embarrass (embarrasses, embarrassing, embarrassed) *verb*

To embarrass someone means to make them feel shy, ashamed or guilty about something.

embryo (embryos) *noun*

An embryo is a human being or animal in the very early stages of its development inside its mother's body.

emerald (emeralds) *noun*

An emerald is a bright green precious stone.

emerge (emerges, emerging, emerged) *verb*

To emerge means to come out from somewhere like a room or vehicle, or from a place where you could not be seen.

emergency (emergencies) *noun*

An emergency is something difficul and sometimes dangerous that happens unexpectedly. If there is an emergency, someone has to do something about it quickly.

employer (employers) *noun*

Employers are people who have other people working for them.

empty (emptier, emptiest) *adjective*
Something, such as a box, vehicle or room, that is empty has no people or things in it.
empty (empties, emptying, emptied) *verb*
If you empty a container, you pour or take everything out of it.
enchanted *adjective*
In stories, someone or something that is enchanted is under a magic spell.
encourage (encourages, encouraging, encouraged) *verb*
If you encourage someone, you tell them that what they are doing is good and they should go on doing it.
end (ends) *noun*
1. The end of something is the last part of it.
2. The ends of something long and narrow are its two short sides: *They sat on each end of the seesaw.*
enemy (enemies) *noun*
Your enemy is someone who fights against you.
energetic *adjective*
Someone who is energetic is lively and determined to succeed.
>**energetically** *adverb*
energy *noun*
1. Energy is the strength to do things.
2. Energy is also the power from things like electricity that makes machines work.
engine (engines) *noun*
1. An engine is a machine that uses heat or other kinds of energy to make a vehicle move.
2. An engine is also a large vehicle that pulls a railway train.
engineer (engineers) *noun*
An engineer is a person who designs or makes things such as instruments, machinery or bridges.
enjoy (enjoys, enjoying, enjoyed) *verb*
If you enjoy doing something, you like doing it very much.
enjoyment *noun*
Enjoyment is the feeling of pleasure that you have when you do something you enjoy.
enormous *adjective*
Something that is enormous is very, very large.
>**enormously** *adverb*
entertain (entertains, entertaining, entertained) *verb*
If you entertain somebody, you do something that they enjoy and find amusing.
entertainment *noun*
Entertainment is things that people watch for pleasure, such as shows and films.
enthusiasm *noun*
Enthusiasm is a lively interest in something.
entire *adjective*
Entire means the whole of something: *Now I shall have to do the entire job again.*
>**entirely** *adverb*
entrance (entrances) *noun*
An entrance is the way into a place.
envelope (envelopes) *noun*
An envelope is a folded paper cover for a letter or card.
envious *adjective*
If you are envious of somebody, you wish you could have the same things that they have.
>**enviously** *adverb*
environment (environments) *noun*
1. The environment is the natural world of land, sea, air, plants and animals, that exists around towns and cities.
2. Someone's environment is the kind of place they live in, and the people and things that have an effect on them.
envy (envies, envying, envied) *verb*
If you envy somebody, you wish you could have the same things that they have.
episode (episodes) *noun*
An episode is one of the parts that a television, radio or magazine serial is divided into.
equal *adjective*
If two things are equal or if one thing is equal to another, they are the same as each other in size, number or amount.
>**equally** *adverb*
equator *noun*
The equator is an imaginary line drawn round the centre of the earth, at an equal

distance from the North Pole and the South Pole.

equipment *noun*
Equipment is the things that are used for a particular purpose: *We need some new kitchen equipment – especially a fridge.*

erupt (erupts, erupting, erupted) *verb*
When a volcano erupts, it sends out a lot of hot molten lava, ash and steam.

escape (escapes, escaping, escaped) *verb*
If a person or animal escapes, they get away from whatever is holding them.

especially *adverb*
1. You say especially when one of a group is special in some way: *You've all behaved badly today, especially Tom.*
2. Especially can also mean 'even more so': *I like cats, especially short-haired ones.*

essay (essays) *noun*
An essay is a short piece of writing on a particular subject.

essential *adjective*
Something that is essential is absolutely necessary.
>**essentially** *adverb*

estimate (estimates, estimating, estimated) *verb*
If you estimate something, you make a guess based on what you know.

evaporation *noun*
Evaporation is when a liquid is gradually changed into a gas, for example by the effects of the sun or the wind, or by being heated.

even *adverb*
You say even when something is rather surprising: *I like you even when you are not very nice to me.*

even *adjective*
1. If something like a path is even, it is smooth and flat.
2. An even number can be divided exactly by two.
>**evenly** *adverb*

evening (evenings) *noun*
The evening is the part of the day between the end of the afternoon and the time when you go to bed.

event (events) *noun*
1. An event is something that happens, especially when it is unusual or important.
2. An event is also a planned and organized occasion such as a sports day.

eventually *adverb*
Eventually means in the end, after a lot of delays or problems.

ever *adverb*
Ever means at any time in the past or future: *Have you ever seen such a big dog?*

evergreen (evergreens) *noun*
An evergreen is a tree or other plant which has leaves all the year round.

evidence *noun*
Evidence is the information which is used in a court of law to try to prove something.

evolution *noun*
Evolution is the change in the form of animals and plants that has taken place gradually over very many generations.

evolve (evolves, evolving, evolved) *verb*
When living things like animals or plants, evolve, they gradually change and develop into different forms.

exactly *adverb*
1. You can say exactly when you mean no more and no less: *My father is exactly two metres tall.*
2. Exactly also means just right: *He found a piece that fitted exactly.*

exaggerate (exaggerates, exaggerating, exaggerated) *verb*
If you exaggerate, you say something is better or worse than it really is.

exam (exams) *noun*
An exam is a test that people take to show how much they have learned. Exam is short for examination.

examination (examinations) *noun*
See exam.

examine (examines, examining, examined) *verb*
1. If you examine something, you look at it carefully or closely.
2. If a doctor examines you, he or she looks at you carefully to see whether there is anything wrong with your health.

example (examples) *noun*
An example is one person or thing that shows what the rest of a set is like: *This is an example of my work.*
>**set an example** *phrase*
If you set an example, you behave so that others will copy you.
excellent *adjective*
Something that is excellent is very, very good.
except *preposition*
Except means apart from: *Everyone went outside except David, who had a cold.*
exception (exceptions) *noun*
An exception is something that does not fit in with a general rule: *With the exception of bats, mammals cannot fly.*
exchange (exchanges, exchanging, exchanged) *verb*
If you exchange something, you replace it with something else.
>**in exchange** *phrase*
If you do something in exchange, you do it because someone has done something for you.
excite (excites, exciting, excited) *verb*
If something excites you, you feel happy and unable to rest.
excitement *noun*
Excitement is a feeling of being very happy and nervous.
exciting *adjective*
Something that is exciting makes you feel very happy and interested.
exclaim (exclaims, exclaiming, exclaimed) *verb*
When you exclaim, you speak suddenly or loudly, because you are excited or angry.
exclamation (exclamations) *noun*
An exclamation is a word or sentence that is spoken suddenly or loudly.
exclamation mark (exclamation marks) *noun*
An exclamation mark is the sign (!) which is used in writing to show that the word, phrase or sentence is an exclamation.
excuse (excuses) *noun*
An excuse is a reason you give for doing something, or not doing it.
excuse (excuses, excusing, excused) *verb*
If you excuse someone for something they have done wrong, you forgive them for it.
exercise (exercises) *noun*
1. Exercises are regular movements you make to keep fit.
2. An exercise is a short piece of work that you do in school to help you learn something, such as arithmetic.
exhausted *adjective*
When you are exhausted, you are so tired you have no energy left.
exist (exists, existing, existed) *verb*
Things that exist are present in the world or universe now.
existence *noun*
Existence is being alive or real.
exit (exits) *noun*
An exit is the way out of a place.
expand (expands, expanding, expanded) *verb*
When something expands, it gets bigger.
expect (expects, expecting, expected) *verb*
If you expect something, you think it will happen.
expedition (expeditions) *noun*
An expedition is an organized journey, usually for a particular purpose, such as exploring a place.
expel (expels, expelling, expelled) *verb*
If someone is expelled from their school, they are told not to come back, because their behaviour has been very bad indeed.
expensive *adjective*
Something that is expensive costs a lot of money.
>**expensively** *adverb*
experience (experiences) *noun*
1. Experience is knowledge or skill someone has gained in a particular job because they have been doing it for a long time.
2. Experience can also be all the events and feelings that make up someone's life.
3. An experience is something that happens to you.
experience (experiences, experiencing, experienced) *verb*
1. If you experience something, you feel it.

2. If you experience a problem, you are affected by it.
experiment (experiments) *noun*
An experiment is a test that you do in order to discover something or to prove or demonstrate something.
expert (experts) *noun*
An expert is someone who is very skilled at doing something or who knows a lot about something.
explain (explains, explaining, explained) *verb*
1. When you explain, you give reasons for something that happened.
2. To explain also means to say something that will help people to understand.
explanation (explanations) *noun*
1. An explanation is something that tells you why something happened: *Sorry I'm late - there is an explanation.*
2. An explanation is also something that helps people to understand something: *She gave us a clear explanation of the way gears work.*
explode (explodes, exploding, exploded) *verb*
If something, such as a firework, explodes, it bursts with a loud bang.
explore (explores, exploring, explored) *verb*
If you explore a place, you go there because you have not been there before, or because nobody has been there before, to find out what it is like.
explosion (explosions) *noun*
An explosion is a sudden, loud burst of energy, for example one caused by a bomb.
express (expresses) *noun*
An express is a fast train or coach which does not stop at many places.
express (expresses, expressing, expressed) *verb*
If you express an idea or feeling, you put it into words or show it by the way you act: *He could only express the way he felt by bursting into tears.*
expression (expressions) *noun*
Your expression is the look on your face that lets people know what you are thinking or feeling.
extension (extensions) *noun*
1. An extension is a new room or building that is added on to an existing building.
2. An extension is also something which is connected to a piece of equipment to make it reach something further away.
3. An extension can also be an extra telephone with the same number as the main telephone.
extinct *adjective*
If an animal or plant family is extinct, it no longer has any living members: *The dodo has been extinct for more than 300 years.*
extra *adjective*
1. You use extra to describe someone or something that is added to others of the same kind: *You'd better take an extra jumper - it's going to be cold.*
2. You can also use extra to describe an amount of money that is more than the expected amount: *You have to send an extra 50p for postage.*
extraordinary *adjective*
Someone or something that is extraordinary is very special or unusual.
>**extraordinarily** *adverb*
extreme *adjective*
Extreme means very great: *Extreme cold can cause many problems.*
>**extremely** *adverb*
eye (eyes) *noun*
1. Your eyes are the part of your body that you use for seeing.
2. The eye of a needle is the small hole at one end that you thread the thread through.
>**catch someone's eye** *phrase*
1. If something catches your eye, you suddenly notice it.
2. If you catch someone's eye, you do something to make them notice you.
eyebrow (eyebrows) *noun*
Your eyebrows are the lines of hair which grow above each eye.
eyelash (eyelashes) *noun*
Your eyelashes are the hairs which grow on the edge of your eyelids.

eyelid (eyelids) *noun*
Your eyelids are the pieces of skin which cover your eyes when you close them.
eyesight *noun*
Eyesight is the ability to see.

F

fable (fables) *noun*
A fable is a story that is meant to teach you something. Fables often have animals as the main characters.
fabric (fabrics) *noun*
A fabric is a material that is made in some way such as weaving or knitting.
face (faces) *noun*
1. Your face is the front part of your head, from your chin to the top of your forehead.
2 The face of a clock or watch is the part with the numbers on it that shows the time.
fact (facts) *noun*
A fact is something that is true.
factory (factories) *noun*
A factory is a large building where a lot of things are made, usually with the help of machines.
fade (fades, fading, faded) *verb*
1. When a colour fades, it gets paler.
2 When the light fades, it get darker, usually because the sun is going down.
fail (fails, failing, failed) *verb*
1. If someone fails when they try to do something, they cannot do it.
2 If something fails, it stops working, or does not do what it is supposed to do: *The brakes failed, and the car hit a wall.*
failure (failures) *noun*
If something is a failure, it is disappointing: *The picnic was a failure – it rained all day.*
faint (faints, fainting, fainted) *verb*
If someone faints, they become unconscious for a short time.
faint (fainter, faintest) *adjective*
Something, like a sound or mark, that is faint is not easy to hear or see.
>**faintly** *adverb*
fair (fairer, fairest) *adjective*
Something that is fair seems reasonable to most people.
fair (fairs) *noun*
A fair is an outside entertainment, where exciting things like roundabouts are set up for a few days so that people can have fun.
fairly *adverb*
Fairly means quite or rather: *We went early and the roads were fairly clear.*
fairy (fairies) *noun*
A fairy is an imaginary creature in children's stories. Fairies are described as tiny women or girls, usually with wings, who have magical powers.
fairy tale (fairy tales) *noun*
A fairy tale is a story for children in which magical things happen.
fake (fakes) *noun*
A fake is something which is not what it seems to be, but has been made to trick people into thinking it is genuine.
fall (falls, falling, fell, fallen) *verb*
1. When someone or something falls, they suddenly drop towards the ground.
2 When night falls, it becomes dark.
3 If someone's face falls, they suddenly look upset or disappointed.
false (falser, falsest) *adjective*
1. If something is false, it is not the real thing: *Her grandfather lost a front tooth and had to have a false one.*
2 If something you say is false, it is not true.
>**falsely** *adverb*
familiar *adjective*
If someone or something is familiar to you, you can recognize them or know them well because you have seen, heard or experienced them before.
family (families) *noun*
1. A family is a group of people made up of parents and their children.
2 A family is also a group of animals or plants of the same kind: *Weasels, stoats and otters all belong to the weasel family.*
famine (famines) *noun*
When there is a famine in a country, there is

little or no food, usually because the crops have failed.

famous *adjective*
Someone or something famous is very well known.

fan (fans) *noun*
1. A fan is a flat object, usually made of folded paper. You wave a fan to move the air and make yourself feel cooler.
2. If you are a fan of a sport or of someone famous, you like them very much and are very interested in them.

fantasy (fantasies) *noun*
1. A fantasy is a story about things that do not exist in the real world.
2. A fantasy is also something pleasant you think about and hope will happen, although it is unlikely.

far (farther/further, farthest/furthest) *adjective*
You use far to describe something that is a long way away: *The Arctic Circle is in the far north.*

far (farther/further, farther/furthest) *adverb*
1. Far means a long way away: *Are you going far?*
2. You use far to ask questions about distance: *How far is the nearest town?*

>**far and wide** *phrase*
Far and wide means in lots of places or over a very large area: *I hunted far and wide for those shoes you wanted.*

fare (fares) *noun*
A fare is the money that you pay for a journey in something like a plane or a train.

farm (farms) *noun*
A farm is a large area of land that is used for growing crops or keeping animals. A farm also has buildings on it, such as a house where the farmer lives, and barns for storing things in.

farmer (farmers) *noun*
A farmer is a person who owns or manages a farm.

farmhouse (farmhouses) *noun*
A farmhouse is the main house on a farm, where the farmer lives.

farmyard (farmyards) *noun*
A farmyard is the small area of land around or between the buildings on a farm.

fascinate (fascinates, fascinating, fascinated) *verb*
If something fascinates you, it interests you very much.

fashion (fashions) *noun*
A fashion is the style of things like clothes that are popular at a particular time.

fast (faster, fastest) *adjective*
1. Someone or something that is fast can move very quickly.
2. If a watch or clock is fast, it is moving too quickly and shows a time that is later than the real time.

fast *adverb*
Something that is held fast is firmly fixed.

fast (fasts, fasting, fasted) *verb*
If someone fasts, they eat no food for a period of time.

fasten (fastens, fastening, fastened) *verb*
When you fasten something, you close it or do it up with something like a button, strap or catch: *Remember to fasten your safety belt.*

fat (fatter, fattest) *adjective*
A person or animal that is fat has too much flesh on their body.

fat (fats) *noun*
1. Fat is the extra flesh that people and animals have under their skin. It is used to store energy and to help keep them warm.
2. Fat is also a solid or liquid that comes from animals or vegetables, which is used in cooking.

fate (fates) *noun*
Someone's fate is what happens to them.

father (fathers) *noun*
Your father is the man who is one of your parents.

fault (faults) *noun*
1. A fault is something wrong with the way something was made.
2. If people say something is your fault, they are blaming you for something bad that has happened.

>**find fault** *phrase*
If you find fault with somebody, you look for mistakes and talk about them unkindly.
favour (favours) *noun*
A favour is something kind you do for someone because they have asked you to.
favourite *adjective*
Your favourite person or thing is the one you like better than all the others: *This teddy is my favourite toy.*
fax (faxes) *noun*
A fax is an exact copy of a document that can be sent to someone by using a special machine.
fear (fears) *noun*
Fear is the nasty feeling you have when you think you are in danger.
feast (feasts) *noun*
A feast is a large and special meal to which lots of people are invited.
feat (feats) *noun*
A feat is an impressive and difficult act.
feather (feathers) *noun*
A feather is one of the very light pieces that make up a bird's coat.
feature (features) *noun*
1. A feature of something is a particular part of it which you notice because it seems important or interesting.
2. A feature is also a special article in a newspaper or magazine, or a special radio or television programme.
3. Someone's features are their eyes, nose, mouth and other parts of their face.
February *noun*
February is the second month of the year. It has 28 days except in a leap year, when it has 29.
feed (feeds, feeding, fed) *verb*
If you feed a person or animal, you give them food.
feel (feels, feeling, felt) *verb*
1. If you feel something, like happy, excited or sad, that is the way you are at that time.
2. If you feel an object, you touch it to find out something about it, such as whether it is rough or smooth.
3. If you feel like doing something, you want to do it.
feeler (feelers) *noun*
An insect's feelers are the two stalks on its head. It uses its feelers to find out things about the objects around it.
feeling (feelings) *noun*
1. A feeling is something you feel, like anger or happiness.
2. Your feelings are things that you think and feel about something, but might not tell people about.
>**hurt someone's feelings** *phrase*
If you hurt someone's feelings, you upset them by something that you say or do.
felt *noun*
Felt is a material made from threads of something, like wool, packed tightly together to make a thick cloth.
female (females) *noun*
A female is an animal that belongs to the sex that can have babies.
fence (fences) *noun*
A fence is something that divides two areas of land. It is usually made of wood or wire stretched between wooden posts.
ferocious *adjective*
An animal or person that is ferocious behaves in a very violent and cruel way.
>**ferociously** *adverb*
ferry (ferries) *noun*
A ferry is a boat that takes passengers and sometimes vehicles across a short stretch of water.
festival (festivals) *noun*
A festival is a date or time of the year when people have a holiday because of something special.
fetch (fetches, fetching, fetched) *verb*
If you fetch something, you go and get it and bring it back.
fever (fevers) *noun*
If you have a fever when you are ill, you have a high temperature.
fibre (fibres) *noun*
A fibre is a thin thread of something, such as wool, cotton or nylon.
fiction *noun*
Fiction is books or stories about people and

events made up by the author.

fidget (fidgets, fidgeting, fidgeted) *verb*
If you fidget, you keep moving your hands or feet or changing your position slightly, for example because you are nervous or bored.

field (fields) *noun*
A field is land where crops are grown, or an area of rough grass where horses, sheep or cattle are kept.

fierce (fiercer, fiercest) *adjective*
1. A person who is fierce looks or sounds angry.
2. An animal that is fierce is dangerous.
>**fiercely** *adverb*

fight (fights, fighting, fought) *verb*
If you fight, you try to hurt someone in some way, such as hitting them with your fists.

figure (figures) *noun*
1. A figure is any of the numbers from 0 to 9.
2. You say you can see a figure when you can see someone, but not very clearly: *It was just getting dark when I saw a small figure coming towards me.*

file (files) *noun*
1. A file is a box or folded piece of card where people keep things like letters.
2. A file is also a metal tool with rough surfaces which is used to make things like wood or metal smooth.

fill (fills, filling, filled) *verb*
If you fill something, you put so much into it there is no room for any more.

film (films) *noun*
1. A film is moving pictures shown on a screen.
2. Film is a long, narrow piece of plastic that is used in a camera to take photographs.

filthy (filthier, filthiest) *adjective*
If something is filthy, it is very, very dirty.

fin (fins) *noun*
A fish's fins are like small wings that stick out of its body. They help the fish to swim and to keep its balance.

final *adjective*
In a series of any kind, the final one is the last one.
>**finally** *adverb*

find (finds, finding, found) *verb*
When you find someone or something, you see the person or thing you have been looking for.

fine (finer, finest) *adjective*
1. Something that is fine is very good indeed.
2. Something like a thread or a nib that is fine is very thin.
3. If you say you are fine, you mean you are well and happy.
4. When the weather is fine, it is dry and sunny.

fine (fines) *noun*
A fine is money that is paid as a punishment.

finger (fingers) *noun*
Your fingers are the four long, jointed parts at the end of your hand. Sometimes when people say fingers they mean thumbs as well.
>**all fingers and thumbs** *phrase*
If you say someone is all fingers and thumbs, you mean they are clumsy at doing something with their hands, such as tying a knot.

fingernail (fingernails) *noun*
Your fingernails are the thin, hard areas that cover the end of each of your fingers.

finish *noun*
The finish of something like a race is the end of it.

finish (finishes, finishing, finished) *verb*
When you finish something, like a meal, you reach the end of it.

fir (firs) *noun*
A fir is a tall, pointed, evergreen tree with leaves like needles. Firs have cones which carry their seeds.

fire (fires) *noun*
1. A fire is a burning pile of coal or wood that people make to keep warm.
2. A fire is also something powered by gas or electricity that gives out heat.
3. A fire can also be when something, like a building or a forest, is burning and being damaged or destroyed by the flames.

fire (fires, firing, fired) *verb*
If someone fires a gun, a bullet is sent from the gun they are using.

fire brigade (fire brigades) *noun*
The fire brigade is an organization which has the job of putting out fires.

fire engine (fire engines) *noun*
A fire engine is a large vehicle that carries firemen and equipment for putting out fires.
fireman (firemen) *noun*
A fireman is a person whose job is to put out fires. Firemen also rescue people or animals who are trapped.
fireplace (fireplaces) *noun*
A fireplace is a space at the bottom of a wall in a room. It has a chimney leading out of it so that the smoke can escape when a fire is lit.
firework (fireworks) *noun*
A firework is a small object that burns with coloured flames or sparks when you light it. Some fireworks make a loud noise, and some shoot up into the air. Sometimes people let off a lot of fireworks when it is a special day.
firm (firmer, firmest) *adjective*
1. Something that is firm does not change much in shape when you press it, but is not completely hard.
2. If someone is firm with you about something, you know they will not change their mind.
>**firmly** *adverb*
first *adjective*
The first person or thing is the one that comes before all the others: *He's always the first child to arrive in the morning.*
first *adverb*
When you say something happened first, you mean it happened before everything else: *First I went to my friend's house, and then to the shops.*
first aid *noun*
First aid is a simple treatment given as soon as possible to a person who is injured or who suddenly becomes ill.
fish (fish/fishes) *noun*
A fish is a creature that lives in water. It has fins and a tail. There are many different kinds of fish.
fisherman (fishermen) *noun*
A fisherman is a person who catches fish, either as a job or for sport.
fishing *noun*
Fishing is the job, sport or hobby of catching fish.
fishmonger (fishmongers) *noun*
A fishmonger is a shopkeeper who sells fish.
fist (fists) *noun*
You make a fist by tucking your fingers into the palm of your hand. You usually do this if you are cross, or are holding something tightly.
fit (fitter, fittest) *adjective*
Someone who is fit is healthy.
fit (fits) *noun*
If you have a fit of something like coughing, you suddenly start doing it and find it hard to stop.
fit (fits, fitting, fitted) *verb*
1. If something such as clothing fits you, it is the right size for you.
2. If something fits something else, it is the right size to go with it: *This is the lid that fits that box.*
3. If one or more things fit into something else, it is big enough to hold them.
fix (fixes, fixing, fixed) *verb*
1. If you fix something that has broken, you make it work again.
2. If you fix something somewhere, you put it there firmly so that it cannot be moved: *She fixed a lamp to the wall outside.*
fizzy (fizzier, fizziest) *adjective*
A fizzy drink or other liquid is full of little bubbles and gas.
flag (flags) *noun*
A flag is a piece of cloth that can be fixed to a pole as a sign, signal or symbol of something. Each country in the world has a different flag, made with special colours or patterns.
flake (flakes) *noun*
A flake of something is a small thin piece of it.
flame (flames) *noun*
A flame is burning gas that comes from anything that is burning or on fire. Flames are very hot and bright.
flannel (flannels) *noun*
1. Flannel is a warm, lightweight cloth woven from something like wool. Suits are

sometimes made of flannel.
2. A flannel is a small piece of towelling that people use to wash themselves with.

flap (flaps) *noun*
A flap is something flat that is fixed along one edge so that the rest of it can move freely: *The cat can get out through a flap in the door.*

flap (flaps, flapping, flapped) *verb*
1. If something like paper or cloth flaps, it moves quickly up and down or from side to side, often making a snapping sound.
2. When a bird flaps its wings, it moves them up and down quickly.

flash (flashes) *noun*
A flash is a very bright light which comes suddenly and only lasts a moment, like lightning in a storm.

flash (flashes, flashing, flashed) *verb*
1. If a light flashes, it shines with a sudden bright light, especially as quick, regular flashes of light.
2. If something flashes past, it moves so fast that you cannot see it properly.

flask (flasks) *noun*
1. A flask is a flat container made of metal or glass for carrying something to drink with you.
2. A Thermos flask is specially made to keep drinks hot or cold.

flat (flatter, flattest) *adjective*
1. Something that is flat is level. It does not slope or curve, or have any bumps or wrinkles in it.
2. Something that folds flat can be folded so that it takes up less space.
3. Flat shoes have low heels, or no heels at all.
4. A flat tyre has very little air in it.
5. A drink that is flat has lost all its bubbles.
6. A battery that is flat has lost its electrical power.

flat (flats) *noun*
A flat is a set of rooms for living in. It is usually on one floor, and is part of a larger building. A flat usually has a kitchen and bathroom.

flavour (flavours) *noun*
The flavour of food or drink is what it tastes like.

flavour (flavours, flavouring, flavoured) *verb*
If you flavour food or drink, you add something to it to give it a special taste.

fleet (fleets) *noun*
1. A fleet is a group of ships which sail together for a special reason, such as to fight battles or to catch fish.
2. A fleet of vehicles is a group of them, especially when they all belong to the same company.

flesh *noun*
1. Flesh is the soft part of a person's or animal's body that covers the bones and is underneath the skin.
2. The flesh of a fruit or vegetable is the soft part of it.

flicker (flickers, flickering, flickered) *verb*
If a light or flame flickers, it does not shine steadily.

flight (flights) *noun*
1. A flight is a journey made in an aircraft.
2. The flight of a bird is the act of flying.
3. A flight of stairs or steps is a set that leads from one level to another without changing direction.

flipper (flippers) *noun*
1. The flippers of an animal such as a seal or a penguin are the flat limbs that it uses for swimming.
2. Flippers are flat pieces of rubber that you can wear on your feet to help you swim more quickly.

float (floats, floating, floated) *verb*
1. If something floats in a liquid, it rests on it, moving slowly.
2. If something floats through the air, it moves gently above the ground.

flock (flocks) *noun*
A flock of birds or sheep is a group of them.

flood (floods) *noun*
A flood is a large amount of water which covers an area that is usually dry.

flood (floods, flooding, flooded) *verb*
If a river floods, it overflows, usually after very heavy rain.

floor (floors) *noun*
1. The floor of a room is the flat part that you walk on.
2. A floor of a building is all the rooms on that level: *Our flat is on the third floor.*
floppy disk (floppy disks) *noun*
A floppy disk is a small magnetic disk used for storing information in a computer.
flour *noun*
Flour is a white or brown powder made by grinding grain such as wheat. Flour is used to make things like bread and cakes.
flow (flows, flowing, flowed) *verb*
If a liquid flows in a certain direction, it moves in a steady stream.
flower (flowers) *noun*
A flower is the part of a plant that has white or coloured petals and that only lasts for a short time.
flu *noun*
Flu is an illness which is like a very bad cold. You get a high temperature and ache all over. Flu is short for influenza.
fluffy (fluffier, fluffiest) *adjective*
1. Something that is fluffy is very soft and woolly.
2. A cake or other food that is fluffy is very light.
fluid (fluids) *noun*
A fluid is a liquid or a gas.
flute (flutes) *noun*
A flute is a musical instrument made of metal or wood, in the shape of a long tube with holes in it. You play it by blowing over a hole at one end while holding the instrument sideways to your mouth and covering the holes with your fingers.
fly (flies) *noun*
A fly is a small insect with two wings.
fly (flies, flying, flew, flown) *verb*
1. When a bird, insect or aircraft flies, it moves through the air.
2. If you fly somewhere, you travel there in an aircraft.
foam *noun*
Foam is lot of small bubbles of air together in a mass, formed when air is mixed in with a liquid.
focus (foci/focuses) *noun*
1. The focus of something is the part of it that most attention is concentrated on.
2. The focus of light rays or sound waves is the point at which they meet.
3. The focus of an earthquake is the point in the earth's crust where the earthquake starts.
focus (focuses, focusing, focused) *verb*
If you focus something like a camera or a telescope, you adjust it so that you can see clearly.
fog *noun*
When there is fog, there are tiny drops of water in the air which make a thick cloud so that it is difficult to see things.
fold (folds) *noun*
Folds in material are the curves in it when it does not hang flat: *The curtains hung in soft folds.*
fold (folds, folding, folded) *verb*
When you fold something, such as paper or cloth, you bend one part of it so that it covers another part, often pressing the edge so that it stays in place.
folder (folders) *noun*
A folder is a piece of folded cardboard for keeping papers in.
follow (follows, following, followed) *verb*
1. If you follow someone who is moving, you move along behind them.
2. If one thing follows another, it happens after it.
3. If you follow something like a path, you go along it.
fond (fonder, fondest) *adjective*
If you are fond of someone, you like them very much.
>**fondly** *adverb*
food *noun*
Food is what people and animals eat to stay alive, and what plants need to grow.
foolish *adjective*
1. If something you do is foolish, it is not sensible.
2. Someone or something that is foolish is so silly that people are likely to laugh at them.
>**foolishly** *adverb*

foot (feet) *noun*
1. Your feet are the parts of your body that touch the ground when you stand or walk.
2. A foot is also a measure of length, equal to 12 inches or 30.48 centimetres.

football (footballs) *noun*
1. Football is a game played on a field, between two teams who use a ball to try to win points against each other by scoring goals.
2. A football is a large ball filled with air that is used in games of football.

footballer (footballers) *noun*
A footballer is someone who plays football.

footprint (footprints) *noun*
A footprint is a mark in the shape of a foot that a person or animal leaves in or on a surface.

footstep (footsteps) *noun*
A footstep is the sound or mark made by someone walking each time their foot touches the ground.

>follow in someone's footsteps *phrase*
If you follow in someone's footsteps, you do the same things as they did earlier: *She followed in her mother's footsteps and became a sculptor.*

forbid (forbids, forbidding, forbade, forbidden) *verb*
If someone forbids you to do something, they mean you must not do it.

force (forces) *noun*
1. The forces are the navy, army and air force.
2. The force of something is the powerful effect it has: *The force of the earthquake damaged hundreds of buildings.*

>force of habit *phrase*
When you do something from force of habit, you do it without thinking, because you have done it so many times before.

force (forces, forcing, forced) *verb*
1. If someone forces someone else to do something, they make them do something they do not want to do.
2. If something forces you to do something, you do something you would not otherwise have done: *The rain forced us to play indoors.*
3. If someone forces their way through something, they push or break things that are in their way: *He forced his way through the brambles.*

forecast (forecasts) *noun*
A weather forecast tells you what sort of weather to expect.

forecast (forecasts, forecasting, forecast) *verb*
If someone forecasts something, they say what they think is going to happen in the future.

forehead (foreheads) *noun*
Your forehead is the front part of your head, between your hair and your eyebrows.

foreign *adjective*
Something that is foreign is to do with a country that is not your own.

forest (forests) *noun*
A forest is a large area where trees grow close together.

forester (foresters) *noun*
A forester is a person whose job is to look after the trees in a forest and to plant new ones.

forget (forgets, forgetting, forgot, forgotten) *verb*
1. If you forget something, you cannot think of it although you knew it before.
2. If you forget to do something, you do not do it because you did not think about it.

forgive (forgives, forgiving, forgave, forgiven) *verb*
If you forgive someone who has done something bad, you stop being cross with them.

fork (forks) *noun*
1. A fork is a tool that you use for eating food. It has three or four prongs on the end of a handle.
2. A fork is also a large tool with prongs, that you use for digging in the garden.
3. A fork in a road or a tree is the point where it divides into two, like the shape of the letter Y.

form (forms) *noun*
1. A form is a piece of paper with questions on it and spaces where you should write the answers.
2. A form in a school is a class: *Her brother is in the sixth form.*
form (forms, forming, formed) *verb*
1. When something forms, it begins to take shape.
2. When something forms a particular shape, it is arranged in such a way that this shape is made.
fortnight (fortnights) *noun*
A fortnight is a period of two weeks.
fortress (fortresses) *noun*
A fortress is a castle or other strong place that is built to keep enemies out.
fortunate *adjective*
Someone who is fortunate has good luck, or has something good.
>**fortunately** *adverb*
fortune (fortunes) *noun*
1. Fortune is good or bad luck.
2. If someone has a fortune, they have a lot of money.
>**tell someone's fortune** *phrase*
Someone who tells your fortune says what they think will happen to you in the future.
forward/forwards *adverb*
If you move forward, you move the way you are facing.
>**look forward** *phrase*
If you look forward to something, you want it to happen because you think you will enjoy it.
forward (forwards, forwarding, forwarded) *verb*
If you forward a letter, you send it on to someone when they have moved house.
fossil (fossils) *noun*
A fossil is the hardened remains of a prehistoric animal or plant that are found inside a rock.
foul (fouler, foulest) *adjective*
If something is foul, it is very unpleasant.
foul (fouls) *noun*
A foul is an act in a game or sport that is against the rules.
foundations *noun*
The foundations of a building are the layers of material, such as bricks or concrete, below the ground, that support the rest of the building.
fountain (fountains) *noun*
A fountain is a jet or spray of water forced up into the air by a pump.
fountain pen (fountain pens) *noun*
A fountain pen is a pen with a container inside which sends ink to the nib.
fowl (fowls) *noun*
A fowl is a bird, especially one that can be eaten, such as duck or chicken.
fox (foxes) *noun*
A fox is a wild animal that looks like a dog. It has reddish-brown fur and a thick tail.
fraction (fractions) *noun*
1. A fraction is a tiny amount or part of something: *The door opened a fraction and the cat put its paw through.*
2. A fraction is also a measured part such as a half or a quarter of something.
fracture (fractures) *noun*
A fracture is a crack or break in something, especially a bone.
fragment (fragments) *noun*
A fragment of something is a small piece or part of it.
frame (frames) *noun*
1. A frame is an object made from long, thin pieces of something such as wood. Frames are usually made with straight sides and a space in the middle. They are used for making things like windows, or to put round pictures.
2. The frame of a pair of glasses is the wire or plastic part which holds the lenses in place.
frantic *adjective*
If you are frantic, you are behaving wildly because you are frightened or worried.
>**frantically** *adverb*
free (freer, freest) *adjective*
1. Someone who is free is not controlled by anybody.

2. An animal that is free is not tied up or kept in a cage.
3. If you are free at a particular time, you are not busy then.
4. If something is free, it does not cost anything.
>**freely** *adverb*
freedom *noun*
You have freedom if you are free.
freeze (freezes, freezing, froze, frozen) *verb*
1. If a liquid freezes, it becomes solid because the temperature is low.
2. If you freeze something, you preserve it by storing it at a very low temperature.
freezer (freezers) *noun*
A freezer is a large container, like a fridge, where you can store food for a long time because the temperature inside is kept very low.
fresh (fresher, freshest) *adjective*
1. If food is fresh, it has been gathered or made recently, and has not become stale or bad.
2. Fresh water is water that is not salty.
3. If you feel fresh, you feel rested and full of energy.
4. Fresh air is the air outside.
>**freshly** *adverb*
freshwater *adjective*
Freshwater means living in or containing water that is not salty: *The lake is full of freshwater fish.*
friction *noun*
Friction is the resistance produced when two surfaces rub against each other.
Friday *noun*
Friday is one of the seven days of the week. It comes after Thursday and before Saturday.
fridge (fridges) *noun*
A fridge is a large metal container. It is kept cool so that the food in it stays fresh longer.
friend (friends) *noun*
A friend is someone you know well and like very much.
friendly (friendlier, friendliest) *adjective*
Someone who is friendly behaves in a pleasant, kind way.
fright *noun*
Fright is a sudden feeling of fear.
frighten (frightens, frightening, frightened) *verb*
If something frightens you, it makes you feel afraid.
frog (frogs) *noun*
A frog is a small creature with smooth skin, big eyes and long back legs which it uses for jumping. Frogs like to live near water, and their hind feet are webbed to help them swim.
front *adjective*
1. A front room or garden is on the side of a building that faces the street.
2. The front page of a newspaper is the outside part, where the name of the newspaper is.
>**in front of** *phrase*
1. If something is in front of you, you are facing it and it is very near you.
2. If you say something in front of someone else, you say it while they are there.
front (fronts) *noun*
1. The front of you is the part of your body that is on the same side as your face.
2. The front of a vehicle is the part where the driver sits.
frost (frosts) *noun*
If there is a frost, the temperature outside is very low, and the ground becomes covered with tiny ice crystals.
frown (frowns, frowning, frowned) *verb*
When you frown, your eyebrows are drawn together. People frown when they are annoyed or worried, or when they are thinking hard.
frozen *adjective*
1. If something like a lake or river is frozen, its surface has turned into ice because the temperature is very low.
2. Frozen food has been preserved by bringing it to a very low temperature.
3. If you are frozen, you are very cold.
fruit (fruit/fruits) *noun*
A fruit is something you can eat that grows on a tree or bush. It contains seeds or a stone. Oranges, plums and grapes are fruit.

fry (fries, frying, fried) *verb*
When you fry food, you cook it in a pan that contains hot fat or oil.

fuel (fuels) *noun*
Fuel is something, like wood or coal, that is burned to provide heat or power.

full (fuller, fullest) *adjective*
If something is full, there is no room for anything more.
>**fully** *adverb*

full stop (full stops) *noun*
A full stop is the punctuation mark (.) which you use at the end of a sentence when it is not a question or an exclamation.

fun *noun*
Fun is something enjoyable that makes you feel happy.

funeral (funerals) *noun*
A funeral is a ceremony that is held when a person has died and their body is being buried or cremated.

funnel (funnels) *noun*
1. A funnel is an object shaped like a cone. It is wide at the top, and has a short tube at the bottom. You can use a funnel to pour things like liquid into containers.
2. A funnel is also a metal chimney on a ship or steam engine.

funny (funnier, funniest) *adjective*
1. Funny people or things make you laugh.
2. Something that is funny is rather strange or surprising.
3. If you say you feel funny, you mean you don't feel very well.
>**funnily** *adverb*

fur *noun*
Fur is the thick hair that grows on the bodies of many mammals.

furious *adjective*
Someone who is furious is extremely angry.
>**furiously** *adverb*

furnace (furnaces) *noun*
A furnace is a container in which a very hot fire is made. Furnaces are used, for example, to melt metal or burn rubbish.

furniture *noun*
Furniture means large objects such as tables, beds and chairs, that people have in rooms.

furry (furrier, furriest) *adjective*
1. An animal or part of an animal that is furry is covered with thick, soft hair.
2. Something that is furry feels soft and rough like fur.

further *adjective*
Further can mean more: *Write to this address for further details.*

further *adverb*
If someone goes further than someone else, they travel a greater distance.

fury *noun*
1. Fury is very strong anger.
2. If you are in a fury, you are very angry.

future *noun*
1. The future is the time that is to come.
2. Your future is what will happen to you, especially in the work that you do: *She has worked very hard and has a promising future as an engineer.*

G

gain (gains) *noun*
A gain is an increase in the amount of something: *He was hoping to lose weight, but the scales showed a gain of two kilos.*

gain (gains, gaining, gained) *verb*
1. If you gain from something, you get something good out of it.
2. If a clock or watch gains, it moves too fast.
3. If you gain on someone who is in front of you in a race, you gradually catch them up.

galaxy (galaxies) *noun*
1. A galaxy is a group of stars and planets that spreads over many millions of miles.
2. The galaxy is the group of stars and planets that the earth belongs to.

gale (gales) *noun*
A gale is a very strong wind.

galleon (galleons) *noun*
A galleon is a large sailing ship with heavy guns. Galleons were used three or four hundred years ago.

gallery (galleries) *noun*
1. A gallery is a place that shows paintings or sculptures.
2. In a hall or theatre, a gallery is a raised area at the back where people can sit and get a good view of what is happening.

galley (galleys) *noun*
A galley is a ship that was used in war hundreds of years ago. It had sails and many oars, and was rowed by slaves or prisoners.

gallon (gallons) *noun*
A gallon is a measure of volume. In Britain, a gallon is equal to eight pints or 4.55 litres.

gallop (gallops, galloping, galloped) *verb*
When a horse gallops, it runs very fast, so that all its legs are off the ground at the same time.

game (games) *noun*
1. A game is a sport or something you play in which you follow fixed rules and try to win.
2. A game can also be something you play where you use toys or pretend to be someone else.

gang (gangs) *noun*
1. A gang is a group of bad people who work together doing things that are against the law.
2. A gang can also mean a group of workers.

gap (gaps) *noun*
1. A gap is an empty space between two things.
2. A gap can be a period of time when you are not doing what you usually do, or when you are not busy.

garage (garages) *noun*
1. A garage is a building in which someone can keep a car.
2. A garage is also a place where people buy petrol or get their cars repaired.

garden (gardens) *noun*
A garden is land next to someone's house where they can grow things such as trees, flowers or grass.

gardener (gardeners) *noun*
1. A gardener is someone who is paid to work in someone else's garden.
2. A gardener can also be someone who enjoys working in their own garden.

garment (garments) *noun*
A garment is a piece of clothing, such as a shirt or coat.

gas (gases) *noun*
1. Gas is something like air that is neither liquid nor solid. It burns easily and is used as a fuel for fires, cookers and central heating in people's homes.
2. A gas can be anything that is neither liquid nor solid. For example, oxygen is a gas.

gasp (gasps, gasping, gasped) *verb*
When you gasp, you take a short, quick breath through your mouth, especially when you are surprised or in pain.

gate (gates) *noun*
A gate is a door that is used at the entrance to a field, garden or grounds of a building.

gather (gathers, gathering, gathered) *verb*
1. If people or animals gather, they come together in a group.
2. If you gather something, you collect a number of things from different places: *Early people used to gather berries for food.*
3. If something gathers speed, it gradually gets faster and faster.

gaze (gazes, gazing, gazed) *verb*
If you gaze, you look steadily at someone or something for a long time, because you find them attractive or interesting, or because you are thinking about something else.

general *adjective*
You use general when you are talking about most people, or most of the people in a group: *There was a general rush for the door when the bell rang.*
>**generally** *adverb*
>**in general** *phrase*
If you say in general, you mean something is true most of the time, or for most people: *In general, people don't like getting cold and wet.*

generous *adjective*
Someone who is generous is kind and willing to help others by giving them what they can.
>**generously** *adverb*

gentle (gentler, gentlest) *adjective*
Someone who is gentle is kind, calm and sensitive.
>**gently** *adverb*

genuine *adjective*
Something that is genuine is real and what it appears to be, and is not a fake or an imitation.

geography *noun*
Geography is the study of the countries of the world, and of such things as climate, towns and population.

gerbil (gerbils) *noun*
A gerbil is a small, furry animal with long back legs. Gerbils live in the deserts of Africa and Asia. They are often kept as pets.

germ (germs) *noun*
A germ is a very small living thing that can make people ill. You cannot see germs without using a microscope.

ghost (ghosts) *noun*
A ghost is a shadowy figure of someone no longer living that some people believe they see.

giant *adjective*
Anything that is much larger than others of its kind can be called giant: *We saw a giant panda on television.*

giant (giants) *noun*
In fairy stories, a giant is someone who is very, very large and strong.

giddy *adjective*
If you feel giddy, you feel unsteady and think that you are about to fall over.

gift (gifts) *noun*
A gift is something you give someone as a present.

gigantic *adjective*
Something that is gigantic is very, very large.

giggle (giggles, giggling, giggled) *verb*
If you giggle, you make quiet, little laughing noises.

ginger *noun*
Ginger is the root of a special plant which has a spicy, hot flavour. Ginger is sometimes sold as a powder.

ginger *adjective*
Ginger hair is a bright orange-brown colour.

giraffe (giraffes) *noun*
A giraffe is a large African animal with a very long neck, long legs, and dark patches on its yellowish skin. It is the tallest of all the mammals and can grow to nearly six metres. Giraffes live in herds in open country, eating leaves and young twigs.

girl (girls) *noun*
A girl is a female child or a young woman.

give (gives, giving, gave, given) *verb*
1. If you give someone something, you offer it to them as a present.
2. If you give someone something they have just asked for, you hand it to them: *Will you give me that pencil, please?*
3. If you give someone information, you tell them what they want to know.
4. If you say you give up, you mean you do not know the answer to a riddle or a puzzle.

glacier (glaciers) *noun*
A glacier is a huge mass of ice which moves very slowly, often down a mountain valley.

glad (gladder, gladdest) *adjective*
1. If you are glad about something, you are happy and pleased about it.
2. If you say you are glad to do something, you mean that you are willing and eager to do it.
>**gladly** *adverb*

glance (glances, glancing, glanced) *verb*
1. If you glance at something, you look at it quickly.
2. If something glances off another object, it hits it at an angle and bounces away in another direction.

glare (glares, glaring, glared) *verb*
If you glare at someone or something, you look at them with an unfriendly or angry expression on your face.

glass (glasses) *noun*
1. Glass is a hard, transparent material that is easily broken. It is used to make windows, and such things as bottles and bowls.

2. A glass is a container that you can drink from.
3. Glasses are two lenses in a metal or plastic frame. People with bad eyesight wear them in front of their eyes to help them see properly.

glide (glides, gliding, glided) *verb*
When something glides, it moves silently and smoothly.

glider (gliders) *noun*
A glider is an aircraft that does not have an engine, but flies by floating on air currents.

glimpse (glimpses) *noun*
A glimpse of someone or something is a very brief sight of them.

glisten (glistens, glistening, glistened) *verb*
If something glistens, it shines or sparkles, usually because it is wet or oily: *Her eyes glistened with tears.*

glitter (glitters, glittering, glittered) *verb*
If something glitters, it shines in a sparkling way: *Her diamond necklace glittered under the lights.*

gloat (gloats, gloating, gloated) *verb*
If you gloat, you show great pleasure in your own success or in other people's failure.

globe (globes) *noun*
1. A globe is a round model of the earth. It is usually fixed on a stand, so that you can spin it round, and it has a map of the world drawn on it.
2. Any object that is round in shape can also be called a globe: *The street lamp was a tall metal pole with a globe on top.*

gloomy (gloomier, gloomiest) *adjective*
1. If a place is gloomy, it is almost dark and you cannot see very well.
2. If people are gloomy, they are unhappy and not at all hopeful.
>**gloomily** *adverb*

glossy (glossier, glossiest) *adjective*
Something that is glossy is smooth and shiny.

glove (gloves) *noun*
A glove is a piece of clothing which covers your hand, with separate places for each finger.

glue *noun*
Glue is a thick, sticky liquid used for joining things together, either when they are being made or if they are broken.

gnat (gnats) *noun*
A gnat is a very small, flying insect that bites people. Gnats usually live near water.

gnaw (gnaws, gnawing, gnawed) *verb*
If people or animals gnaw something, they bite on something hard for a long time.

gnome (gnomes) *noun*
In fairy stories, a gnome is like a very small, old man with a beard and pointed hat. Gnomes are usually described as living underground.

goal (goals) *noun*
1. A goal in games such as football or hockey is the space into which players try to get the ball so that they can score a point for their team.
2. If you score a goal, you win a point by getting the ball into the goal.
3. If something is your goal, you hope to succeed in doing it one day.

goat (goats) *noun*
A goat is an animal with short, coarse hair, horns, and a short tail.

goblin (goblins) *noun*
In fairy stories, a goblin is a small, ugly creature who likes to make trouble.

goggles *noun*
Goggles are large glasses that fit closely round your eyes to protect them from things like dust, sparks or water.

gold *adjective*
Something that is gold in colour is bright yellow.

gold *noun*
Gold is a valuable yellow-coloured metal that is used for making things like jewellery.

goldfish *noun*
A goldfish is a gold or orange-coloured fish which is often kept as a pet in a bowl or a garden pond.

golf *noun*
Golf is a game in which people use long sticks called clubs to hit a small ball into special holes.

good (better, best) *adjective*
1. Someone who is good is kind and caring, and can be trusted.
2. A child or animal that is good is well-behaved and obedient.
3. Good music, art or literature is of high quality.
4. Something such as a film or a show that is good is pleasant and enjoyable.
5. Someone who is good at something is skilful and successful at it.
goose (geese) *noun*
A goose is a large bird that has a long neck and webbed feet. Its cry is a loud, honking noise.
gorilla (gorillas) *noun*
The gorilla is the largest of the apes. It lives in African forests, feeding on fruit and the shoots of young trees. Gorillas live in family groups.
government (governments) *noun*
A government is the group of people in a country or a state who make laws and decide about things that are important, such as medical care and old-age pensions.
grab (grabs, grabbing, grabbed) *verb*
If you grab something, you pick it up suddenly and roughly.
graceful *adjective*
Someone or something that is graceful moves in a smooth way which is pleasant to watch.
>**gracefully** *adverb*
gradual *adjective*
Something that is gradual happens slowly.
>**gradually** *adverb*
graffiti *noun*
Graffiti is words or pictures that are scribbled on walls in public places.
grain (grains) *noun*
1. Grain is a cereal crop, especially wheat or corn, that has been harvested for food.
2. A grain of something like rice, wheat or other cereal is a seed from it.
3. A grain of something such as sand or salt is a tiny, hard piece of it.
gram (grams) *noun*
A gram is a very small unit of weight. One sheet of writing paper weighs about four grams.
grammar *noun*
Grammar is the rules of a language.
grand (grander, grandest) *adjective*
1. Buildings that are grand are large and look important.
2. People who are grand seem very important.
>**grandly** *adverb*
grandfather (grandfathers) *noun*
Your grandfather is the father of one of your parents.
grandmother (grandmothers) *noun*
Your grandmother is the mother of one of your parents.
grandparent (grandparents) *noun*
Your grandparents are the parents of one of your parents.
granite *noun*
Granite is a very hard rock which is often used for building large buildings.
grape (grapes) *noun*
A grape is a small, sweet, round fruit. It can be either pale green or dark purple in colour. Grapes grow in bunches on vines. They can be eaten raw, used for making wine, or dried to make raisins, sultanas or currants.
grapefruit (grapefruit/grapefruits) *noun*
A grapefruit is a large, round fruit. It is like an orange, but it is larger and has a pale yellow skin. It has a sharp, slightly bitter taste.
graph (graphs) *noun*
A graph is a diagram, usually a line or curve, which brings together two or more sets of numbers or measurements.
grasp (grasps, grasping, grasped) *verb*
1. If you grasp something, you take it with your hand and hold it very firmly.
2. If you grasp something that is difficult to understand, you understand it.
grass *noun*
Grass is a very common, green plant with long, thin, spiky leaves.
grasshopper (grasshoppers) *noun*
A grasshopper is an insect. It has long back legs and can jump well. The male makes a high-pitched sound by rubbing its back legs against its short, leathery wings.

grate (grates) *noun*
A grate is a framework of metal bars in a fireplace, which holds the coal or wood.
grate (grates, grating, grated) *verb*
If you grate food, such as cheese or carrots, you rub a piece of it over a metal tool so that the food is shredded into very small pieces.
grateful *adjective*
If you are grateful for something nice that someone has done, you have warm feelings towards them and want to thank them.
>**gratefully** *adverb*
grave (graves) *noun*
A grave is a place where a dead person is buried.
grave (graver, gravest) *adjective*
1. Something that is grave is very important, serious and worrying.
2. Someone who is grave is quiet and serious.
>**gravely** *adverb*
gravel *noun*
Gravel is made up of very small stones. It is used to cover paths.
gravity *noun*
Gravity is the force which makes things fall to the ground when you drop them, and makes things stay on the ground instead of floating in the air.
gravy *noun*
Gravy is a thin sauce made from the juices that come out of meat when you cook it.
graze (grazes, grazing, grazed) *verb*
When an animal grazes, it eats grass and other plants as they are growing.
graze (grazes) *noun*
A graze is a small wound caused by scraping your skin against something.
grease *noun*
Grease is a thick oil which is put on the moving parts of cars and other machines to make them work smoothly.
great (greater, greatest) *adjective*
1. You say something is great when it is very large in size, number or amount: *The waves threw a great shower of pebbles on to the seafront.*
2. Great can also mean important: *It is interesting to hear about great scientists.*
greedy (greedier, greediest) *adjective*
Someone who is greedy is eager for something like money or food. They want more than they need, or more than their fair share.
>**greedily** *adverb*
green (greener, greenest) *adjective*
Something that is green is the colour of grass.
green (greens) *noun*
1. A green is an area of land covered with grass, especially in the middle of a town or village.
2. Greens are the green leaves of vegetables such as spinach or cabbage, which are cooked and eaten.
greengrocer (greengrocers) *noun*
A greengrocer is a shopkeeper who sells fruit and vegetables.
greenhouse (greenhouses) *noun*
A greenhouse is a building which has glass walls and roof. It is used to grow plants in.
greet (greets, greeting, greeted) *verb*
When you greet someone, you look pleased to see them, and say something friendly.
greeting (greetings) *noun*
A greeting is something you say or do to show your pleasure when you meet someone.
grey (greyer, greyest) *adjective*
Something that is grey is the colour of ashes, or clouds on a rainy day.
grief *noun*
Someone who feels grief is very, very sad, often because a person or animal they love has died.
grill (grills) *noun*
A grill is part of a cooker where food is cooked by strong heat from above.
grim (grimmer, grimmest) *adjective*
1. Something that is grim is unpleasant or difficult and makes people feel unhappy.
2. If someone looks grim, they are very serious, because they are worried or angry about something.
>**grimly** *adverb*

grin (grins, grinning, grinned) *verb*
If you grin, you give a broad smile.
grind (grinds, grinding, ground) *verb*
1. If you grind something such as corn or pepper, you crush it between two hard surfaces until it becomes a powder.
2. If you grind your teeth, you rub your upper and lower teeth together as though you are chewing.
>**grind to a halt** *phrase*
If a vehicle grinds to a halt, it stops slowly.
grip (grips, gripping, gripped) *verb*
1. If you grip something, you take hold of it firmly.
2. If something grips you, you find it very interesting and give it your full attention.
groan (groans, groaning, groaned) *verb*
If you groan, you make a long, low sound, because you are in pain or unhappy, or because you do not approve of something.
groceries *noun*
Groceries are foods such as flour, sugar and tinned foods.
groove (grooves) *noun*
A groove is a wide, deep line cut into a surface.
ground (grounds) *noun*
1. The ground is the surface of the earth or the floor of a room.
2. A ground is an area of land where people play sports such as football or cricket.
group (groups) *noun*
1. A group is a number of people or things which are together in one place.
2. A group can also mean a set of people who are interested in the same thing, or have something in common.
grow (grows, growing, grew, grown) *verb*
1. When a person, animal or plant grows, they get bigger.
2. If you grow plants, you put seeds or young plants in the ground and look after them.
3. When someone grows up, they gradually change from being a child into being an adult.
growth *noun*
Growth is the process of increasing in size.
growl (growls, growling, growled) *verb*
If a dog or other animal growls, it makes a low, rumbling noise, usually because it is angry.
grub (grubs) *noun*
A grub is a young insect which has just come out of an egg.
grumble (grumbles, grumbling, grumbled) *verb*
If you grumble, you complain about something, usually in a low voice.
grunt (grunts, grunting, grunted) *verb*
When a pig grunts, it makes a low, rough noise.
guarantee (guarantees) *noun*
A guarantee is a written promise that if something does not work properly, it will be replaced or repaired.
guard (guards) *noun*
A guard is a person who watches over people, places or objects to keep them safe.
guess (guesses) *noun*
A guess is an answer that you give when you do not have all the information you need.
guest (guests) *noun*
A guest is someone who is staying with you because you have invited them.
guide (guides) *noun*
A guide is a person who takes people round places such as cities or museums.
guidebook (guidebooks) *noun*
A guidebook is a book which tells tourists about a town, area or country.
guilty (guiltier, guiltiest) *adjective*
1. If someone is guilty of something, they have done something wrong.
2. If you feel guilty, you feel unhappy because you think you have done something wrong, or have not done something you were supposed to do.
>**guiltily** *adverb*
guinea pig (guinea pigs) *noun*
A guinea pig is a small, furry animal without a tail. Guinea pigs are often kept as pets.

guitar (guitars) *noun*
A guitar is a musical instrument made of wood, usually with six strings. You play it by plucking or strumming the strings.

gulf (gulfs) *noun*
A gulf is a large area of sea which stretches a long way into the land.

gum (gums) *noun*
1. Your gums are the layers of firm, pink flesh inside your mouth. They cover the bone that your teeth are fixed into.
2. Gum is a kind of sweet that you chew but do not swallow.
3. Gum is also a sticky liquid which can be used to fix paper on to something else, such as card.
4. A gum is a chewy sweet, flavoured so that it tastes like fruit.

gun (guns) *noun*
A gun is a weapon with a long, metal tube and a place for bullets. The bullets are forced out of the gun by a small explosion and they fly through the air at great speed.

gunpowder *noun*
Gunpowder is a mixture that explodes when a flame is put near it. It is used for making things such as fireworks.

gutter (gutters) *noun*
A gutter is an open drain for carrying water away. There are gutters on the edges of roofs and at the sides of roads.

H

habit (habits) *noun*
A habit is something that you do often or regularly, sometimes without thinking about it: *She had a habit of rubbing her ear when she was worried.*

>in the habit of *phrase*
If you are in the habit of doing something, you do it often or regularly: *We are in the habit of going camping whenever we can.*

haddock *noun*
A haddock is a sea fish that you can eat. Haddock are found in the North Atlantic.

hail *noun*
Hail is small balls of ice that fall like rain from the sky.

hailstone (hailstones) *noun*
A hailstone is one of the small balls of ice that fall from the sky when there is hail.

hair (hairs) *noun*
Your hair is made up of a large number of long fine threads that grow on your head. Each thread is called a hair. Hair also grows on the bodies of some other animals.

hairy (hairier, hairiest) *adjective*
Someone or something that is hairy is covered with hair.

half (halves) *noun*
A half is one of two equal parts of something.

hall (halls) *noun*
1. The hall of a house is the area inside the front door that leads to other rooms.
2. A hall is a large room or building that is used for such things as concerts or meetings.
3. The town hall is the place where the local government has its main offices.

ham *noun*
Ham is meat from the back leg of a pig. It is specially treated so that it can be kept for a long time.

hamburger (hamburgers) *noun*
A hamburger is a piece of minced meat which has been shaped into a flat disc. Hamburgers are fried or grilled and then eaten, often in a bread roll.

hammer (hammers) *noun*
A hammer is a tool that is used for hitting things, such as nails into wood.

hammock (hammocks) *noun*
A hammock is a piece of strong cloth or netting which is hung between two supports and used as a bed.

hamster (hamsters) *noun*
A hamster is a small, furry animal which is often kept as a pet. Hamsters belong to the same family as mice. They have very short tails, and large cheek pouches for carrying food.

hand (hands) *noun*
Your hand is the part of your body which is at the end of your arm. It has four fingers and a thumb.
hand (hands, handing, handed) *verb*
If you hand something to someone, you pass it from your hand to theirs.
handbag (handbags) *noun*
A handbag is a small bag that women use for holding things, such as money and keys.
handkerchief (handkerchiefs) *noun*
A handkerchief is a small, square piece of fabric that you use for wiping your nose.
handle (handles) *noun*
1. The handle of a door or window is a small, round knob or lever that is used for opening or closing it.
2. The handle of something such as a tool or cup is the part that you hold so that you can pick it up and use it.
handlebars *noun*
Bicycle handlebars are made from a metal bar. They are fixed to the front of the bicycle and used to steer it.
handsome *adjective*
A handsome man has an attractive face.
handwriting *noun*
A person's handwriting is the way in which they write when they are using a pen or pencil.
handy (handier, handiest) *adjective*
Something that is handy is useful and easy to use.
hang (hangs, hanging, hung) *verb*
1. If you hang something up, you fix it there so that it does not touch the ground: *Please hang your coat on the hook.*
2. Something that hangs is heavy or loose so that it swings slightly: *Her long hair hangs over her shoulders.*
hangar (hangars) *noun*
A hangar is a large building in which aircraft are kept.
hang glider (hang gliders) *noun*
A hang glider is a glider for one person with which they can fly into the air. It is made of fabric stretched over a frame, with a harness underneath.
happen (happens, happening, happened) *verb*
1. Something that happens takes place as a result of something else: *What will happen if I press this button?*
2. Someone who happens to do something does it by chance: *I happened to be near the phone when it rang.*
happiness *noun*
Happiness is the feeling you have when you are happy.
happy (happier, happiest) *adjective*
Someone who is happy has feelings of pleasure because something nice has happened or because most things are the way they want.
>**happily** *adverb*
harbour (harbours) *noun*
A harbour is an area of water on a coast which is protected from the open sea by land or strong walls so that boats can stay there safely.
hard (harder, hardest) *adjective*
1. An object that is hard is very firm and stiff.
2. If something is hard to do, you cannot do it without a lot of work.
3. If you find something hard to understand, it does not make sense to you unless you think very carefully.
hard *adverb*
If it rains hard, a lot of rain falls.
harden (hardens, hardening, hardened) *verb*
When something hardens, it becomes stiff or firm.
>**can hardly** *phrase*
When you say you can hardly do something, you mean you can only just do it.
hardware *noun*
Hardware is the pieces of machinery that make up a computer.
hare (hares) *noun*
A hare is an animal like a rabbit but larger, with long ears and long legs. It does not live in a burrow, but rests in grass or in a ploughed field. Hares even have their babies in the open.

harm *noun*
Harm is injury to a person or animal.
harness (harnesses) *noun*
1. A harness is a set of straps which fit under a person's arms to fasten round their body. It is used to keep a piece of equipment in place, or to hold the person firmly in place.
2. A horse's harness is a set of leather straps fastened round its head or body.
harsh (harsher, harshest) *adjective*
1. A harsh way of life is very difficult.
2. Weather that is harsh is cold and unpleasant.
3. A person who is harsh is unkind.
4. A voice or other sound that is harsh sounds rough and unpleasant.
harvest (harvests) *noun*
The harvest is the cutting or picking of crops when they are ripe.
hat (hats) *noun*
A hat is a head covering for wearing outside. Hats often have a brim round them.
hatch (hatches, hatching, hatched) *verb*
When a baby bird, insect or other animal hatches, it comes out of its egg by breaking the shell.
hatchet (hatchets) *noun*
A hatchet is a small axe that a person can use in one hand.
hate (hates, hating, hated) *verb*
1. If you hate someone or something, you have a very strong feeling of dislike for them.
2. When you say you hate doing something, you mean you find it very unpleasant.
hatred *noun*
Hatred is an extremely strong feeling of dislike for someone or something.
haul (hauls, hauling, hauled) *verb*
If you haul someone or something that is heavy, you move them with a long, steady pull.
haunt (haunts, haunting, haunted) *verb*
A ghost that haunts a place appears there regularly.
hawk (hawks) *noun*
A hawk is a large bird with a short, hooked beak, sharp claws and very good eyesight. Hawks catch and eat small birds and animals.
hay *noun*
Hay is grass which has been cut and dried to feed animals.
head (heads) *noun*
1. Your head is the part of your body which has your eyes, nose and mouth in it.
2. Someone who is the head of something, such as a company or a school, is in charge of it and in charge of the people in it.
headlight (headlights) *noun*
Headlights are large, powerful lights at the front of a vehicle.
headline (headlines) *noun*
A headline is the title of a newspaper story, printed in large letters at the top of the story.
headquarters *noun*
The headquarters of an organization is a building or other place where the leaders of the organization work.
headstrong *adjective*
Someone who is headstrong is determined to do what they want and will not let anyone stop them.
head teacher (head teachers) *noun*
The head teacher of a school is the teacher who is in charge of the school.
health *noun*
A person's health is how their body is, and whether they are well or ill.
healthy (healthier, healthiest) *adjective*
1. Someone who is healthy is well and not suffering from any illness.
2. Something that is healthy is good for you and should help you to stay healthy: *You need some healthy, outdoor exercise.*
heap (heaps) *noun*
A heap of things is a lot of things piled up, usually rather untidily.
hear (hears, hearing, heard) *verb*
When you hear sounds, you notice them by using your ears.
heart (hearts) *noun*
Your heart is the organ that pumps the blood round inside your body.

heat *noun*
Heat is warmth.
heat (heats, heating, heated) *verb*
If you heat something, you make it warmer, often by using a special piece of equipment: *Heat the milk in a saucepan.*
heather *noun*
Heather is a low plant with woody stems, very small spiky leaves, and small purple, pink or white flowers. Heather grows wild, especially on hills or moorland.
heavy (heavier, heaviest) *adjective*
1. Something that is heavy weighs a lot or weighs more than usual.
2 If a person or an animal has a heavy build, their body is large, solid and strong-looking.
Hebrew (Hebrews) *noun*
The Hebrews were a people of ancient Israel.
hedge (hedges) *noun*
A hedge is a row of bushes or small trees. Hedges can be used to divide two areas of land. They also shelter people and plants from strong winds.
hedgehog (hedgehogs) *noun*
A hedgehog is a small, brown animal with sharp spikes all over its back. It defends itself by rolling up into a ball.
heel (heels) *noun*
1. Your heel is the back part of your foot.
2 The heel of a shoe is the raised part underneath, at the back.
height *noun*
1. The height of a person is how tall they are.
2 The height of an object is its measurement from bottom to top: *A Coast Redwood tree can grow to a height of more than 100 metres.*
3. When something is in the air, its height is its distance from the ground.
helicopter (helicopters) *noun*
A helicopter is an aircraft without wings. It has one or two sets of large blades which go round above it. It can use the blades to take off straight up into the air, to fly, and to hover.
helmet (helmets) *noun*
A helmet is a very hard hat that is worn to protect the head. Hundreds of years ago, knights going into battle wore helmets made of iron or steel.
help (helps, helping, helped) *verb*
1. If you help someone to do a job, you do part of it for them so that it can be finished more easily or more quickly.
2 If you help someone who is worried or unhappy, you do whatever you can to make them feel better.
helpful *adjective*
People who are helpful do whatever they can to make things easier for other people.
>**helpfully** *adverb*
helping (helpings) *noun*
A helping of food is the amount of it that you get in a single serving.
hem (hems) *noun*
The hem of a garment is the bottom edge of it. It is folded over and sewn to make it neat.
hen (hens) *noun*
1. A hen is a female chicken. Some people keep hens for their eggs.
2 A hen can also be any female bird.
herd (herds) *noun*
A herd is a large group of animals of one kind that live together.
here *adverb*
You say here when you mean the place where you are: *I'll stand here and wait.*
hero (heroes) *noun*
1. A hero is a man or boy who has done something brave and good.
2 The hero of a story is the man or boy that the story is about.
heroine (heroines) *noun*
1. A heroine is a woman or girl who has done something brave and good.
2 The heroine of a story is the woman or girl that the story is about.
heron (herons) *noun*
A heron is a wading bird that has very long legs, a long beak and grey and black feathers.
herring (herrings) *noun*
A herring is a long silver-coloured fish that

lives in large groups in the sea. Herrings are caught as food.

hesitate (hesitates, hesitating, hesitated) *verb*
If you hesitate, you pause slightly while you are doing something, or just before you do it.

hexagon (hexagons) *noun*
A hexagon is a shape that has six straight sides.

hibernate (hibernates, hibernating, hibernated) *verb*
When certain animals, such as bears, hibernate, they spend the winter in a sleeplike state.

hidden *adjective*
Something that is hidden is not easily noticed.

hide (hides, hiding, hid, hidden) *verb*
1. If you hide somewhere, you go where you cannot easily be seen.
2. If you hide something, you put it in a place where it cannot easily be seen.

high (higher, highest) *adjective*
1. Something that is high is a long way from the bottom to the top: *The wall round the garden is quite high.*
2. If something is high, it is a long way up: *There was an aircraft high above her.*
3. If the quality of something is high, it is very good.

hill (hills) *noun*
A hill is an area of land that is higher than the land around it. A hill is not as high as a mountain.

Hindu (Hindus) *noun*
A Hindu is a person who believes in the Indian religion Hinduism.

hinge (hinges) *noun*
Hinges are pieces of metal, wood or plastic that are used to hold a door so that it can swing freely.

hint (hints, hinting, hinted) *verb*
If you hint, or hint at something, you suggest it in a roundabout way: *I hinted that I would like a bicycle for my birthday.*

hip (hips) *noun*
Your hip is the area at the side of your body, between the top of your leg and your waist.

hippopotamus (hippopotamuses/ hippopotami) *noun*
A hippopotamus is a large African animal with short legs. It has thick, wrinkled skin without any fur. Hippopotamuses live in herds on the banks of large rivers, and spend a lot of time in the water. They are often called hippos for short.

hire (hires, hiring, hired) *verb*
If you hire something, you pay money to be allowed to use it for a period of time.

history *noun*
History is the study of things that happened in the past.

hit (hits, hitting, hit) *verb*
1. If a person hits someone, they touch them quickly and hard, usually to try to hurt them.
2. If you hit a ball, you make it move by swinging something like a bat to touch it hard.
3. If someone hits something when they are in a car, they move towards it and touch it. This usually causes damage.

hive (hives) *noun*
A hive is a house for bees, made so that the beekeeper can collect the honey.

hoard (hoards, hoarding, hoarded) *verb*
If you hoard things, you save or store them because they are important to you.

hoard (hoards) *noun*
A hoard is a store of things you have saved that are important to you and that you do not want other people to have.

hoarse (hoarser, hoarsest) *adjective*
If your voice is hoarse, it sounds rough.
>**hoarsely** *adverb*

hobby (hobbies) *noun*
A hobby is something you enjoy doing in your spare time, such as collecting stamps or birdwatching.

hockey *noun*
Hockey is an outdoor game, played between teams of 11 players. They use long curved sticks to hit a small ball, and they try to score goals.

hold (holds, holding, held) *verb*
1. When you hold something, you keep it in your hand.
2. If something holds a particular amount of something, it can contain that amount: *This jug holds one litre.*
hole (holes) *noun*
1. A hole is a hollow space in something solid like the ground: *The dog buried his bone in a hole in the garden.*
2. A hole can also be an opening that goes right through something: *I watched the birds through a hole in the fence.*
holiday (holidays) *noun*
A person's holiday is a period of time when they are not at work or at school.
hollow (hollower, hollowest) *adjective*
Something that is hollow has a space inside it: *The owl lived in a hollow tree trunk.*
hollow (hollows) *noun*
A hollow is an area that is lower than the ground around it.
holly *noun*
Holly is a small tree which has prickly leaves all the year round. Female trees often have bright red berries.
home *adjective*
A home game is one that is played on your team's own ground.
home (homes) *noun*
Your home is the place where you live and feel you belong.
>**at home** *phrase*
If you feel at home somewhere, you feel comfortable and like being there.
homework *noun*
Homework is school work that children do at home.
honest *adjective*
Someone who is honest tells the truth and can be trusted.
>**honestly** *adverb*
honey *noun*
Honey is a sweet, sticky, golden liquid that is made by bees. People often eat honey spread on bread.
honeycomb (honeycombs) *noun*
A honeycomb is the place inside a hive where the honey is stored. It has lots of six-sided holes made by worker bees from wax.
hood (hoods) *noun*
1. A hood is part of a garment such as a coat or cloak which you can pull up to cover your head.
2. A hood is also a covering on a vehicle. It is usually made of strong fabric and can be raised or lowered: *It began to rain, so she put the hood up on the pram.*
hoof (hoofs/hooves) *noun*
The hoof of an animal such as a horse is the hard bony part of its foot.
hook (hooks) *noun*
1. A hook is a bent piece of something like metal or plastic that is used for holding things, or hanging things up.
2. A hook made for fishing is a bent piece of thin metal.
hoot (hoots, hooting, hooted) *verb*
1. If you hoot the horn on a vehicle, it makes a loud noise.
2. When an owl hoots, it makes a sound like a long 'oo'.
hop (hops, hopping, hopped) *verb*
1. If you hop, you move in small jumps using only one foot.
2. When birds and some small animals hop, they move in small jumps using both feet together.
hope *noun*
Hope is a feeling that you want things to go well in the future, and believe that they will.
hopeful *adjective*
If you are hopeful, you feel sure that something you want to happen will happen.
hopeless *adjective*
You say something is hopeless when it is very bad, and you do not feel there is any chance that it will get better.
horizon (horizons) *noun*
The horizon is the line in the far distance where the sky seems to touch the land or the sea.
horizontal *adjective*
Something that is horizontal is flat and parallel with the ground.
>**horizontally** *adverb*

horn (horns) *noun*
1. Horns are the hard, pointed growths that stick out of the tops of the heads of animals such as goats and bulls.
2. A horn is an object that is built into vehicles such as cars. It makes a loud noise as a signal or warning.
horrible *adjective*
Something that is horrible is awful or very unpleasant.
>**horribly** *adverb*
horrify (horrifies, horrifying, horrified) *verb*
If something horrifies you, you feel dismayed or shocked.
horse (horses) *noun*
A horse is a large animal which people ride for pleasure, or to get from one place to another. Horses are also used for pulling things such as ploughs and carts.
horseshoe (horseshoes) *noun*
A horseshoe is a piece of metal shaped like a U. It is fixed with nails to the underneath of a horse's hoof, to protect it.
hose (hoses) *noun*
A hose is a long pipe made of rubber or plastic which carries water. People use hoses for things like putting out fires, watering gardens and washing cars.
hospital (hospitals) *noun*
A hospital is a place where people who are ill or injured are looked after by doctors and nurses.
hot (hotter, hottest) *adjective*
1. Something that is hot has a high temperature.
2. If you are hot, you feel too warm to be comfortable.
3. Hot food is food that is meant to be eaten as soon as it is cooked.
4. You say food is hot if it has a strong taste caused by spices: *This curry is too hot for me.*
hotel (hotels) *noun*
A hotel is a building where people pay to stay, usually for a few nights.
hour (hours) *noun*
An hour is a period of 60 minutes. There are 24 hours in a day.
house (houses) *noun*
A house is a building where people live.
hover (hovers, hovering, hovered) *verb*
To hover means to stay in one place in the air. Many birds and insects can hover by moving their wings very quickly.
hovercraft (hovercraft/hovercrafts) *noun*
A hovercraft is a vehicle that glides over water or land on a cushion of air.
howl (howls, howling, howled) *verb*
1. If an animal such as a dog or a wolf howls, it makes a long, loud, wailing sound.
2. When the wind howls, it makes a wailing noise, usually because it is blowing through a narrow gap.
hug (hugs, hugging, hugged) *verb*
When you hug someone, you put your arms round them tightly because you like them.
huge (huger, hugest) *adjective*
Something that is huge is very, very big.
>**hugely** *adverb*
hum (hums, humming, hummed) *verb*
If you hum, you sing a tune with your lips closed.
human being (human beings) *noun*
A human being is a man, woman or child.
hump (humps) *noun*
A hump is a large lump on the back of an animal such as a camel, which is used for storing fat and water.
hungry (hungrier, hungriest) *adjective*
When you are hungry, you want to eat because your stomach is empty.
>**hungrily** *adverb*
hunt (hunts, hunting, hunted) *verb*
1. When people or animals hunt, they chase wild animals to kill them, usually for food.
2. If you hunt for something, you try to find it by looking carefully.
hurricane (hurricanes) *noun*
A hurricane is a very violent wind or storm.
hurry (hurries, hurrying, hurried) *verb*
1. If you hurry somewhere, you go there as quickly as you can.
2. If you hurry to do something, you do it faster than usual.
3. If someone tells you to hurry up, they want you to move faster than you are.

hurt (hurts, hurting, hurt) *verb*
1. When part of your body hurts, you feel pain.
2. If you have been hurt, you have been injured.

husband (husbands) *noun*
When two people are married, the man is the woman's husband.

hut (huts) *noun*
A hut is a small house with only one or two rooms.

hutch (hutches) *noun*
A hutch is a cage made of wood and wire netting. Pets such as rabbits are kept in hutches.

hygiene *noun*
Hygiene means keeping yourself and the things around you clean, to prevent illness or the spread of diseases.

hyphen (hyphens) *noun*
A hyphen is a punctuation mark (-) which can be used to join two words together to make one word, for example 'blast-off'.

I

ice *noun*
Ice is water that has frozen and become solid.

iceberg (icebergs) *noun*
An iceberg is a huge block of ice that floats in the sea in very cold places. Only the top of an iceberg shows. Most of it is underwater.

ice cream *noun*
Ice cream is a very cold, sweet-tasting, creamy food.

ice skate (ice skates) *noun*
An ice skate is a boot with a metal blade fixed underneath it. You wear it when you skate on ice.

icicle (icicles) *noun*
An icicle is a piece of ice shaped like a pointed stick. Icicles hang from roofs, or wherever water has been dripping and freezing.

icing *noun*
Icing is a mixture of powdered sugar and water or egg whites. It is used to cover cakes as a decoration.

idea (ideas) *noun*
If you have an idea, you suddenly think of a way of doing something.

identical *adjective*
Two or more things that are identical are exactly the same in every detail.

idle (idler, idlest) *adjective*
1. Machines or factories that are idle are not being used.
2. An idle person is someone who does not do very much even if there is plenty to do.
>**idly** *adverb*

ignore (ignores, ignoring, ignored) *verb*
If you ignore something, you take no notice of it.

ill (worse, worst) *adjective*
Someone who is ill has something wrong with their health.

illness (illnesses) *noun*
An illness is something like a cold or measles that people can suffer from.

imaginary *adjective*
Something that is imaginary is not real. It is only in your mind: *She liked to have imaginary talks with famous people.*

imagine (imagines, imagining, imagined) *verb*
When you imagine something, you think about it and form a picture of it in your mind.

imitate (imitates, imitating, imitated) *verb*
If you imitate someone, you copy the way they speak or behave.

imitation (imitations) *noun*
1. An imitation is something that is supposed to be like something else, although it is usually not as good as the original.
2. An imitation is also something you do to copy the way someone else speaks or behaves.

immediately *adverb*
If you do something immediately, you do it without doing anything else in between.

impatient *adjective*
Someone who is impatient does not like to be kept waiting for anything. They get annoyed if they think people are doing things too slowly.
>**impatiently** *adverb*
important *adjective*
1. An important discovery or invention is one that is very useful to a lot of people.
2. Someone who is important has a lot of power in a particular group.
3. If someone says something is important, they mean it matters a lot.
>**importantly** *adverb*
impossible *adjective*
Something that is impossible cannot be done.
>**impossibly** *adverb*
impressive *adjective*
Something that is impressive causes people to admire it, usually because it is large or important.
>**impressively** *adverb*
improve (improves, improving, improved) *verb*
If something improves, it gets better.
improvement (improvements) *noun*
An improvement is a change in something that makes it better.
inch (inches) *noun*
An inch is a measure of length, equal to about 2.54 centimetres. There are 12 inches in a foot.
include (includes, including, included) *verb*
If you include something in a whole thing, you make it part of the whole thing: *Batteries are not included with this torch.*
increase (increases, increasing, increased) *verb*
If something increases, it becomes greater: *As he rode down the hill, his speed increased.*
index (indexes) *noun*
An index is an alphabetical list at the back of a book that helps you find the things you want to read about.
indignant *adjective*
If you are indignant, you feel you have a right to be angry because someone has done something unfair.
>**indignantly** *adverb*
indigo *adjective*
Something that is indigo is a dark colour between blue and violet.
individual *adjective*
Individual means to do with one particular person, rather than a whole group.
>**individually** *adverb*
indoors *adverb*
When you are indoors, you are inside a building.
infant (infants) *noun*
An infant is a baby or a very young child.
influence *noun*
Someone who is a particular kind of influence on people has that kind of effect on them: *You mustn't play with him any more - he's a bad influence on you.*
information *noun*
If someone gives you information about something, they tell you about it.
infuriate (infuriates, infuriating, infuriated) *verb*
If something or someone infuriates you, they make you extremely angry.
ingredient (ingredients) *noun*
Ingredients are the things that are used to make something.
inhabitant (inhabitants) *noun*
The inhabitants of a place are the people who live there.
initial (initials) *noun*
1. An initial is the first letter of a word, especially a name.
2. Your initials are the set of capital letters which stand for each of your names.
initiative *noun*
If you have initiative, you can see what needs to be done and get on with it in a sensible way.
injection (injections) *noun*
If you have an injection, someone, like a doctor or nurse, pricks your skin with a special needle. Injections are usually to prevent illnesses.
injure (injures, injuring, injured) *verb*
If something injures a person or animal, it damages some part of their body.

injury (injuries) *noun*
If a person or animal has an injury, part of their body has been damaged.
ink *noun*
Ink is the coloured liquid that is used for writing and printing.
inland *adverb*
If you go inland, you go away from the coast towards the middle of a country.
inn (inns) *noun*
An inn is a small, old hotel, usually in the country, where people can pay for food and somewhere to sleep. Inns often have a bar where people can buy drinks.
innocent *adjective*
1. If someone is innocent, they are not guilty of something they have been accused of.
2. If something you do or say is innocent, you do not realize it may offend people.
>innocently *adverb*
insect (insects) *noun*
An insect is a small animal that has six legs. Most insects have wings. Ants, flies, butterflies and beetles are all insects.
insert (inserts, inserting, inserted) *verb*
If you insert an object into something, you put it inside it.
insist (insists, insisting, insisted) *verb*
If you insist on doing something, you refuse to give in, even if other people do not want you to do it.
insistent *adjective*
Someone who is insistent keeps on saying that something must be done.
>insistently *adverb*
inspect (inspects, inspecting, inspected) *verb*
If you inspect something, you look at every part of it carefully.
inspire (inspires, inspiring, inspired) *verb*
If something or someone inspires you to do something, they make you want to do it by giving you new ideas and making you feel excited about it.
instant *adjective*
1. You use instant to describe food or drink that can be prepared quickly and easily: *This instant coffee is quite good.*
2. You can also use instant to describe something that happens immediately: *The play was an instant success.*
>instantly *adverb*
instead *adverb*
Instead means in place of something else: *I don't want to go to the fair. I'd rather stay here instead.*
instructions *noun*
Instructions are information on how to do something.
instrument (instruments) *noun*
1. An instrument is a tool that is used to do a particular job.
2. An instrument is also an object, such as a piano or guitar, which you play to make music.
insult (insults, insulting, insulted) *verb*
If you insult someone, you offend them by saying something rude.
intelligent *adjective*
1. A person who is intelligent can understand, learn, and think things out quickly and well.
2. An animal that is intelligent shows that it can think and understand.
>intelligently *adverb*
intend (intends, intending, intended) *verb*
If you intend to do something, you have decided or planned to do it.
interest (interests) *noun*
If you have an interest in something, you want to learn or hear more about it.
interesting *adjective*
If you find something interesting, it attracts your attention.
>interestingly *adverb*
interfere (interferes, interfering, interfered) *verb*
If something interferes with something else, it gets in the way: *You shouldn't watch so much television. It interferes with your homework.*
interrupt (interrupts, interrupting, interrupted) *verb*
If you interrupt someone, you start talking before they have finished what they were saying.

interview (interviews) *noun*
1. An interview is a meeting at which someone asks you questions about yourself.
2. An interview can also be a conversation between a reporter and a well-known person. Interviews are published in newspapers or magazines, or broadcast on television or radio.
invent (invents, inventing, invented) *verb*
If someone invents something, such as a machine or an instrument, they are the first person to think of it.
invention (inventions) *noun*
An invention is something that is a completely new idea: *She is working on an invention that will help disabled people.*
inventor (inventors) *noun*
An inventor is someone who thinks of new ideas and tries them out to see if they will work.
investigate (investigates, investigating, investigated) *verb*
If you investigate something, you examine all the details to find out what happened.
invisible *adjective*
1. If something is invisible, it cannot be seen because it is hidden, or too small: *Germs are invisible unless you use a microscope.*
2. In stories, invisible people or things cannot be seen by anybody.
invitation (invitations) *noun*
When you get an invitation, someone asks you to come to something such as a party.
invite (invites, inviting, invited) *verb*
If you invite someone to something, like a meal or a party, you ask them to come to it.
iron (irons) *noun*
1. Iron is a metal that is found in rocks. It is used to make lots of things, such as gates and railings. It is also mixed with other things to make steel.
2. An iron is an object that has a handle and a flat base. You can heat it and use it to smooth clothes after they have been washed and dried.
irritable *adjective*
If you are feeling irritable, you are in a mood in which you easily become annoyed.
>**irritably** *adverb*
Islam *noun*
Islam is the religion of the Muslims.
island (islands) *noun*
An island is a piece of land with water all round it.
itch (itches, itching, itched) *verb*
When you itch, or part of your body itches, you have a feeling on your skin that makes you want to scratch it.
ivory *noun*
Ivory is the hard, smooth, creamy-white material that forms part of the tusks of some animals, such as elephants.

J

jacket (jackets) *noun*
1. A jacket is a short coat. It has long sleeves and opens at the front.
2. The jacket of a potato is its skin.
jam (jams) *noun*
1. Jam is a food that is made by cooking fruit with a lot of sugar. You usually spread jam on bread.
2. A jam is when there are so many people or vehicles in a place it is impossible for them to move.
jam (jams, jamming, jammed) *verb*
If something jams, it becomes fixed and will not move.
January *noun*
January is the first month of the year. It has 31 days.
jar (jars) *noun*
A jar is a container. It is usually shaped like a cylinder and is made of glass. Jars are used for storing food such as jam.
jaw (jaws) *noun*
Your jaw is the lower part of your face, below your mouth. It moves up and down when you eat or talk.

jealous *adjective*
Someone who is jealous feels upset because someone else has what they want: *He felt jealous of the new baby, because everyone was paying attention to it instead of him.*
>**jealously** *adverb*

jeans *noun*
Jeans are trousers that are usually made from a strong cotton cloth.

jelly *noun*
Jelly is clear food that wobbles when you move it. You can eat it as a cold pudding.

jellyfish *noun*
A jellyfish is a creature that lives in the sea. It has an umbrella-shaped body that looks like clear jelly.

jerk (jerks) *noun*
If something happens with a jerk, it happens suddenly with a quick movement.

jersey (jerseys) *noun*
A jersey is a piece of clothing knitted from something like wool. You wear a jersey on the top half of your body, sometimes over a shirt.

jet (jets) *noun*
1. A jet is an aircraft with special engines. It can fly very fast and high up.
2. A jet of something such as water is a thin, forceful stream of it.

Jew (Jews) *noun*
A Jew is a person descended from the Hebrews, or one who believes in Judaism.

jewel (jewels) *noun*
A jewel is a precious stone, such as a diamond or a ruby. Jewels are often used to make things like rings and necklaces.

jewellery *noun*
Jewellery is the name for ornaments, like rings and necklaces, that people can wear. Jewellery is often made of valuable metal such as gold or silver. It is sometimes decorated with precious stones.

jigsaw (jigsaws) *noun*
A jigsaw is a game which uses a picture cut into a lot of pieces. You have to put the picture back together again by finding the right place for all the pieces.

job (jobs) *noun*
1. A job is the work that someone does to earn money.
2. A job can also be anything that has to be done: *There are always plenty of jobs to do when I get home.*

join (joins, joining, joined) *verb*
1. If you join two things, you fix them together.
2. If you join something like a club, you become a member of it.

joiner (joiners) *noun*
A joiner is a person who works with wood, making doors for example.

joint (joints) *noun*
1. A joint is a part of your body, such as your elbow or knee, where two bones meet and are able to move.
2. A joint can also be any place where two things are fastened together.

joke (jokes) *noun*
A joke is something that is done or said to make you laugh.

journey (journeys) *noun*
If you go on a journey, you travel from one place to another.

Judaism *noun*
Judaism is the religion of the Jews.

judge (judges) *noun*
1. In law, a judge is a person who has the power to decide how the law should be used.
2. The judge of a competition is a person who has been asked to choose the winner.

jug (jugs) *noun*
A jug is a container shaped like a cylinder, with a handle and a spout.

juice *noun*
Juice is the liquid that comes from fruit such as oranges when you squeeze them.

juicy (juicier, juiciest) *adjective*
Something that is juicy has a lot of juice in it and is very enjoyable to eat.

July *noun*
July is the seventh month of the year. It has 31 days.

jumble sale (jumble sales) *noun*
A jumble sale is an event that is held to raise money. People bring things they do not want any more, and other people buy them for small amounts of money.

jump (jumps, jumping, jumped) *verb*
When you jump, you move quickly and suddenly up in the air, using your own strength.
jumper (jumpers) *noun*
A jumper is a piece of clothing, usually made of wool, that covers the top part of your body. It has long sleeves and does not open at the front.
junction (junctions) *noun*
A junction is a place where roads or railway lines meet.
June *noun*
June is the sixth month of the year. It has 30 days.
jungle (jungles) *noun*
A jungle is a forest in a hot country, that has very large numbers of tall trees and other plants growing closely together.
junior *adjective*
Junior means younger.
junk (junks) *noun*
1. Junk is a group of objects that someone thinks are old or useless: *Will you please clear that junk out of the cupboard.*
2. A junk is a Chinese sailing boat that has a flat bottom and square sails.
just *adverb*
1. If you say that something has just happened, you mean it happened a short time ago.
2. If you say that you are just going to do something, you mean you will do it very soon.
justice *noun*
Justice is fairness in the way that people are treated.

K

kangaroo (kangaroos) *noun*
A kangaroo is a large Australian animal which moves forward by jumping on its back legs. Female kangaroos carry their babies in a special pouch on their stomachs.
keel (keels) *noun*
The keel of a boat is a long piece of wood or metal which is specially shaped to fit the bottom of the boat. It helps to keep the boat steady.
keen (keener, keenest) *adjective*
Someone who is keen to do something wants to do it very much.
keep (keeps, keeping, kept) *verb*
1. If you keep something for somebody, you save it for them.
2. If you keep doing something, you do it over and over again.
3. If something keeps you a certain way, you stay that way because of it: *That dog is keeping me awake.*
kennel (kennels) *noun*
A kennel is a small building made for a dog to sleep in.
kerb (kerbs) *noun*
The kerb is the edge of the pavement.
kernel (kernels) *noun*
The kernel of a nut is the part that is inside the shell.
kettle (kettles) *noun*
A kettle is a covered container used for boiling water. It has a handle and a spout.
key (keys) *noun*
1. A key is a specially shaped piece of metal that you use for locking things such as doors and padlocks.
2. The keys on a piece of equipment, such as a computer keyboard or a piano, are the parts that you press to make it work.
keyboard (keyboards) *noun*
The keyboard of a piece of equipment, such as a computer or a piano, is the flat part with keys that you press to make it work.
keyhole (keyholes) *noun*
A keyhole is a hole in a lock where you put the key to open something like a door or a case.
kick (kicks, kicking, kicked) *verb*
If you kick something, you hit it hard with your foot.
kid (kids) *noun*
A kid is a young goat.
kidnap (kidnaps, kidnapping, kidnapped) *verb*
If someone kidnaps another person, they take them away by force.

kill (kills, killing, killed) *verb*
To kill someone or something means to cause them to die.
kilogram (kilograms) *noun*
A kilogram is a measure of weight. It is called a kilo for short. It is equal to 1000 grams.
kilometre (kilometres) *noun*
A kilometre is a measure of distance. It is equal to 1000 metres.
kilt (kilts) *noun*
A kilt is a pleated skirt worn by men as part of the national costume of Scotland. It is made of woollen material woven in a special squared pattern called tartan.
kind (kinder, kindest) *adjective*
Someone who is kind behaves in a gentle, caring way.
>**kindly** *adverb*
kind (kinds) *noun*
If you talk about a kind of object, you mean that sort of object: *I want that kind of pen, please. The ballpoint.*
kindness *noun*
Kindness is when someone is being friendly and helpful towards someone else.
king (kings) *noun*
A king is a man who rules a country. Kings are not chosen by the people, but are born into a royal family. The eldest son of the king becomes king when his father dies.
kingdom (kingdoms) *noun*
1. A kingdom is a country or region that is ruled by a king or queen.
2. People say the animal kingdom when they mean all the animals in the world: *This creature is the largest in the whole animal kingdom.*
kingfisher (kingfishers) *noun*
A kingfisher is a brightly coloured bird that lives by the banks of rivers.
kiss (kisses, kissing, kissed) *verb*
If you kiss someone, you touch them with your lips as a sign of affection.
kit (kits) *noun*
1. A kit is a set of things that are used for a particular purpose: *Have you seen my first-aid kit?*
2. A kit is also a set of parts that can be put together to make something: *I'd like a model aircraft kit for my birthday.*
kitchen (kitchens) *noun*
A kitchen is a room that is used for cooking and washing up in.
kite (kites) *noun*
A kite is an object made from a light frame covered with paper or cloth, with a long string fixed to it. If you hold the end of the string, the kite can fly in the air.
kitten (kittens) *noun*
A kitten is a young cat.
kiwi (kiwis) *noun*
A kiwi is a bird that lives in New Zealand. Kiwis cannot fly, but they can run fast.
knee (knees) *noun*
Your knee is the joint where your leg bends.
kneel (kneels, kneeling, kneeled/knelt) *verb*
When you kneel, or kneel down, you sit down with your weight on your knees and your legs bent underneath you.
knife (knives) *noun*
A knife is an object that you use for cutting. It is made from a sharp, flat piece of metal which is fixed into a handle.
knight (knights) *noun*
1. Hundreds of years ago, a knight was a man who fought battles for his king. He rode a horse and wore armour.
2. Now a knight is a man who is allowed to put 'Sir' in front of his name.
knit (knits, knitting, knitted) *verb*
If you knit, you make something, such as a jumper, from wool or a similar thread.
knob (knobs) *noun*
1. A knob is a round handle on a door or a drawer.
2. A knob is also a round button on a piece of equipment such as a radio.
knock (knocks, knocking, knocked) *verb*
1. If you knock at a door, you hit is so that someone will hear and open the door to you.
2. If you knock something over, you touch it roughly, usually by accident, and it falls over.

knot (knots) *noun*
1. A knot is the place where a piece of something such as string or cloth is tied.
2. A knot in a piece of wood is a small hard area where a branch once grew.
3. A knot is also a measure of speed for ships.

know (knows, knowing, knew, known) *verb*
If you know something, you have it in your mind and you are sure it is true.

knowledge *noun*
Knowledge is what people know about things.

knuckle (knuckles) *noun*
Your knuckles are the rounded pieces of bone where your fingers join your hands. Sometimes the bony places where your fingers bend are also called knuckles.

koala (koalas) *noun*
A koala is an Australian animal. It looks like a small bear and has grey fur and large ears. Koalas live in trees and eat leaves.

L

label (labels) *noun*
A label is a piece of paper or cloth that is fixed to an object. The label tells you things about the object. For example, the label on a medicine bottle tells you what the medicine is called and how you should take it.

laboratory (laboratories) *noun*
A laboratory is a building or a room that contains special equipment. Scientists use laboratories for their work.

lace *noun*
Lace is an ornamental fabric with a lot of holes in it. It is made by looping or twisting fine threads.

laces *noun*
Laces are pieces of cord that are put through holes along two edges of something. The laces are pulled tight and tied to fasten the two edges together.

ladder (ladders) *noun*
A ladder is a piece of equipment that is used for climbing up things like walls or trees.

lady (ladies) *noun*
1. You say lady when you are talking about a woman: *I think this lady was in front of me.*
2. A woman who is married to a knight can put 'Lady' in front of her name: *Sir John and Lady Brown.*

ladybird (ladybirds) *noun*
A ladybird is a small, round beetle with spots on its wings. Ladybirds are usually orangey-red, with black spots.

lake (lakes) *noun*
A lake is a large area of fresh water with land all round it.

lamb (lambs) *noun*
A lamb is a young sheep.

lamp (lamps) *noun*
A lamp is an object that gives light by burning oil or gas, or by using electricity.

lamp-post (lamp-posts) *noun*
A lamp-post is a tall metal or concrete pole with a light on top. Lamp-posts are fixed by the sides of roads.

lampshade (lampshades) *noun*
A lampshade is a covering that is fitted round or over an electric light bulb.

land *noun*
Land is the part of the world that is solid, dry ground. It is not covered by sea.

land (lands, landing, landed) *verb*
If something such as an aircraft lands, it comes down from the air on to land or water.

landing (landings) *noun*
A landing is an area in a house. It is at the top of the stairs, and has rooms leading off it.

landmark (landmarks) *noun*
A landmark is a building or feature of the land which can be used to find out where you are.

landscape (landscapes) *noun*
A landscape is everything you can see when you look across an area of land.

lane (lanes) *noun*
1. A lane is a narrow road, especially in the country.
2. A lane is also part of a main road or motorway. It is marked with lines to show drivers where to go.
language (languages) *noun*
A language is the words that are used by the people of a country when they speak or write to each other.
lantern (lanterns) *noun*
A lantern is a kind of lamp. It has a metal frame with glass sides. Lanterns usually hold oil and have a special piece of string inside called a wick. When the wick is lit, it burns the oil slowly to give a light.
lap (laps) *noun*
Your lap is the top of your legs when you are sitting down.
lap (laps, lapping, lapped) *verb*
When an animal laps a drink, it flicks liquid into its mouth with its tongue.
large (larger, largest) *adjective*
Something that is large is bigger than others of its kind.
larva (larvae) *noun*
A larva is an insect at an early stage of its life. It looks like a short, fat worm.
laser (lasers) *noun*
A laser is a narrow beam of light produced by a special machine. Lasers are used for many different things, including surgery.
last *adjective*
The last person or thing is the one that comes after all the others: *I came last in the sack race.*
late (later, latest) *adjective*
If you are late arriving somewhere, you get there after the time you were supposed to.
lately *adverb*
If something has happened lately, it has happened during the last few days or weeks: *I haven't seen him lately – I think he must be on holiday.*
laugh (laughs, laughing, laughed) *verb*
When you laugh, you make the sound people make when they are happy or when they think something is very funny.
laughter *noun*
Laughter is the act of laughing or the sound of people laughing, especially because they are very amused or happy.
launch (launches, launching, launched) *verb*
When something such as a rocket or satellite is launched, it is sent into the air or into space.
launderette (launderettes) *noun*
A launderette is a shop where people can pay to use washing machines to wash clothes in.
lava *noun*
Lava is a kind of rock. It comes out of volcanoes as a very hot liquid. Then it cools and becomes solid.
lavatory (lavatories) *noun*
1. A lavatory is the same as a toilet. It is a deep bowl which is joined to a drain. It has a seat on top with a large hole in the middle.
2. A lavatory is also the room where the lavatory is. Sometimes there is a washbasin in the room as well.
law (laws) *noun*
A law is a rule that is made by the government.
lawn (lawns) *noun*
A lawn is an area of grass that is kept short. It is usually part of someone's garden.
lawnmower (lawnmowers) *noun*
A lawnmower is a machine for cutting the grass on lawns.
lawyer (lawyers) *noun*
A lawyer is a person who understands the law and can advise people about it.
lay (lays, laying, laid) *verb*
1. If you lay something somewhere, you put it there carefully.
2. If you lay the table, you put things like knives and forks on the table ready for a meal.
layer (layers) *noun*
A layer is a single thickness of something that lies on top of or underneath something else.
lazy (lazier, laziest) *adjective*
1. Someone who is lazy does not want to work or do anything hard.
2. If you do something in a lazy way, you do it gently or easily without making much effort.

>**lazily** *adverb*
lead (leads) *noun*
A dog's lead is a long, thin piece of leather or a chain. You fix one end of it to the dog's collar and hold the other end.
lead (leads, leading, led) *verb*
1. Someone who leads a group of people is in charge of them.
2. If you lead someone to a particular place, you go with them to show them where it is.
3. If something like a path leads to a particular place, it goes to that place.
4. If you are leading in a race or game, you are winning at that point.
lead *noun*
1. Lead is a grey, heavy metal.
2. The lead in a pencil is the centre part of it that makes a mark on paper.
leader (leaders) *noun*
The leader of a group of people is the person who is in charge.
leaf (leaves) *noun*
A leaf is one of the thin, flat parts of a plant. Leaves are usually green. Different sorts of plant have differently shaped leaves.
leaflet (leaflets) *noun*
A leaflet is a little book or piece of paper containing information about a particular subject.
leak (leaks, leaking, leaked) *verb*
If something such as water leaks, it gets through a hole that should not be there.
lean (leans, leaning, leaned/leant) *verb*
If you lean a certain way, you bend your body in that direction.
lean (leaner, leanest) *adjective*
Lean meat does not have much fat.
leap (leaps, leaping, leaped/leapt) *verb*
If you leap somewhere, you jump a long way.
leap year (leap years) *noun*
A leap year is a year which has 366 days. There is a leap year every four years.
learn (learns, learning, learned/learnt) *verb*
When you learn something, you get to know it or find out how to do it.
leather *noun*
Leather is the specially treated skin of animals. It is used for making things like shoes and furniture.
leave (leaves, leaving, left) *verb*
1. If you leave a place, you go away from it.
2. If you leave something in a particular place, you let it stay there when you go away.
3. If you leave an amount of something, it is there when the rest is gone: *I've only got ten pence left.*
4. If you leave something a certain way, you let it stay as it is: *Leave the television on, please.*
5. If you leave something until a particular time, you do not do it before that time: *Why do you leave everything to the last minute?*
ledge (ledges) *noun*
1. A ledge is a piece of rock on the side of a cliff or mountain which is in the shape of a narrow shelf.
2. A ledge is also a small narrow shelf attached to a wall.
left *noun*
The left is the side that you begin reading on in English.
leg (legs) *noun*
1. Your legs are the two long parts of your body that you use for walking.
2. The legs of an animal are the thin parts of its body that it uses for standing and moving.
3. The legs of a piece of furniture, such as a table or chair, are the parts that rest on the floor and support the main part.
legend (legends) *noun*
A legend is a very old and popular story that may or may not be true.
lemon (lemons) *noun*
A lemon is an oval-shaped fruit with a thick yellow skin. Lemons are juicy but they taste sour.
lemonade *noun*
Lemonade is a drink that is made from lemons, sugar and water.
lend (lends, lending, lent) *verb*
If you lend something to someone, you let them have something of yours for a while.

length (lengths) *noun*
1. The length of something is the distance that it measures from one end to the other.
2. The length of something like a holiday is the period of time that it lasts.
3. If you swim a length in a swimming pool, you swim from one end to the other.

lens (lenses) *noun*
A lens is a thin piece of clear material such as glass. It has a curved surface which makes things look clearer, larger or smaller.
Lenses are used in spectacles, cameras and microscopes.

leopard (leopards) *noun*
A leopard is a member of the cat family. Leopards live in the forests of Africa and Asia. Their coats are yellow with black spots in the shape of circles. Leopards are about two metres long from nose to tip of tail.

lesson (lessons) *noun*
A lesson is a short period of time when you are taught something.

letter (letters) *noun*
1. A letter is a message that is written down on paper. You usually put a letter in an envelope and post it.
2. A letter is also a written symbol which stands for one of the sounds in a language: *She went for an eye test and was asked to read the letters on the card.*

letterbox (letterboxes) *noun*
1. A letterbox is a rectangular hole in a door at the entrance to a building. The postman delivers letters by pushing them through the letterbox.
2. A letterbox is also a large, metal container in the street. It has a slot in it so that you can put letters inside. The letters are collected and sent to the addresses written on the envelopes.

lettuce (lettuces) *noun*
A lettuce is a plant with large, green leaves. You can eat it raw in salads.

level *adjective*
1. Something that is level is completely flat with no part higher than any other part.
2. If one thing is level with another, they are both the same height.

lever (levers) *noun*
1. A lever is a long handle that is fixed to a piece of machinery. The lever is pulled or pushed to make the machine work.
2. A lever is also a long bar which can help lift heavy weights.

library (libraries) *noun*
A library is a place where you can go to read the books and newspapers that are kept there. Most libraries allow people to borrow books for certain periods.

lick (licks, licking, licked) *verb*
If you lick something, you move your tongue across it.

lid (lids) *noun*
A lid is the top of a box or other container. It can be raised or taken off when you want to open the container.

lie (lies) *noun*
A lie is something that someone says which they know is not true.

lie (lies, lying, lay, lain) *verb*
If you lie somewhere, your body is flat on the ground or on a bed of some kind.

life *noun*
Life is being alive. All living things - humans, animals and plants - have life.

lifeboat (lifeboats) *noun*
1. A lifeboat is a medium-sized boat which is sent out to sea to rescue people who are in danger.
2. A lifeboat is also a small boat which is carried on a ship. If the ship is in danger of sinking, people can use the lifeboat to escape.

lift (lifts) *noun*
A lift is something like a small room that moves up and down inside a tall building. It can carry people from one level to another.

lift (lifts, lifting, lifted) *verb*
1. If you lift something, you take it in your hands and move it upwards.
2. If you lift your eyes or your head, you look up.

liftoff *noun*
Liftoff is the moment when a rocket or spaceship leaves the ground to begin its journey into space.

light (lights, lighting, lit) *verb*
If you light something, you make it start burning: *They decided to light the fire.*
light (lighter, lightest) *adjective*
1. Something that is light to carry does not weigh very much.
2. Light colours are very pale.
3. Light winds blow gently.
4. A light sound is one that is not loud.
>**lightly** *adverb*
light (lights) *noun*
1. Light is the thing that lets you see. It comes from the sun and moon, and from things such as lamps and torches.
2. A light is anything that makes light.
lighthouse (lighthouses) *noun*
A lighthouse is a tower containing a powerful, flashing light. Lighthouses are built on the coast or on small islands in the sea. They are used to guide ships or to warn them of danger.
lightning *noun*
Lightning is a very bright flash of light in the sky that happens during a thunderstorm.
like *preposition*
1. If you say that one person or thing is like another, you mean they are similar in some way: *He looks like his father but he doesn't act like him.*
2. If you ask someone what something is like, you want them to describe it to you or tell you what they think of it.
like (likes, liking, liked) *verb*
If you like something, you enjoy it and find it pleasant.
likely (likelier, likeliest) *adjective*
If someone is likely to do something, they will very probably do it.
lilac *adjective*
Something that is lilac is a pale purple colour.
limb (limbs) *noun*
1. Your limbs are your arms and legs.
2. The limbs of a tree are its branches.
limit (limits) *noun*
A limit is the largest or smallest amount of something that is allowed: *I mustn't spend more than three pounds - that's my limit.*
limp (limper, limpest) *adjective*
1. If someone is limp, they have no strength or energy.
2. Something that is limp is soft and not crisp or firm: *I'm going to throw this lettuce away - it's gone limp.*
>**limply** *adverb*
limp (limps, limping, limped) *verb*
If a person or animal limps, they walk unevenly, usually because there is something wrong with one foot or leg.
line (lines) *noun*
1. A line is a long, thin mark on a surface. Some writing paper has lines on it to show you where to write.
2. A line of people or things is a number of them in a row.
3. A clothes line is a piece of rope on which you hang clothes to dry.
4. A railway line is one of the heavy, metal rails that trains run on.
linen *noun*
1. Linen is a kind of cloth that is made from a plant called flax.
2. Linen is also the name for things like sheets and pillowcases that are used in the house.
link (links) *noun*
1. A link is one of the rings in a chain.
2. A link is also a connection between two things that makes it possible to mix or work together: *Our school has close links with the two other schools in the area.*
lion (lions) *noun*
A lion is a large animal of the cat family. Lions live in parts of Africa and Asia, in groups called prides.
lioness (lionesses) *noun*
A lioness is a female lion.
lip (lips) *noun*
Your lips are the top and bottom outer edges of your mouth.
liquid (liquids) *noun*
A liquid is something, like water, which is not solid and can be poured.
list (lists) *noun*
A list is a set of things that are written down one below the other.

listen (listens, listening, listened) *verb*
If you listen to a sound that you can hear, you give it your attention.

litre (litres) *noun*
A litre is a measure of the amount of space that something takes up. Liquids such as orange juice and milk are sold in litres.

litter (litters) *noun*
1. Litter is rubbish, such as bits of paper and bottles that are left lying untidily outside.
2. A litter is a group of animals born to the same mother at the same time.

little *adjective*
1. Something or someone that is little is small in size.
2. A little period of time is short: *She only waited a little while.*

live *adjective*
1. Live animals or plants are alive.
2. A live television programme is one that is being broadcast at the same time as it is happening.
3. Live music is music that is played by people who are there, rather than music on tapes or records.

live (lives, living, lived) *verb*
1. To live means to be alive.
2. If someone lives in a particular place, that is where their home is.

lively (livelier, liveliest) *adjective*
1. Someone who is lively is cheerful and full of energy.
2. A place that is lively has a lot of interesting and exciting things happening.

liver (livers) *noun*
Your liver is a large organ in your body. Its job is to clean your blood.

living *adjective*
1. Living things are things which can have life. Humans, animals and plants are all living things.
2. Someone who is living is alive now.

living *noun*
Someone who earns a living doing something earns enough money to buy all the things they need for living: *She earns a living as an artist.*

living room (living rooms) *noun*
The living room in a house is the room where the family spend most of their time.

lizard (lizards) *noun*
A lizard is a small reptile with four short legs and a long tail. It has a rough, dry skin. Lizards' babies hatch from eggs.

llama (llamas) *noun*
A llama is a South American animal of the camel family, with thick, long hair. Llamas are used by people to carry things. People also use their wool to make clothes.

load (loads) *noun*
A load is things which are being carried somewhere.

load (loads, loading, loaded) *verb*
1. If someone loads a vehicle, they put things in it to be taken somewhere.
2. If someone loads a gun, they put a bullet in it.
3. When you load a camera, you put film into it so that it is ready to use.

loaf (loaves) *noun*
A loaf of bread is bread that has been baked in a special shape. You can cut loaves into slices.

lobster (lobsters) *noun*
A lobster is a sea creature that has a hard shell, two large claws and eight legs. Lobsters live in shallow water where it is rocky.

local *adjective*
Local means belonging to the area where you live or work, or the area which you are talking about: *I read about it in the local paper.*
>**locally** *adverb*

lock (locks) *noun*
A lock is an object which is used to keep something such as a door or a case shut. Only a person with the right key can open a lock.

locomotive (locomotives) *noun*
A locomotive is a railway engine driven by steam, electricity or diesel power. It is used to pull trains along railway tracks.

locust (locusts) *noun*
A locust is an insect with long legs and wings that belongs to the same family as a

grasshopper. It lives mainly in hot countries. Locusts fly in large groups called swarms and cause great damage by eating crops.

loft (lofts) *noun*
A loft is the space inside the sloping roof of a house or other building. People sometimes store things in lofts.

log (logs) *noun*
1. A log is a piece of a thick branch from a tree.
2. A log is also a record of things that happen, especially on a ship or aircraft.

lonely (lonelier, loneliest) *adjective*
1. Someone who is lonely is unhappy because they do not have any friends, or do not have anyone to talk to.
2. A lonely place is a place that not many people go to.

long (longer, longest) *adjective*
1. Something that is long lasts for a great period of time: *We had a long holiday this year.*
2. Something long is far from one end to the other: *It's a long way from London to New York.*

long (longs, longing, longed) *verb*
If you long for something, you want it very much, especially if you are not likely to get it: *I long for a cream bun, but I'm on a diet.*

look (looks, looking, looked) *verb*
1. If you look in a particular direction, you direct your eyes that way so that you can see what is there.
2. If you say how someone looks, you tell them how they seem to you: *You look a bit tired.*
3. If you ask what someone looks like, you want a description of their appearance.
4. If you look after someone, you care for them.
5. If you look forward to something, you want it to happen because you think you will enjoy it.

loom (looms) *noun*
A loom is a machine that is used for weaving thread into cloth.

loom (looms, looming, loomed) *verb*
If something looms, it appears as a tall, unclear shape, often in a frightening way: *The trees loomed above him in the fog.*

loop (loops) *noun*
A loop is a circular shape in something long and thin. When you tie shoelaces, the bow has two loops in it.

loose (looser, loosest) *adjective*
1. Something that is loose is not firmly fixed in place: *I have a loose tooth.*
2. Things that are loose are not fixed together: *She had four loose sheets of paper in her bag.*

lord (lords) *noun*
1. Hundreds of years ago, a lord was a man who owned large areas of land and a lot of buildings. He had power over many other people. People worked for him and in exchange he protected them.
2. Now, 'Lord' is a title which is put in front of some important men's names in Britain.

lorry (lorries) *noun*
A lorry is a large vehicle that is used to carry loads by road.

lose (loses, losing, lost) *verb*
1. If you lose something, you do not know where it is.
2. If someone loses weight, they become thinner.
3. If a clock or watch loses time, it goes slower than it should do.
4. If you lose something like a game or a race, someone does better than you.

lost *adjective*
1. If you are lost, you cannot find your way or do not know where you are.
2. If something is lost, you cannot find it.

loud (louder, loudest) *adjective*
A loud sound is one that makes a lot of noise and is easy to hear.
>**loudly** *adverb*
>**out loud** *phrase*
If you read out loud, you speak the words you are reading instead of just thinking them.

loudspeaker (loudspeakers) *noun*
A loudspeaker is a piece of equipment that is used so that sounds can be heard. Microphones, radios and record players all need loudspeakers.

lounge (lounges) *noun*
A lounge is a room in a house or hotel where people sit and relax.
love *noun*
Love is a very strong feeling of affection for someone.
love (loves, loving, loved) *verb*
If you love someone, you like them very much and they are very important to you.
lovely (lovelier, loveliest) *adjective*
Something that is lovely is very pleasing to look at or listen to.
low (lower, lowest) *adjective*
1. Something that is low measures only a short distance from the ground to the top: *There was a low wall that they used to jump over.*
2. If the sun or moon is low, it is close to the horizon.
3. If a river is low, there is less water in it than usual.
4. If the price of something is low, it is cheaper than usual.
5. If an amount of something is low, there is less than there needs to be: *We're getting very low on exercise books.*
lower (lowers, lowering, lowered) *verb*
1. If you lower something, you move it slowly downwards: *As it was getting dark, she lowered the blind.*
2. If you lower your voice, you speak more quietly.
loyal *adjective*
Someone who is loyal stays firm in their friendship for someone.
>**loyally** *adverb*
luck *noun*
Luck is something that seems to happen without any reason. Luck can be good or bad.
lucky (luckier, luckiest) *adjective*
Someone who is lucky seems to have good luck.
>**luckily** *adverb*
luggage *noun*
Luggage is made up of the suitcases, bags and things that you take with you when you are travelling.
luminous *adjective*
Something which is luminous shines or glows with light, especially in the dark.
lump (lumps) *noun*
1. A lump is a piece of something solid: *She took a lump of modelling clay and started to make an animal.*
2. A lump on someone's body is a small swelling.
3. A lump of sugar is a small amount of it, shaped like a cube.
lunar *adjective*
If someone says lunar they are talking about the moon.
lunch *noun*
Lunch is a meal that you have in the middle of the day.
lunchtime *noun*
Lunchtime is the time in the middle of the day when most people have lunch.
lung (lungs) *noun*
Your lungs are the two parts of your body inside your chest that fill with air when you breathe.
luxurious *adjective*
Something that is luxurious is very comfortable and expensive.
luxury (luxuries) *noun*
A luxury is something quite expensive to buy, which is not necessary but which gives you pleasure.

M

machine (machines) *noun*
A machine is a piece of equipment which does a particular kind of work. It is usually powered by an engine or by electricity.
magazine (magazines) *noun*
A magazine is a thin book which comes out regularly, usually once a week or once a month. It has articles, stories and pictures.
maggot (maggots) *noun*
A maggot is a tiny creature that looks like a very small worm. As maggots develop they turn into flies.

magic *noun*
In fairy stories, magic is the thing that makes impossible things happen.
magician (magicians) *noun*
1. In fairy stories, a magician is a man who has magic powers.
2. A magician is also a real person who entertains people by doing tricks which look as though they were done by magic.
magnet (magnets) *noun*
A magnet is a piece of iron or other material which attracts iron towards it.
magnetic *adjective*
Something that is magnetic has the power of a magnet to attract iron or other metal towards it.
>**magnetically** *adverb*
magnificent *adjective*
Something that is magnificent is very grand.
>**magnificently** *adverb*
magnifying glass (magnifying glasses) *noun*
A magnifying glass is a piece of glass, usually in a frame, which makes objects appear to be bigger than they really are.
magpie (magpies) *noun*
A magpie is a bird of the crow family. It has black and white markings and a long tail.
mahogany *noun*
Mahogany is a dark reddish-brown wood that is used to make furniture.
mail *noun*
Mail is things like letters and parcels that the post office delivers to you.
main *adjective*
The main part of something is the most important part.
>**mainly** *adverb*
You use mainly when you want to say that something is true in most cases: *The vet's waiting room was full of animals, mainly dogs and cats.*
mains *noun*
The mains are the pipes or wires that supply gas, water and electricity to buildings.
major *adjective*
You use major to describe something important: *This is a major discovery.*
make (makes, making, made) *verb*
1. If you make something, you use your skill to shape it or put it together.
2. If you make a mistake, you do something wrong.
3. If you make an effort, you try hard.
4. If you make someone do something, you cause them to do it.
5. If you make friends with someone, you get to know them and like them.
>**make up your mind** *phrase*
If you make up your mind, you decide what you are going to do.
male (males) *noun*
A male is an animal that belongs to the sex that cannot have babies.
mammal (mammals) *noun*
A mammal is a warm-blooded animal. Female mammals do not lay eggs. They feed their babies with milk from their own bodies. Human beings, cats and whales are all mammals.
mammoth (mammoths) *noun*
A mammoth was an animal like an elephant. It had very long tusks and long hair. Mammoths have been extinct for thousands of years.
mammoth *adjective*
Mammoth means very large indeed.
man (men) *noun*
1. A man is an adult male human.
2. You can say man to mean human beings in general: *Man is a mammal that walks on two legs.*
manage (manages, managing, managed) *verb*
If you manage to do something, you do something that is difficult.
mane (manes) *noun*
The mane of an animal such as a horse or a male lion is the long, thick hair that grows from its neck.
manner (manners) *noun*
1. Your manner is the way you behave and speak on a particular occasion.
2. Good manners are a polite way of behaving or speaking.

mantelpiece (mantelpieces) *noun*
A mantelpiece is a shelf over a fireplace.
manufacture (manufactures, manufacturing, manufactured) *verb*
When people manufacture something, they make it in a factory.
map (maps) *noun*
A map is a drawing of a particular area as it would look from above.
maple (maples) *noun*
A maple is a tree with five-pointed leaves. Maples grow in cool areas. They lose their leaves in winter.
marathon (marathons) *noun*
A marathon is a race in which people have to run about 42 kilometres along roads.
marathon *adjective*
A marathon task is one that takes a long time to do and is very tiring.
marble (marbles) *noun*
1. Marble is a type of very hard rock that shines when it is polished. Statues and parts of buildings are sometimes made of marble.
2. A marble is one of the very small, coloured, glass balls used by children in the game of marbles.
marbles *noun*
Marbles is a children's game, played with very small balls usually made of coloured glass. You roll a ball along the ground and try to hit the other players' balls with it.
march (marches, marching, marched) *verb*
If you march, you walk with regular steps like a soldier.
March *noun*
March is the third month of the year. It has 31 days.
margarine *noun*
Margarine is a soft, yellow mixture that looks like butter. It is made with vegetable oil. You can spread it on bread or use it in cooking.
margin (margins) *noun*
The margin on a written or printed page is the space at the edge of the page.
mark (marks) *noun*
1. A mark is a small part of a surface which is a different colour because something has been dropped on it or because it has been damaged in some way.
2. A mark is also something which has been written or drawn: *He made a lot of little marks on the paper with his pencil.*
3. Teachers sometimes give marks to show how good or bad a student's work is.
market (markets) *noun*
A market is a place where things are bought and sold. Markets are often held somewhere outside, such as in the centre of a town. In some towns, markets are held regularly, for example once a week.
marmalade *noun*
Marmalade is a food rather like jam. It is made from fruit like oranges or lemons. It is usually eaten for breakfast, spread on toast.
marriage *noun*
Marriage is the relationship between a husband and wife.
marry (marries, marrying, married) *verb*
A man and woman who marry become husband and wife.
marsh (marshes) *noun*
A marsh is an area of land which is always very wet and muddy. This is usually because water cannot drain from it properly.
marsupial (marsupials) *noun*
A marsupial is an animal whose babies are carried in a pouch at the front of their mother's body. Kangaroos and koalas are marsupials.
marvellous *adjective*
Something that is marvellous is wonderful, and even better than you expected.
>**marvellously** *adverb*
mask (masks) *noun*
A mask is something that you wear over your face. There are usually holes that you can see through. Some masks are funny and some are frightening.
mass (masses) *noun*
1. A mass of things is a large number of them grouped together.
2. A mass is an amount of a solid, liquid or gas, especially a large amount which has no definite shape.

mast (masts) *noun*
A mast is a long, vertical pole on a sailing ship. It is used to hold the sails and flags.
mat (mats) *noun*
A mat is a small piece of carpet or other material that is put on the floor.
match (matches) *noun*
1. A match is an organized game of something like tennis or football.
2. A match is also a small, thin stick of wood or card. One end is specially treated so that when you brush it hard against something rough, it makes a flame.
match (matches, matching, matched) *verb*
If you match one thing with another, you decide there is some connection between them. In some tests or puzzles, you are asked to match things from a list: *Can you match the animals with the countries they come from?*
material (materials) *noun*
1. A material is anything solid that can be used to make something else. Wood, iron and stone are all materials.
2. Material is fabric that you can use to make things like clothes and curtains.
mathematics *noun*
See maths.
maths *noun*
Maths is the study of numbers, quantities and shapes. Maths is short for mathematics.
matter (matters, mattering, mattered) *verb*
If something matters to you, you care about it and feel it is important.
matter *noun*
Matter is what the world is made of. Solids, liquids and gases are all matter.
>**the matter** *phrase*
You say 'What's the matter?' or 'Is anything the matter?' to someone when you want to know what their problem is.
mattress (mattresses) *noun*
A mattress is a large, flat cushion which is the same size as a bed. It is put on a bed to make it comfortable to lie on.
May *noun*
May is the fifth month of the year. It has 31 days.
may (might) *verb*
1. When you say something may be true, you mean it could be true but you are not sure.
2. If someone says you may do something, you are allowed to do it.
maybe *adverb*
You say maybe when something is possible but you are not sure.
mayor (mayors) *noun*
The mayor of a town or city is the man or woman who has ben chosen to be its head.
meadow (meadows) *noun*
A meadow is a field of grass and flowers.
meal (meals) *noun*
A meal is food that people eat, usually at set times during the day.
mealtime (mealtimes) *noun*
A mealtime is a period when you eat a meal.
mean (means, meaning, meant) *verb*
If you ask what something means, you want it explained to you.
mean (meaner, meanest) *adjective*
1. Someone who is mean is too careful with something such as money.
2. If you are mean to someone, you are unkind to them.
>**meanly** *adverb*
means *noun*
The means of doing something is the way it is done: *The car has broken down. We shall have to find some other means of getting there.*
meanwhile *adverb*
Meanwhile means while a particular thing is happening.
measles *noun*
Measles is an illness caught especially by children. It gives you a high temperature and red spots on your skin.
measure (measures, measuring, measured) *verb*
If you measure something, you find out how large or heavy it is.

meat *noun*
Meat is flesh taken from an animal that has been killed for eating.
mechanic (mechanics) *noun*
A mechanic is someone whose job is to repair and look after machines and engines.
mechanical *adjective*
A mechanical object is one that has moving parts and is used to do a particular kind of work.
>mechanically *adverb*
medal (medals) *noun*
A medal is a small piece of metal in the shape of a circle or a cross. It is given for bravery or as a prize.
medical *adjective*
Medical means to do with medicine or the care of people's health.
>medically *adverb*
medicine *noun*
Medicine is something that is given to a person who is ill to make them better.
meet (meets, meeting, met) *verb*
If you meet someone, you go to the same place at the same time as they do.
meeting (meetings) *noun*
A meeting is when a group of people meet to talk about particular things.
melody (melodies) *noun*
A melody is a tune.
melon (melons) *noun*
A melon is a large fruit which is sweet and juicy inside. It has a thick, hard, green or yellow skin.
melt (melts, melting, melted) *verb*
When something melts, it changes from a solid into a liquid.
member (members) *noun*
A member of a group is one of the people, animals or things belonging to that group.
membership *noun*
Membership of an organization is belonging to it.
memory (memories) *noun*
1. Your memory is being able to remember things: *If you want to be an actor, you need a good memory.*
2. A memory is something you remember from the past: *The memory of the holiday was still fresh in her mind.*
mend (mends, mending, mended) *verb*
If you mend something that is broken or does not work, you put it right so that it can be used again.
mental *adjective*
Mental arithmetic is sums that you work out in your mind, without using a pencil and paper or a calculator.
>mentally *adverb*
mention (mentions, mentioning, mentioned) *verb*
If you mention something, you say it, but do not spend very long talking about it.
menu (menus) *noun*
1. A menu is a list of food that you can order in a restaurant.
2. A menu is also a list on a computer that tells you what you can do.
mercury *noun*
Mercury is a silver-coloured metal, usually in liquid form. It is used in thermometers to measure temperature.
mermaid (mermaids) *noun*
In stories, a mermaid is a woman who lives in the sea. She has a fish's tail instead of legs.
mess *noun*
1. If you say something is a mess, you mean it is very untidy.
2. A mess is also something that has been spilt.
message (messages) *noun*
A message is words that you send or leave when you cannot speak directly to someone.
messenger (messengers) *noun*
A messenger is a person who takes a message to someone. Some people take messages regularly because it is their job.
metal (metals) *noun*
A metal is a hard material such as iron, steel or copper. Metals are used for making things like tools or machinery.
meteorology *noun*
Meteorology is the scientific study of the weather, used in making weather forecasts.

meter (meters) *noun*
A meter is an instrument for measuring something, such as the amount of gas or electricity that you have used.
method (methods) *noun*
A method is a particular way of doing something.
metre (metres) *noun*
A metre is a measure of length. It is equal to 100 centimetres or 39.37 inches.
mew (mews, mewing, mewed) *verb*
When a cat mews, it makes a soft high-pitched noise.
micro- *prefix*
If a word begins with micro-, it means something very small. For example, a microcomputer is a very small computer.
microchip (microchips) *noun*
A microchip is a very tiny piece of silicon, a special material that is used in computers.
microphone (microphones) *noun*
A microphone is an instrument that you speak into when you want to make your voice louder. You also need a microphone if you want to record what you are saying.
microscope (microscopes) *noun*
A microscope is an instrument which helps you to see very tiny things. You look at things through a special lens which makes them seem much bigger.
microwave (microwaves) *noun*
A microwave is a kind of oven which cooks food very quickly.
mid-air *noun*
If something happens in mid-air, it happens in the air rather than on the ground.
midday *noun*
Midday is 12 o'clock in the middle of the day.
middle *noun*
The middle of an area is the part that is furthest from all its sides.
midnight *noun*
Midnight is 12 o'clock in the middle of the night.
might *verb*
1. If you say something might happen, you mean you are not sure if it will.
2. If you say something might be true, you are not sure about it.
might *noun*
Might is power or strength.
mighty (mightier, mightiest) *adjective*
Something that is mighty is very powerful or strong.
migrate (migrates, migrating, migrated) *verb*
1. If people migrate, they move from one place to another, especially to find work or to live there for a short time.
2. When birds, fish or animals migrate, they move at a particular time or season from one place to another.
mild (milder, mildest) *adjective*
1. If someone is mild, they are gentle and kind.
2. Mild weather is warmer than usual.
mile (miles) *noun*
A mile is a measure of distance. It is equal to 1760 yards or 1.6 kilometres.
military *adjective*
Military means to do with the armed forces of a country.
milk *noun*
Milk is the white liquid that female mammals make in their bodies to feed their young. People drink milk.
milkman (milkmen) *noun*
A milkman is a person who delivers milk regularly to people's houses.
mill (mills) *noun*
1. A mill is a building in which grain is crushed to make flour.
2. A mill is also a factory used for making a particular material such as cotton or steel.
millilitre (millilitres) *noun*
A millilitre is a measure of volume for liquids and gases. There are 1000 millilitres in a litre.
millimetre (millimetres) *noun*
A millimetre is a measure of length. There are 10 millimetres in a centimetre, and 1000 millimetres in a metre.

million (millions) *noun*
A million is a thousand thousands. In figures it is written 1,000,000.

millionaire (millionaires) *noun*
A millionaire is a very rich person who has money, buildings or other valuable things, that are worth more than a million pounds.

mimic (mimics, mimicking, mimicked) *verb*
If you mimic the actions or voice of someone, you imitate them in a way that is meant to be amusing or entertaining.

mince *noun*
Mince is beef which has been put through a special machine. The machine cuts it into very small pieces.

mince (minces, mincing, minced) *verb*
If you mince meat, you cut it into very small pieces.

mincemeat *noun*
Mincemeat is a sticky mixture of dried fruit and other sweet things. Mincemeat is usually cooked in pastry to make mince pies.

mind (minds) *noun*
Your mind is where your thoughts are.

mind (minds, minding, minded) *verb*
1. If you mind something or somebody, you look after them for a while.
2. If you do not mind something, it does not worry you.

mine (mines) *noun*
A mine is a place where people dig deep holes to find something like coal or diamonds.

mineral (minerals) *noun*
1. A mineral is a material that is formed naturally in rocks and the earth. Tin, salt and sulphur are minerals.
2. Minerals are also sweet, fizzy drinks.

minister (ministers) *noun*
1. A minister is an important member of the government of a country.
2. A minister is also a person who is in charge of a church.

minor (minors) *noun*
A minor is a person who is not yet an adult. In Britain, anyone under the age of 18 is a minor.

minor *adjective*
Something that is minor is not very important or serious.

mint (mints) *noun*
1. Mint is a small plant. Its leaves have a strong taste and smell. Mint is used in cooking.
2. A mint is the place where the coins of a country are made.

minute (minutes) *noun*
A minute is a measure of time. There are 60 minutes in one hour.

minute *adjective*
Something that is minute is extremely small.
>**minutely** *adverb*

miracle (miracles) *noun*
A miracle is something wonderful and surprising that cannot be explained.

mirror (mirrors) *noun*
A mirror is a flat piece of glass that reflects light. When you look in a mirror, you can see yourself.

mischief *noun*
Mischief is silly things that some children do to annoy other people.

mischievous *adjective*
A mischievous child is often naughty but does not do any real harm.
>**mischievously** *adverb*

miserable *adjective*
Someone who is miserable is very unhappy.
>**miserably** *adverb*

misery *noun*
Misery is great unhappiness.

mishap (mishaps) *noun*
A mishap is something that happens to you which you do not like, but which is not very serious.

miss (misses, missing, missed) *verb*
1. If you are aiming at something and miss, you fail to hit it.
2. If you miss something, you do not notice it: *We missed our turning and had to go back.*
3. If you miss a bus or train, you are too late to get on it.
4. If you miss somebody, you are lonely without them.

missile (missiles) *noun*
1. A missile is a weapon like a rocket.
2. A missile is also any object that is thrown at someone.
missing *adjective*
If something is missing, it is not in its usual place and you cannot find it.
mist (mists) *noun*
A mist is a large number of tiny drops of water in the air. When there is a mist, you cannot see very far.
mistake (mistakes) *noun*
A mistake is something which is not quite right: *There are two spelling mistakes on this page.*
mistletoe *noun*
Mistletoe is a plant with white berries. It grows on the branches of trees instead of in the soil.
misunderstand (misunderstands, misunderstanding, misunderstood) *verb*
If you misunderstand someone, you do not understand them properly.
mix (mixes, mixing, mixed) *verb*
If you mix two things, you stir them or put them together in some way. Then they become one thing: *The children made paste by mixing flour and water.*
mixture (mixtures) *noun*
A mixture is something that is made by mixing two or more things. A mixture is usually a liquid or a rather sticky solid.
moan (moans) *noun*
A moan is a low, miserable cry that people give if they are in pain or are very unhappy.
mob (mobs) *noun*
A mob is a large, disorganized crowd of people, especially people who are angry about something.
model (models) *noun*
1. A model is a small copy of something. It shows what it looks like or how it works.
2. A model is also someone who shows clothes to people by wearing them.
modern *adjective*
1. Modern means to do with the period of history that you live in.
2. Modern also describes something which is new and which uses the latest ideas.
modest *adjective*
1. People who are modest do not boast about their own qualities or possessions.
2. A house or flat that is modest is not large or expensive.
>**modestly** *adverb*
moist (moister, moistest) *adjective*
Something that is moist is slightly wet.
moisten (moistens, moistening, moistened) *verb*
If you moisten something, you make it slightly wet.
moisture *noun*
Moisture is tiny drops of water in the air or on a surface.
mole (moles) *noun*
1. A mole is a small, dark lump on someone's skin.
2. A mole is also a small animal. It has tiny eyes and short, dark, silky fur. Moles have strong front claws and are very good at digging. They live most of the time on their own in tunnels in the ground. Moles eat insects and worms.
molehill (molehills) *noun*
A molehill is a small pile of earth on the ground which has been left by a mole that has been digging.
moment (moments) *noun*
1. A moment is a very short period of time.
2. A moment is also a point in time when something happens: *At that moment, the teacher came into the room.*
Monday *noun*
Monday is one of the seven days of the week. It comes after Sunday and before Tuesday.
money *noun*
Money is the coins or bank notes you use when you buy something.
mongrel (mongrels) *noun*
A mongrel is a dog which is a mixture of two or more breeds.
monkey (monkeys) *noun*
A monkey is an animal that lives in hot countries. It has a long tail and strong hands.

monsoon *noun*
1. The monsoon is the season in southern Asia when there is a lot of very heavy rain.
2. The monsoon is also the wind that brings the monsoon rains in southern Asia.
monster (monsters) *noun*
A monster is a large, imaginary creature that looks very frightening.
month (months) *noun*
A month is a measure of time. There are 12 months in a year.
mood (moods) *noun*
Your mood is the way you are feeling about things at a particular time, especially how cheerful or angry you are.
moon *noun*
The moon is a round object in the sky. It goes round the earth once every four weeks.
moonlight *noun*
Moonlight is the light that comes from the moon at night.
moor (moors) *noun*
A moor is an area of land with poor soil. It is covered mainly with grass and heather.
moose *noun*
A moose is a large North American deer. Moose have very flat, branch-shaped horns called antlers.
mop (mops) *noun*
A mop is a tool for washing dishes. It has a short handle with sponge or pieces of string fixed to the end. Some mops are used for cleaning the floor. These have longer handles.
morning *noun*
Morning is the part of the day before noon.
morsel (morsels) *noun*
A morsel is a very small amount of something, especially a very small piece of food.
mortar *noun*
Mortar is a mixture of cement, sand and water. It is used in building to hold bricks together.
mosque (mosques) *noun*
A mosque is a building where Muslims worship.
mosquito (mosquitoes/mosquitos) *noun*
A mosquito is a small, flying insect which lives in damp places. It bites people and animals.
moss (mosses) *noun*
Mosses are very small green plants without roots. They grow on damp soil, stone or wood.
moth (moths) *noun*
A moth is an insect with large wings. Moths often fly at night, and they are attracted to bright lights.
mother (mothers) *noun*
1. A mother is a woman who has children of her own.
2. Any female animal who has a baby is also called a mother.
motion (motions) *noun*
A motion is a movement.
motionless *adjective*
Someone or something that is motionless is not moving at all.
>**motionlessly** *adverb*
motor (motors) *noun*
A motor is part of a vehicle or machine. The motor uses fuel to make the vehicle or machine work.
motorbike (motorbikes) *noun*
A motorbike is a two-wheeled vehicle that is like a bicycle, but is much heavier and is driven by an engine.
motorway (motorways) *noun*
A motorway is a large road. Motorways are specially built for fast travel over long distances.
mountain (mountains) *noun*
A mountain is a raised part of the earth's surface. Mountains are very high with steep sides. They are usually difficult to climb.
mouse (mice) *noun*
A mouse is a small, furry animal with a long tail. There are different kinds of mouse.
moustache (moustaches) *noun*
A man's moustache is the hair that grows above his upper lip.
mouth (mouths) *noun*
Your mouth is the opening in your face that you put your food into when you eat. People, animals, fish and insects have mouths. Birds have beaks.

move (moves, moving, moved) *verb*
1. When someone or something moves, they change their position. They do not stay still.
2. When you move an object, you put it somewhere else.
3. If you move house, you leave the house where you have been living. You take your furniture and other things with you and go to live in a different house.
movement (movements) *noun*
1. When you make a movement, you move part of your body.
2. If you see or hear a movement, you notice someone or something moving.
mow (mows, mowing, mowed, mown) *verb*
If a person mows an area of grass, they cut it with a lawnmower.
mud *noun*
Mud is a wet, sticky mixture of earth and water, which becomes hard when it dries. In some countries, it is used to build houses.
muddle *noun*
If something, such as papers, is in a muddle, they are all mixed up.
muffle (muffles, muffling, muffled) *verb*
If you muffle something, you make it quieter: *She put her hand over her mouth to muffle her laughter.*
mug (mugs) *noun*
A mug is a large deep cup, usually with straight sides and a handle.
multiply (multiplies, multiplying, multiplied) *verb*
1. When animals and insects multiply, the number of them gets bigger. This is because they have large numbers of babies which grow up and have babies of their own.
2. If you multiply a number, you add it to itself. For example, to multiply two by three, you add three lots of two together, like this: 2 + 2 + 2. Then you have six.
mumble (mumbles, mumbling, mumbled) *verb*
If you mumble, you speak very quietly and do not open your mouth properly, so that the words are difficult to hear.
mumps *noun*
Mumps is an illness caught especially by children. If you get mumps, your neck swells and your throat hurts.
murder (murders, murdering, murdered) *verb*
To murder someone means to kill someone on purpose.
murmur (murmurs, murmuring, murmured) *verb*
If you murmur, you say something very quietly.
muscle (muscles) *noun*
Muscles are things in your body that loosen and tighten to help you move.
museum (museums) *noun*
A museum is a place or building where you can see collections of important things. Some museums have works of art. Some have stuffed animals and birds. Many museums tell the story of something, such as photography, vehicles or fabrics. Most big towns have a museum.
mushroom (mushrooms) *noun*
A mushroom is a small vegetable with a short, thick stem and a round top. It looks like a tiny umbrella.
music *noun*
Music is made up of sounds which are put together in a pattern. The sounds are usually made by a special instrument, such as a piano or guitar. When music is made by a human voice, it is called singing.
musician (musicians) *noun*
A musician is a person who plays a musical instrument well.
Muslim (Muslims) *noun*
A Muslim is someone who follows the teachings of Mohammed.
mustard *noun*
Mustard is a yellow or brown paste which tastes hot and spicy. People often eat a small amount of mustard with meat.
mutton *noun*
Mutton is the meat from an adult sheep.
mysterious *adjective*
Something that is mysterious is strange and cannot be explained or understood.
>**mysteriously** *adverb*

mystery (mysteries) *noun*
1. A mystery is something strange that cannot be explained.
2. A mystery story is one in which strange things happen. These things are usually explained at the end of the story.

N

nail (nails) *noun*
1. A nail is a small piece of metal with a point on one end. It usually has a flat top that you can hit with a hammer. Nails are sometimes used to join two pieces of wood together.
2. Your nails are the thin hard areas that cover the end of each of your fingers and toes.
naked *adjective*
1. Someone who is naked is not wearing any clothes.
2. Something that is naked does not have any cover over it when you would normally expect it to be covered: *There was nothing in the room but a naked light bulb.*
name (names) *noun*
A name is what someone or something is called.
nappy (nappies) *noun*
A nappy is a thick piece of soft material wrapped round a baby's bottom to help keep it dry and clean.
narrator (narrators) *noun*
A narrator is a person in something like a book or a film, who tells the story or explains what is happening.
narrow (narrower, narrowest) *adjective*
Something that is narrow is a very short distance from one side to the other.
nasty (nastier, nastiest) *adjective*
1. Something that is nasty is very unpleasant.
2. Someone who is nasty is very unkind.
>nastily *adverb*
national *adjective*
Something that is national is to do with the whole of a country or nation.
>nationally *adverb*
native *adjective*
Your native country is the country where you were born.
native (natives) *noun*
A native of a particular country is someone who was born there.
natural *adjective*
Natural is used to describe things that are not made by people. Trees, rocks and rivers are natural things.
>naturally *adverb*
nature *noun*
Nature is everything in the world that is not caused by human beings.
naughty (naughtier, naughtiest) *adjective*
A child who is naughty behaves badly.
>naughtily *adverb*
navigate (navigates, navigating, navigated) *verb*
Someone who navigates a ship or aircraft works out which way to go.
navy (navies) *noun*
A navy is one of the forces that a country uses for fighting. Navies use ships to fight at sea.
near (nearer, nearest) *adjective*
Something that is near is not far away: *Where is the nearest supermarket?*
near *preposition*
If something happens near a particular point in time, it happens close to it: *It happens somewhere near the beginning of the story.*
nearby *adjective*
If something is nearby, it is close to where you are or close to the place you are talking about.
nearly *adverb*
Nearly means almost but not quite: *I nearly caught him but he ran off at the last moment.*
neat (neater, neatest) *adjective*
Something that is neat is very tidy and clean.
>neatly *adverb*
necessary *adjective*
Something that is necessary is needed to get the result you want.
>necessarily *adverb*

neck (necks) *noun*
Your neck is the part of your body which joins your head to the rest of your body.

necklace (necklaces) *noun*
A necklace is a piece of jewellery which is worn round the neck.

need (needs, needing, needed) *verb*
1. If you need something, you must have it in order to live and be healthy.
2. Sometimes you need something to help you do a particular job: *Now I need a paintbrush.*
3. If someone says you need not do something, they mean you do not have to do it.

needle (needles) *noun*
1. A needle is a small, very thin piece of metal used for sewing. It has a hole in one end and a sharp point at the other. You put thread through the hole.
2. A needle can also be a thin, hollow metal rod with a sharp point, which people like doctors use to give injections.
3. Knitting needles are long, thin pieces of metal or plastic that are used for knitting.
4. The thin leaves on pine trees are also called needles.

negative *adjective*
A negative sentence is one that has the word 'no' or 'not' in it.

negative (negatives) *noun*
A negative is a piece of film from a camera. You can get your photographs printed from a negative.

neighbour (neighbours) *noun*
A neighbour is someone who lives near you.

neighbourhood (neighbourhoods) *noun*
The neighbourhood of a place or person is the area or the people around them.

nephew (nephews) *noun*
Someone's nephew is a son of their sister or brother.

nerve (nerves) *noun*
Your nerves are the long, thin threads in your body that carry messages between your brain and the other parts of your body.

nervous *adjective*
1. Someone who is nervous is easily frightened.
2. If you are nervous about something, you are slightly worried about it.
>**nervously** *adverb*

nest (nests) *noun*
A nest is a home that a bird or other animal makes for its babies.

nestle (nestles, nestling, nestled) *verb*
If you nestle somewhere, you move into a comfortable position, especially by pressing against someone or something soft.

net (nets) *noun*
1. Net is material made from threads which are knotted or woven together, leaving holes in between.
2. A net is a piece of netting which is used in games like tennis, football, and netball.
3. A net is also a bag made from netting which is sometimes fixed to the end of a pole and is used to catch animals, especially fish or butterflies.

netball *noun*
Netball is a game played by two teams of seven players. Each team tries to score goals by throwing a ball through a net. The net is on a hoop above the players' heads.

never *adverb*
Never means at no time in the past or future: *You must never cross the road without looking carefully.*

new (newer, newest) *adjective*
1. Something that is new has just been made or built: *They have just built some new houses close to us.*
2. A new discovery is something that has not been noticed before: *Scientists have found a new star.*
>**newly** *adverb*

newcomer (newcomers) *noun*
A newcomer is a person who has recently arrived to live somewhere or to join an organization.

news *noun*
News is information about something that has just happened.

newspaper (newspapers) *noun*
A newspaper is sheets of paper which are printed and sold regularly. Daily newspapers are printed every day from Monday to Saturday. Others are sold once a week. Newspapers give information about things that have happened and are happening. They also have other interesting things such as puzzles and cartoons.
newt (newts) *noun*
A newt is a small creature rather like a lizard. It has a moist skin, short legs and a long tail. Newts live partly on land and partly in water. Female newts lay eggs which hatch into tadpoles. The tadpoles gradually turn into tiny newts.
next *adjective*
1. The next period or thing is the one that comes immediately after the present one: *The next programme will follow after the break.*
2. The next place is the one that is nearest to you: *She is in the next room.*
next *adverb*
You use next to say what happens immediately after something else: *We couldn't guess what would happen next.*
nib (nibs) *noun*
A nib is a small pointed piece of metal at the end of a pen. It holds ink and the ink comes out of it as you write.
nibble (nibbles, nibbling, nibbled) *verb*
1. If you nibble something, you eat it slowly by taking small bites out of it.
2. If a small animal, like a mouse, nibbles something, it takes small bites out of it quickly.
nice (nicer, nicest) *adjective*
1. You say something is nice when you like it: *This cake is nice.*
2. If the weather is nice, it is warm and pleasant.
3. If you are nice to people, you are friendly and kind.
>**nicely** *adverb*
nickname (nicknames) *noun*
A nickname is a name that is given to a person by friends or family.
niece (nieces) *noun*
Someone's niece is a daughter of their sister or brother.
night (nights) *noun*
The night is the time between evening and morning when it is dark outside.
nightdress (nightdresses) *noun*
A nightdress is a piece of clothing shaped like a dress, that women and girls wear in bed.
nightfall *noun*
Nightfall is the time of day when it starts to get dark.
nightie (nighties) *noun*
Nightie is short for nightdress.
nightingale (nightingales) *noun*
A nightingale is a small, brown European bird. The male has the most beautiful song of all birds. Nightingales sing after dark as well as during the day.
nightmare (nightmares) *noun*
A nightmare is a very frightening dream.
nocturnal *adjective*
An animal that is nocturnal is active mostly at night.
nod (nods, nodding, nodded) *verb*
If you nod, you move your head quickly down and up to show that you are answering 'yes' to a question, or to show that you understand or agree with what someone is saying.
noise (noises) *noun*
1. A noise is a sound that someone or something makes.
2. Noise is loud or unpleasant sounds.
nonsense *noun*
Nonsense is words that do not make sense.
noon *noun*
Noon is 12 o'clock in the middle of the day.
normal *adjective*
Something that is normal is usual and ordinary, and what you would expect.
>**normally** *adverb*
north *noun*
North is one of the four main points of the compass. If you face the point where the sun rises, north is on your left.
nose (noses) *noun*
Your nose is the part of your face that sticks out above your mouth. It is used for smelling and breathing.

nostril (nostrils) *noun*
Your nostrils are the two openings at the end of your nose. You breathe through your nostrils.
note (notes) *noun*
1. A note is a short letter.
2. A note is also a sound made by singing or by playing a musical instrument.
3. A bank note is a printed piece of paper that is used as money.
notebook (notebooks) *noun*
A notebook is a small book for writing notes in.
notice (notices, noticing, noticed) *verb*
If you notice something, you pay attention to it: *They suddenly noticed it was getting late, and began to run.*
notice (notices) *noun*
A notice is a sign which tells people something: *There was a notice which said 'Cameras are not allowed in the museum.'*
noun (nouns) *noun*
In grammar, a noun is a word which names something: *'James', 'newt' and 'success' are all nouns.*
nourishment *noun*
Nourishment is the food that living things need in order to grow and stay healthy.
novel (novels) *noun*
A novel is a long written story about people and events that have been made up by the author.
novel *adjective*
Something that is novel is new and interesting.
November *noun*
November is the eleventh month of the year. It has 30 days.
now *adverb*
Now means at the present time.
>**just now** *phrase*
Just now means a very short time ago.
nuclear *adjective*
Nuclear energy is the energy that is released when the nuclei of atoms are either split or joined together.
nucleus (nuclei) *noun*
The nucleus of an atom is the middle part, which is made up of tiny particles called protons and neutrons.
nuisance (nuisances) *noun*
If you say that someone or something is a nuisance, you mean they annoy you.
>**make a nuisance** *phrase*
If you make a nuisance of yourself, you behave in a way that annoys other people.
numb *adjective*
If part of your body is numb, it does not feel anything.
number (numbers) *noun*
1. You use numbers when you are counting or saying how many things there are. Numbers can be written as words; for example, one, two or three. They can also be written as symbols; for example, 7, 8 or 23.
2. You also use numbers for things like addresses and telephones.
nurse (nurses) *noun*
A nurse is a person whose job is to care for people who are ill or injured. Many nurses work in hospitals.
nursery (nurseries) *noun*
1. A nursery is a place where young children can be looked after during the day.
2. A nursery can also be a place where plants are grown and sold.
nut (nuts) *noun*
1. A nut is the hard fruit of certain trees such as walnuts and chestnuts.
2. A nut is also a small piece of metal with a hole in it. It screws on to a bolt to fasten things together.
nylon *noun*
Nylon is a strong man-made material. It can be used for making fabrics for things like curtains or clothes.

oak (oaks) *noun*
An oak is a large tree which loses its leaves in the winter. The fruit of an oak tree is an acorn.

oar (oars) *noun*
An oar is a long pole that is used for rowing a boat. It has a wide flat piece on the end that goes in the water. The flat piece is called the blade.
oasis (oases) *noun*
An oasis is a place in a desert where there is water, so that plants can grow.
oats *noun*
Oats are the grains of a cereal. They are used especially for making porridge or for feeding animals.
obey (obeys, obeying, obeyed) *verb*
If you obey someone, you do as they say.
object (objects) *noun*
An object is a thing that you can touch and see, for example a toy or a book. Living things such as people and animals are not called objects.
oblong (oblongs) *noun*
An oblong is a shape with four straight sides and square corners. It has two equal long sides and two equal short sides.
observe (observes, observing, observed) *verb*
If you observe someone or something, you watch them carefully.
obstinate *adjective*
Someone who is obstinate is very determined to do what they want and will not change their mind.
>obstinately *adverb*
obvious *adjective*
Something that is obvious is easy to see or understand.
>obviously *adverb*
occasion (occasions) *noun*
An occasion is an important event or celebration.
occasionally *adverb*
If something happens occasionally, it happens sometimes but not very often.
occupant (occupants) *noun*
1. The occupant of a building or room is the person who lives or works there.
2. An occupant can also be someone who is occupying something like a seat or a room at a particular time.
occupy (occupies, occupying, occupied) *verb*
1. To occupy a place means to live, stay or work in it.
2. If something like a chair is occupied, someone is using it.
3. If something occupies you, you are busy doing it or thinking about it.
occur (occurs, occurring, occurred) *verb*
1. When something occurs, it happens.
2. If something occurs to you, you suddenly think of it or realize it.
ocean (oceans) *noun*
An ocean is one of the five very large seas on the earth's surface.
o'clock *adverb*
You say o'clock after numbers when you tell the time.
October *noun*
October is the tenth month of the year. It has 31 days.
octopus (octopuses) *noun*
An octopus is a sea creature with eight long arms called tentacles. It uses its tentacles to catch its food.
odd (odder, oddest) *adjective*
1. Odd numbers are those which cannot be divided exactly by two: *13, 25 and 79 are odd numbers.*
2. Odd things are those which do not belong in a pair or a set: *You can't go out like that - you're wearing odd socks.*
3. If you say something is odd, you mean it is strange or unusual.
>oddly *adverb*
odour (odours) *noun*
An odour is a particular smell.
offence (offences) *noun*
An offence is something which is against the law.
offend (offends, offending, offended) *verb*
1. If you offend someone, you upset or embarrass them by doing or saying something rude.
2. To offend also means to commit a crime.
offer (offers, offering, offered) *verb*
1. If you offer something to someone, you ask them if they would like to have it.

2. If you offer to do something, you say you will do it without being asked: *Their neighbour was ill, so they offered to do his shopping.*

>**on offer** *phrase*
If something is on offer, it is for sale at a lower price than usual.

office (offices) *noun*
An office is a room where someone works. Offices usually have lots of papers and books in them.

officer (officers) *noun*
1. An officer is an important person in an organization such as the armed forces.
2. Members of the police force are also called officers.

official *adjective*
Something that is official is written or done by the government or by someone else in authority.

>**officially** *adverb*

offspring *noun*
Someone's offspring are their children.

often *adverb*
If something happens often, it happens many times or most of the time.

ogre (ogres) *noun*
In fairy tales, an ogre is a man who is large, cruel and frightening, and often eats people.

oil *noun*
1. Oil is a smooth, thick liquid that is found under the ground. It is used to keep machines running smoothly, and also for fuel.
2. Oil can also be made from plants or animals. This oil can sometimes be used for cooking.

ointment (ointments) *noun*
An ointment is a smooth, thick mixture that you put on sore skin to help it get better.

old (older, oldest) *adjective*
1. Someone who is old has lived for many years.
2. Something that is old has been in the world for many years.
3. You say something is old if it has been used a lot: *These are my old shoes.*
4. If you ask how old someone is, you want to know how many months or years they have lived: *How old is your baby?*

old-fashioned *adjective*
Something that is old-fashioned belongs to the past and has been replaced by something more modern.

olive (olives) *noun*
An olive is a small, green or black, oily fruit with a stone in the middle. Olives can be eaten, but they have a bitter taste. They can also be pressed to make olive oil.

omelette (omelettes) *noun*
An omelette is a food made by beating eggs and cooking them in a flat pan.

once *adverb*
1. If you do something once, you do it one time only.
2. If something happens once in a period it happens regularly at one time in that period: *This comic comes out once a week, on Fridays.*
3. Once means at some time in the past: *Once, the Romans ruled in Britain.*

>**at once** *phrase*
1. If you do something at once, you do it without doing anything else first.
2. If several things happen at once, they all happen at the same time.

onion (onions) *noun*
An onion is a small round vegetable which grows underground. It has a strong, sharp smell and taste. Onions are made up of thin, white layers with a papery, brown skin on the outside.

only *adjective*
1. Only means one and no more: *He was the only boy in the group.*
2. An only child is someone who has no brothers or sisters.

only *adverb*
1. You say only when you mean one person or thing and not others: *He's only interested in football.*
2. You can say only when something is not very important: *I thought it was an unusual bird, but it was only a sparrow.*
3. Only can be used when something was less than you expected: *I only paid two pounds for it.*

opaque *adjective*
If something, like a window, is opaque, you cannot see through it.
open (opens, opening, opened) *verb*
1. If you open a door, you move it so that people can go through it.
2. If you open a box or a bottle, you take the lid off or unfasten it.
3. When flowers open, they change from being buds and their petals spread out.
4. When a place, such as a shop or library, opens, you can use it.
opening (openings) *noun*
An opening is a hole or space that things or people can go through.
opera (operas) *noun*
An opera is a musical play in which most of the words are sung.
operate (operates, operating, operated) *verb*
1. When someone operates a machine, they make it work.
2. When doctors operate, they cut open a person's body so that they can put things right inside.
operation (operations) *noun*
1. An operation is a plan that needs a lot of people or actions.
2. An operation can also be when doctors cut open a person's body to put things right inside.
opinion (opinions) *noun*
An opinion is what someone thinks about something.
opposite (opposites) *noun*
The opposite of something is the thing that is most different from it: *Hot is the opposite of cold.*
opposite *preposition*
If one person or thing is opposite another, they are on the other side of something: *In the train I sat opposite a small boy.*
orange *adjective*
Something that is orange has a colour between red and yellow.
orange (oranges) *noun*
An orange is a round fruit with a thick skin. Oranges are juicy and sometimes sweet. They can be eaten raw or used to make marmalade.
orbit (orbits) *noun*
An orbit is the curved path in space that is followed by one object going round a larger object; for example, a planet going round the sun.
orchard (orchards) *noun*
An orchard is an area of land where fruit trees are grown.
orchestra (orchestras) *noun*
An orchestra is a large group of musicians who play different instruments together.
order (orders) *noun*
1. Order is the way a set of things is organized. Names are often written in alphabetical order.
2. An order is something you are told to do.
order (orders, ordering, ordered) *verb*
If you order something, for example in a restaurant, you ask for it to be brought to you.
ordinary *adjective*
Something that is ordinary is not special in any way.
ore *noun*
Ore is rock or earth with metal such as tin or iron in it.
organ (organs) *noun*
1. An organ is a part of your body that does a special job. For example, your heart, lungs and stomach are organs.
2. An organ is also a large musical instrument which has a lot of pipes of different lengths. It is played rather like a piano. As you press the keys, air is forced through the pipes to make different sounds.
organization/organisation (organizations) *noun*
An organization is a large group of people who have particular aims. The police force and the Post Office are organizations.
organize/organise (organizes, organizing, organized) *verb*
If you organize something, you make all the arrangements for it, so that everything happens as planned.

original *adjective*
If you say someone's ideas are original, you mean they are very clever at thinking of new ways of doing things.

original (originals) *noun*
The original of something, like a work of art, is the one the artist made themselves, and not a copy.

ornament (ornaments) *noun*
1. An ornament is a small object that you have in your home because you think it is attractive and pleasant to look at.
2. An ornament is also something, such as jewellery, that a person wears to make them look more attractive.

orphan (orphans) *noun*
An orphan is a child whose parents are dead.

ostrich (ostriches) *noun*
An ostrich is the largest living bird. It cannot fly, but it can run very fast. Ostriches live in sandy places in Africa. Their eggs are very large, weighing more than a kilo each.

other *adjective*
1. When you say other things or other people, you can mean more of the same kind: *He found it hard to make friends with other children.*
2. You can also use other to mean different: *We got lost last time. I think we'll try some other way.*

>every other day *phrase*
Every other day means one day in every two: *We meet every other day, on Mondays, Wednesdays and Fridays.*

>the other day *phrase*
If you say something happened the other day, you mean it happened a few days ago.

otherwise *adverb*
You say otherwise to explain what will happen if you don't do something: *I'd better take an umbrella, otherwise I'll get soaked.*

otter (otters) *noun*
An otter is an animal with brown fur, short legs and a long tail. Otters live in and around lakes and rivers. They swim well with their webbed feet, and catch fish for food. Otters are very playful, even when they are adults.

outdoor *adjective*
Outdoor activities or clothes happen or are used outside and not in a building.

outdoors *adverb*
Outdoors means in the open air rather than in a building.

outer *adjective*
Outer is used to describe things which contain or enclose something else: *An onion is made up of a number of layers. The outer layer is brown and papery.*

outline (outlines) *noun*
1. An outline is the shape of something, especially when you cannot see any details: *As it grew darker, they could only see the outlines of the trees against the sky.*
2. An outline is also a kind of drawing which shows the outside shape of something.

oval (ovals) *noun*
An oval is a shape like an egg.

oven (ovens) *noun*
An oven is part of a cooker. It is like a metal box with a door. Food is put in an oven to be baked or roasted.

overboard *adverb*
If someone falls overboard, they fall over the side of a ship into the water.

overcoat (overcoats) *noun*
An overcoat is a thick, warm coat that people wear in winter.

overgrown *adjective*
If a place is overgrown, it is thickly covered with plants and weeds, usually because it has not been looked after for a long time.

overhead *adjective*
You say something is overhead when it is above you, or above the place that you are talking about.

overhear (overhears, overhearing, overheard) *verb*
If you overhear someone, you hear what they are saying when they are not talking to you and do not know that you are listening.

overjoyed *adjective*
If you are overjoyed about something, you are extremely pleased about it.

overlap (overlaps, overlapping, overlapped) *verb*
If one thing overlaps another, or if two things overlap, a part of one thing covers a part of the other.

overload (overloads, overloading, overloaded) *verb*
If you overload something, such as a vehicle, you put more things or people into it than it was designed to carry.

overseas *adverb*
If you go overseas, you go to a country which is on the other side of a sea or ocean.

overtake (overtakes, overtaking, overtook, overtaken) *verb*
If you overtake someone, you pass them because you are moving faster than they are.

owe (owes, owing, owed) *verb*
1. If you owe money to someone, you need to pay it back because they have lent it to you.
2. If you owe someone something such as thanks, you feel grateful to them. Usually this is because they have been kind or helpful to you.

owl (owls) *noun*
An owl is a bird with a flat face and large eyes. There are many kinds of owl. Usually owls hunt at night for small animals.

own (owns, owning, owned) *verb*
1. If you own something, it belongs to you.
2. If you own up to something wrong, you say that you did it.

>on your own *phrase*
1. If you are on your own, you are alone.
2. If you do something on your own, you do it without any help.

owner (owners) *noun*
The owner of something is the person it belongs to.

oxygen *noun*
Oxygen is a gas that forms part of the air we breathe. Oxygen is needed by most plants, animals and insects, and things will not burn without it.

oyster (oysters) *noun*
An oyster is a flat shellfish. Some oysters can be eaten, and some make pearls.

ozone *noun*
Ozone is a form of oxygen. There is a layer of ozone high above the earth's surface which gives protection against dangerous rays from the sun.

P

pace (paces) *noun*
1. The pace of something is the speed at which it happens.
2. A pace is a step that you take when you walk.

pack (packs) *noun*
1. A pack is a bag holding your belongings.
2. A pack is also a set of playing cards.
3. A pack of wolves or other animals is a group that hunts together.

pack (packs, packing, packed) *verb*
When you pack, you put your clothes in a case or bag.

package (packages) *noun*
A package is a small parcel.

packaging *noun*
Packaging is the container that something is sold or sent in.

packet (packets) *noun*
A packet is a box or small bag, usually made from card or plastic. Foods such as cereals are often sold in packets.

pad (pads) *noun*
1. A pad is a number of pieces of paper which are fixed together on one side. You write on the paper and then tear it off the pad.
2. An animal's pads are the soft parts under its paws.

paddle (paddles) *noun*
A paddle is a pole with a flat part at one or both ends.

paddle (paddles, paddling, paddled) *verb*
1. If you paddle in the sea, you stand or walk in the shallow water.
2. If you paddle a small boat such as a canoe, you use a paddle to move the boat along.

padlock (padlocks) *noun*
A padlock is a special kind of lock. It is used for fastening two things together.
page (pages) *noun*
A page is one side of a piece of paper in a book, newspaper or magazine.
pageant (pageants) *noun*
A pageant is a show. It is usually about history, with people dressed in colourful costumes.
pagoda (pagodas) *noun*
A pagoda is a tall building which is used as a temple. Pagodas can be seen in China, Japan and South East Asia.
pail (pails) *noun*
A pail is a bucket, especially one made of metal or wood.
pain (pains) *noun*
A pain is an unpleasant feeling that you have in part of your body if you have been hurt or are ill.
painful *adjective*
If part of your body is painful, it hurts. This is because it is injured or because there is something wrong with it.
>**painfully** *adverb*
paint *noun*
Paint is a coloured liquid that you put on to a surface.
paint (paints, painting, painted) *verb*
1. When you paint a picture, you use paint to make a picture on paper or canvas.
2. When someone paints a room or a piece of furniture they cover it with paint, to protect it or to make it look fresh and clean.
paintbrush (paintbrushes) *noun*
A paintbrush is a brush that you use for putting paint on to something.
painting (paintings) *noun*
A painting is a picture that has been painted.
pair (pairs) *noun*
1. A pair is a set of two things that are to be used together: *I need a new pair of shoes.*
2. Some objects, such as trousers and scissors, have two main parts which are the same size and shape. This sort of object is also called a pair: *Have you got a pair of scissors?*
palace (palaces) *noun*
A palace is a very large, important house, especially one which is the home of a king, queen, or president.
pale (paler, palest) *adjective*
1. Something that is pale is light in colour, and not strong or bright.
2. If someone looks pale, the skin on their face looks whiter than usual, often because they are not well.
palm (palms) *noun*
1. The palm of your hand is the inside surface of it. Your fingers and thumb are not part of your palm.
2. A palm is a tree which grows in hot countries. It has long pointed leaves that grow out of the top of a tall trunk. Palm tree trunks have no branches.
pan (pans) *noun*
1. A pan is a container with a long handle that is used for cooking.
2. A lavatory pan is the bowl-shaped part of a toilet.
panda (pandas) *noun*
A giant panda is a large, black and white animal the size of a bear. Giant pandas live in the bamboo forests of China.
panic (panics, panicking, panicked) *verb*
If you panic, you suddenly get so worried you cannot act sensibly and calmly.
pant (pants, panting, panted) *verb*
If you pant, you breathe quickly and loudly, with your mouth open. You usually pant when you have been doing something, like running, which uses a lot of energy.
panther (panthers) *noun*
Panther is another name for a leopard. Black leopards are usually called panthers.
pantomime (pantomimes) *noun*
A pantomime is a funny musical play for children. The stories for pantomimes are taken from fairy tales.
pants *noun*
Pants are a piece of clothing that you wear under your other clothes. They have two holes for your legs and elastic round the waist.

paper (papers) *noun*
1. Paper is the material that you write on or wrap things with.
2. A newspaper is also called a paper.

parachute (parachutes) *noun*
A parachute is a large piece of thin cloth shaped like an umbrella. It has strings fixed to it so that a person or object that is attached to it can float down to the ground from an aircraft.

parade (parades) *noun*
A parade is a lot of people marching in the road on a special day.

paraffin *noun*
Paraffin is a liquid which is used as a fuel in things like heaters and lamps.

paragraph (paragraphs) *noun*
A paragraph is a series of sentences that are all about one idea. The first sentence in a paragraph always begins on a new line.

parallel *adjective*
Two lines or other things that are parallel are the same distance apart all the way along:
The road along the sea front is parallel with the sea.

parcel (parcels) *noun*
A parcel is one or more objects wrapped in paper. This is usually done so that it can be sent by post.

parchment *noun*
Parchment is the yellowish-cream skin of a sheep or goat. A long time ago, people used to write on parchment.

parent (parents) *noun*
Your parents are your mother and father.

park (parks) *noun*
A park is an area of land with grass and trees, usually in a town. People go there to relax or enjoy themselves.

park (parks, parking, parked) *verb*
When someone parks a vehicle, they put it where it will not get in the way. Then they often leave it for a short period.

parliament (parliaments) *noun*
The parliament of a country is a group of people who meet to make the country's laws.

parrot (parrots) *noun*
A parrot is a tropical bird with a curved beak. Parrots are usually brightly coloured.

part (parts) *noun*
1. A part of something is one of the pieces that it is made from: *We need a new part for the washing machine.*
2. A part is also a particular bit of something: *I don't know this part of London.*
3. If you have a part in a play, you go on stage and act.

particular *adjective*
When you talk about a particular person or thing, you mean just that person or thing and not others of the same kind.

partly *adverb*
Partly means not completely: *The table was partly covered with a small cloth.*

partner (partners) *noun*
Your partner is the person you are doing something with, for example in dancing or playing games.

party (parties) *noun*
A party is a group of people having fun together.

pass (passes) *noun*
1. A pass is a route between two mountains.
2. A pass is also a piece of paper that allows you to do something.

pass (passes, passing, passed) *verb*
1. If you pass someone, you go past them without stopping.
2. If you pass something to someone, you hand it to them.
3. If you pass a test or an exam, you are successful in it.

passage (passages) *noun*
A passage is a long, narrow space with walls on both sides.

passenger (passengers) *noun*
A passenger is a person who travels in a vehicle but is not the driver. In aircraft and ships, a passenger is anyone on board who is not part of the crew.

passport (passports) *noun*
A passport is a special pass that you need when you go to a foreign country.

password (passwords) *noun*
A password is a secret word or phrase that you must say to be allowed into a particular place.

pasta *noun*
Pasta is a type of food made from a mixture of flour, eggs and water, which is formed into different shapes. Spaghetti, macaroni and noodles are all types of pasta.

paste *noun*
1. Paste is a thick, wet mixture that can be used to stick paper.
2. Paste is also a smooth mixture of food. You usually spread paste on bread or toast.

pastry *noun*
Pastry is a food made of flour, fat and water, which is mixed into a dough and then rolled flat. Pastry is used for making pies.

pasture *noun*
Pasture is land that is used for farm animals to graze on.

pat (pats, patting, patted) *verb*
If you pat something, you hit it gently, usually with your open hand.

patch (patches) *noun*
A patch is a piece of material that you use to cover a hole in something, such as clothing.

path (paths) *noun*
A path is a strip of ground that people walk on.

patience *noun*
Patience is being able to wait calmly for something, or to do something difficult or boring without giving up.

patient *adjective*
If you are patient, you are able to wait calmly for something, or to do something difficult or boring without giving up.
>**patiently** *adverb*

patient (patients) *noun*
A patient is someone who is being treated by a doctor.

patrol (patrols, patrolling, patrolled) *verb*
When people, like the police, patrol a particular area, they go round it to make sure there is no trouble or danger.

pattern (patterns) *noun*
A pattern is the particular way that something is organized. For example, lines and shapes can be organized to make patterns on fabric.

pause (pauses, pausing, paused) *verb*
If you pause while you are doing something, you stop for a moment.

pavement (pavements) *noun*
A pavement is a path with a hard surface. In towns there are usually pavements on each side of a street so that people can walk in safety.

paw (paws) *noun*
The paw of an animal such as a cat or dog is its foot. Paws have claws at the front and soft pads underneath.

pay (pays, paying, paid) *verb*
When a person pays someone, they give them money in exchange for work or for things that have been bought.

payment *noun*
Payment is the act of paying money or of being paid.

pea (peas) *noun*
Peas are round green seeds which are eaten as a vegetable. They grow inside a covering called a pod.

peace *noun*
1. Peace is a feeling of quiet and calm.
2. When a country has peace or is at peace, it is not fighting a war.

peaceful *adjective*
A peaceful place or time is very quiet and calm.
peacefully *adverb*

peach (peaches) *noun*
A peach is a round, juicy fruit with a large stone in the centre. It has sweet, yellow flesh and a furry yellow and red skin. Peaches grow in warm countries.

peacock (peacocks) *noun*
A peacock is a large male bird of the pheasant family. The female is called a peahen. Peacocks have bright blue and green feathers, and very long tail feathers which they spread in a large fan to attract the females.

peak *adjective*
Peak times are periods which are very busy.
peak (peaks) *noun*
1. The peak of a mountain is the pointed top of it.
2. The peak of a cap is the part that sticks out at the front.
peanut (peanuts) *noun*
Peanuts are small, hard seeds which grow under the ground in a covering called a pod. The pods are usually about four centimetres long and hold two or three seeds.
pear (pears) *noun*
A pear is a sweet, juicy fruit which grows on trees. It is narrow near its stalk, and wider and rounded at the bottom.
pearl (pearls) *noun*
A pearl is a small, hard, round object which grows inside the shell of an oyster. It is creamy-white in colour. Pearls are used to make valuable jewellery.
pebble (pebbles) *noun*
A pebble is a smooth, rounded stone which is found on sea shores and river beds.
peck (pecks, pecking, pecked) *verb*
When a bird pecks, it bites at something with a sudden forward movement of its beak.
peculiar *adjective*
If you say something is peculiar, you mean it is strange or unusual.
pedal (pedals) *noun*
The pedals on a cycle are the two parts that you push with your feet to make it move.
pedestrian (pedestrians) *noun*
A pedestrian is a person who is walking rather than travelling in a vehicle.
peel *noun*
The peel of a fruit or vegetable is its skin.
peel (peels, peeling, peeled) *verb*
1. If you peel, you lose small pieces of skin because of sunburn.
2. If a painted surface is peeling, pieces of paint are coming off it.
peep (peeps, peeping, peeped) *verb*
If you peep at something, you look at it very quickly, and usually secretly.
peg (pegs) *noun*
1. A peg on a wall or door is a thin piece of wood, metal or plastic that is used to hang things on.
2. A peg is also a small plastic or wooden object that is used to hold washing on a line.
pelican (pelicans) *noun*
A pelican is a large water bird. It has a long beak with a soft lower part like a pouch.
pen (pens) *noun*
1. A pen is a long, thin tool with which you write in ink. There are different sorts of pen, such as ballpoint, felt-tip and fountain pens.
2. A pen is also a small, fenced area where farm animals are kept for a short time.
pencil (pencils) *noun*
A pencil is an object that you use for writing or drawing. It is made from a long, thin piece of wood with a material called graphite in the middle. The graphite makes a dark mark on paper.
pendulum (pendulums) *noun*
A pendulum is a large weight which hangs from a clock. It swings from side to side to keep the clock going at the right speed.
penguin (penguins) *noun*
A penguin is a large, black and white bird found in the Antarctic. Penguins cannot fly. They use their wings for swimming in the water.
penis (penises) *noun*
Boys and men have a penis. It is used to get rid of waste liquid from the body. Men can also use their penis to help make babies.
penknife (penknives) *noun*
A penknife is a small knife with blades that fold back into the handle.
penny (pennies/pence) *noun*
A penny is a small British coin. A hundred pence are worth one pound. Penny and pence are often called p for short.
pension (pensions) *noun*
A pension is money that someone receives regularly without having to work. Pensions are paid to people who have retired.
pentagon (pentagons) *noun*
A pentagon is a shape which has five straight sides.
people *noun*
People are men, women and children.

pepper (peppers) *noun*
1. Pepper is a hot-tasting powder which is used to flavour food.
2. A pepper is a vegetable. Peppers are hollow, and they are red, green or yellow in colour. They can be cooked, or eaten raw in salads.
>**per cent** *phrase*
If you say a number followed by 'per cent', you mean that number as a proportion of 100. For example, ten per cent means ten out of every hundred.
perch (perches) *noun*
1. A perch is a fish that lives in lakes, ponds and rivers.
2. A perch is also a short piece of wood for a bird to stand on.
perch (perches, perching, perched) *verb*
When a bird perches on something, like a branch or a fence, it stands there.
perfect *adjective*
1. Something that is perfect is done so well that it could not be done better.
2. Perfect also means new or undamaged.
3. If you say something is perfect, you mean it is wonderful and you are very pleased with it.
>**perfectly** *adverb*
perform (performs, performing, performed) *verb*
1. When you perform a difficult task, you do it.
2. If someone performs, they do something to entertain an audience.
performance (performances) *noun*
A performance is doing something in front of people; for example, acting or dancing.
perfume (perfumes) *noun*
1. A perfume is a pleasant smell: *The roses filled the air with perfume.*
2. Perfume is also a liquid that smells pleasant. Some people put it on their skin to make them smell nice.
perhaps *adverb*
1. If you say perhaps something will happen, you mean it might happen but you are not sure.
2. You also say perhaps when you are suggesting a reason which you are not sure is right: *Why is Christopher so late? I don't know - perhaps he missed the bus.*
period (periods) *noun*
1. A period is a particular length of time: *Mrs Smith will be away for a period of six months.*
2. A period can also be a particular time in history; for example, the Victorian period.
periscope (periscopes) *noun*
A periscope is a tube with mirrors in it. The mirrors are arranged so that when you look in one end of the tube you can see things that would otherwise be out of sight.
permanent *adjective*
Something that is permanent lasts for ever or for a very long time.
>**permanently** *adverb*
permission *noun*
If you are given permission to do something, someone has said you may do it.
permit (permits) *noun*
A permit is an official piece of paper which says you may do something, such as work in a foreign country.
permit (permits, permitting, permitted) *verb*
1. If someone permits you to do something, they allow you to do it.
2. If something permits a particular thing, it makes it possible to happen: *We'll have the party in the garden, weather permitting.*
persist (persists, persisting, persisted) *verb*
If you persist, you go on doing something even when it is difficult or other people have told you to stop.
person (people) *noun*
A person is a man, woman or child.
persuade (persuades, persuading, persuaded) *verb*
If someone persuades you to do something you did not want to do, they cause you to do it by giving you a good reason.
pest (pests) *noun*
A pest is an insect, rat or other small animal, which damages food supplies or crops.

pet (pets) *noun*
A pet is a tame animal that you keep and look after in your home.
petal (petals) *noun*
The petals of a flower are the white or coloured main parts.
petrol *noun*
Petrol is a liquid which is used as fuel in motor vehicles.
pheasant (pheasants) *noun*
A pheasant is a long-tailed bird that is often hunted for food by human beings.
phone (phones) *noun*
A phone is an instrument for talking to someone who is in another place. Phone is short for telephone.
photo (photos) *noun*
Photo is short for photograph.
photocopier (photocopiers) *noun*
A photocopier is a machine that makes copies of documents by photographing them.
photograph (photographs) *noun*
A photograph is a picture that is made using a camera and film.
photographer (photographers) *noun*
A photographer is someone who takes photographs.
phrase (phrases) *noun*
A phrase is a short group of words that people often use together.
physical *adjective*
1. Physical means to do with things that can be touched or seen.
2. Physical qualities, actions or things are to do with a person's body, rather than their mind.
>**physically** *adverb*
pianist (pianists) *noun*
A pianist is a person who plays the piano.
piano (pianos) *noun*
A piano is a large musical instrument with a row of black and white keys. When the keys are pressed down, little hammers hit wire strings inside the piano. Each string makes a different sound.
pick (picks, picking, picked) *verb*
1. If you pick something or someone, you choose them: *We need to pick three more people for our team.*
2. When you pick things such as flowers or fruit, you gather them.
3. If you pick something up, you lift it up from where it is.
pickle (pickles) *noun*
Pickles are vegetables or fruit which have been kept in vinegar or salt water. They have a strong, sharp taste.
picnic (picnics) *noun*
A picnic is a meal that you take with you and eat out of doors. People often have a picnic on the beach or in a field.
picture (pictures) *noun*
1. A picture is a drawing, painting or photograph of people, places or things.
2. Film and television cameras also take pictures, and show them on screens.
pie (pies) *noun*
A pie is fruit, vegetables or meat baked in pastry.
piece (pieces) *noun*
1. A piece is a bit or a part of something.
2. The pieces in a board game are the specially shaped objects that you move on the board when you play.
pier (piers) *noun*
A pier is a long platform which sticks out over the sea at some seaside towns. Piers usually have some kind of entertainment on them.
pierce (pierces, piercing, pierced) *verb*
1. If a sharp object pierces something, it goes through it and makes a hole in it.
2. If you have your ears pierced, you have holes made so that you can wear earrings in them.
piercing *adjective*
A piercing sound or voice is high-pitched and very sharp and clear in an unpleasant way.
pig (pigs) *noun*
A pig is a farm animal. Pigs are rather fat with short legs, large ears and tiny tails. They do not have much hair on their skin. Male pigs are called boars and female pigs are sows. Their babies are called piglets.

pigeon (pigeons) *noun*
A pigeon is a bird, usually grey in colour, with a fat body and a small head. Pigeons make a soft, cooing sound.
pigsty (pigsties) *noun*
A pigsty is a hut with a yard where pigs are kept on a farm.
pile (piles) *noun*
1. A pile is a lot of things heaped up together.
2 A pile is also a number of things, such as books, which have been put one on top of the other.
pill (pills) *noun*
A pill is medicine which is made into a small, round object that can be swallowed whole.
pillar (pillars) *noun*
A pillar is a tall post made of something such as stone or brick. It usually helps to hold up a building.
pillar box (pillar boxes) *noun*
A pillar box is an iron cylinder with a narrow slot in it. Pillar boxes stand on pavements. You can put letters through the slot to be collected by the postman.
pillow (pillows) *noun*
A pillow is a bag filled with soft material to rest your head on in bed.
pillowcase (pillowcases) *noun*
A pillowcase is a cover for a pillow, made of cotton or other material, that can be taken off and washed.
pilot (pilots) *noun*
1. A pilot is a person who is trained to fly an aircraft.
2 A pilot is also a person who guides a ship through a difficult stretch of water; for example, into a harbour.
pimple (pimples) *noun*
A pimple is a small, red spot, especially on your face.
pin (pins) *noun*
A pin is a very small, thin piece of metal with a point at one end. Pins can be pushed through things such as pieces of paper or cloth, to hold them together.
pincer (pincers) *noun*
The pincers of an animal such as a crab or lobster are their two curved front claws.
pinch (pinches, pinching, pinched) *verb*
If someone pinches you, they squeeze part of you quickly between their thumb and first finger.
pinch (pinches) *noun*
A pinch of something, such as salt, is the amount that you can hold between your thumb and first finger.
pine (pines) *noun*
A pine is a tall, evergreen tree. It has thin, sharp leaves called needles. The seeds of pine trees are held in cones on the branches of the tree.
pineapple (pineapples) *noun*
A pineapple is a large, oval fruit that is sweet and juicy. Pineapples grow in the tropics on plants which have stiff fleshy leaves.
pink (pinker, pinkest) *adjective*
Something that is pink has a colour between white and red.
pint (pints) *noun*
A pint is a measure for liquids. There are eight pints in one gallon. A pint is equal to 568 cubic centimetres.
pipe (pipes) *noun*
A pipe is a long, hollow tube, usually made of metal or plastic. Pipes are used to carry liquids or gas.
pirate (pirates) *noun*
In the past, a pirate was a robber who sailed on the sea and stole from other ships.
pistol (pistols) *noun*
A pistol is a small gun that can be fired from one hand.
pit (pits) *noun*
1. A pit is a large hole that has been dug in the ground.
2 A pit is also a coal mine.
pitch (pitches) *noun*
1. A pitch is an area of ground where a game such as hockey or football is played.
2 The pitch of a sound is how high or low it is.
pitch (pitches, pitching, pitched) *verb*
When you pitch a tent, you put it up, so that you can use it.

pity (pities, pitying, pitied) *verb*
If you pity someone, you feel very sorry for them.
pity *noun*
If you say something is a pity, you mean it is disappointing: *My friend can't come after all. – Oh dear, that's a pity.*
pizza (pizzas) *noun*
A pizza is a flat, round piece of dough or pastry, spread with things like tomatoes and cheese, and then baked in an oven.
place (places) *noun*
A place is somewhere such as a particular area or building: *Let's find a place where we can eat.*
>**take place** *phrase*
If something takes place, it happens, especially in an organized way: *The prize giving will take place in the school hall.*
plague (plagues) *noun*
1. A plague is a disease that spreads quickly and kills large numbers of people.
2. A plague of unpleasant things is a large number of them that arrive at the same time and are difficult to deal with: *The crops were destroyed by a plague of locusts.*
plaice *noun*
A plaice is a sea fish with a flat body, which is caught for food.
plain (plainer, plainest) *adjective*
1. A plain object or surface is in one colour and has no writing or pattern on it.
2. Plain things such as food or clothing are simple in style.
3. If something is plain, it is clear and easy to see.
>**plainly** *adverb*
plain (plains) *noun*
A plain is a large, flat area of land with very few trees on it.
plait (plaits, plaiting, plaited) *verb*
If you plait a length of hair, you divide it into three lengths. Then you twist them together, putting them over and under until they make one thick length.
plan (plans) *noun*
1. If you say you have a plan, you mean you have thought of a way of doing something.
2. A plan is also a drawing that shows what something looks like from above.
plan (plans, planning, planned) *verb*
If you plan what you are going to do, you decide exactly how you are going to do it.
plane (planes) *noun*
A plane is a flying vehicle. It has wings and one or more engines.
planet (planets) *noun*
A planet is a large, round object in space that goes round a star. Earth is one of the nine planets that go round the sun.
plank (planks) *noun*
A plank is a long, flat piece of wood.
plant (plants) *noun*
A plant is anything that grows in the soil.
plant (plants, planting, planted) *verb*
When you plant things, such as flowers or trees, you put them in the ground so that they will grow.
plaster (plasters) *noun*
1. Plaster is a smooth paste that dries and forms a hard layer. It is used to cover walls and ceilings inside buildings.
2. A plaster is a strip of sticky material used for covering small cuts on your body.
plastic *noun*
Plastic is a man-made material which is light in weight. It can be made into different shapes and does not break easily. Plastic is used to make all sorts of things, such as buckets, bowls and plates.
Plasticine *noun*
Plasticine is a soft material like clay, which can be used to make models.
plate (plates) *noun*
A plate is a flat dish that is used to hold food.
platform (platforms) *noun*
1. A platform is a raised area in a hall. It is for people to stand on so that they can be seen more easily.
2. A platform is also the area in a railway station where you wait for the train.
play (plays, playing, played) *verb*
1. When you play, you spend time doing enjoyable things.

2. When one person or team plays another, they take part in a game and each side tries to win.
3. If you play a musical instrument, you make musical sounds with it.
4. If you play a record, a compact disc or a tape, you put it on a piece of equipment so that you can hear it.
play (plays) *noun*
A play is a story which is acted on the stage, or on radio or television.
player (players) *noun*
1. A player is a person who takes part in a sport or game.
2. A player can also be someone who plays a musical instrument.
playground (playgrounds) *noun*
A playground is a piece of land for children to play on.
pleasant (pleasanter, pleasantest) *adjective*
1. You say someone is pleasant when they are friendly and easy to talk to.
2. Something that is pleasant is nice to look at or listen to.
>**pleasantly** *adverb*
please (pleases, pleasing, pleased) *verb*
If you please someone, you make them feel happy.
pleasure *noun*
Pleasure is a feeling of happiness or enjoyment.
plenty *noun*
If there is plenty of something, there is more than enough of it: *Help yourself to some apples. We've got plenty.*
pliers *noun*
Pliers are a tool used for pulling out small things like nails, or for bending or cutting wire.
plot (plots) *noun*
1. A plot is a secret plan by a number of people to do something that is wrong.
2. The plot of a film, novel or play is the story and the way it develops.
3. A plot of land is a small piece of land that has been marked out for a special purpose such as building houses or growing vegetables.
plot (plots, plotting, plotted) *verb*
If people plot something, they plan secretly to do it.
plough (ploughs) *noun*
A plough is a large farming tool with sharp blades, which is attached to a tractor or an animal such as a horse. A plough is pulled across the soil to turn it over, usually before seeds are sown.
pluck (plucks, plucking, plucked) *verb*
When someone plucks a musical instrument, such as a guitar, they pull the strings with their fingers and then let them go.
plug (plugs) *noun*
1. A plug is a thick piece of rubber or plastic that fits in the drain hole of a bath or washbasin.
2. A plug is also a small object that joins pieces of equipment to the electricity supply.
plum (plums) *noun*
A plum is a small fruit with a thin, dark red or yellow skin and juicy flesh. It has a large stone in the middle.
plumber (plumbers) *noun*
A plumber is a person who fits and mends water pipes.
plunge (plunges, plunging, plunged) *verb*
If someone plunges into the water, they dive or throw themselves into it.
plural (plurals) *noun*
In grammar, the plural of a word is the one that you use when you are talking about two or more people, things or groups: *The plural of child is children.*
poach (poaches, poaching, poached) *verb*
1. If you poach an egg, you remove its shell and cook the egg gently in boiling water.
2. If someone poaches fish, animals or birds, they catch them on someone else's land without permission.
pocket (pockets) *noun*
A pocket is a small bag that is sewn into clothing. Pockets are used to carry small things, such as handkerchiefs or coins.
pod (pods) *noun*
A pod is a seed cover. Peas and beans grow inside pods.

poem (poems) *noun*
A poem is a piece of writing. Poems often have short lines, which sometimes rhyme. The lines usually have a particular rhythm.
poet (poets) *noun*
A poet is a person who writes poems.
poetry *noun*
Poetry is a kind of writing in which the lines have a particular rhythm and sometimes rhyme.
point (points) *noun*
1. A point is a particular spot or place.
2. The point of something such as a pin is the sharp end of it.
3. In a game or sport, a point is part of the score.
point (points, pointing, pointed) *verb*
If you point at something, you show it to someone by using your finger.
pointed *adjective*
Something that is pointed has a point at one end.
poison *noun*
Poison is something that harms or kills people or animals if it is taken into their body.
poisonous *adjective*
Something that is poisonous will kill people or animals or make them ill if it is taken into their body.
polar *adjective*
You use polar to talk about the areas around the North and South Poles: *These animals live in the polar regions.*
polar bear (polar bears) *noun*
A polar bear is a large, white bear that lives near the North Pole.
pole (poles) *noun*
1. A pole is a long, thin piece of wood or metal, used especially for holding things up.
2. A pole is also one of the two points on the earth that are the furthest from the equator.
police *noun*
The police are an organization whose job is to protect people and their belongings. It is also their job to make sure that people obey the law.
policeman (policemen) *noun*
A policeman is a man who is a member of the police.
policewoman (policewomen) *noun*
A policewoman is a woman who is a member of the police.
polish *noun*
Polish is something that you put on the surface of an object to clean and protect it and make it shine.
polite (politer, politest) *adjective*
Someone who is polite is well behaved and thinks about other people's feelings.
>**politely** *adverb*
politics *noun*
Politics is the study of the way in which a country is governed.
pollen *noun*
Pollen is a fine powder found in flowers. It helps to make seeds grow.
pollution *noun*
Pollution is making things like the air and water dirty and dangerous for people and animals to live in and to use.
polythene *noun*
Polythene is a thin, plastic material that is often made into bags.
pond (ponds) *noun*
A pond is a small lake.
pony (ponies) *noun*
A pony is a kind of horse which is smaller than an ordinary horse.
pool (pools) *noun*
A pool is a small area of still or slow-moving water.
poor (poorer, poorest) *adjective*
1. Someone who is poor has very little money and few belongings.
2. If someone has poor eyesight, they cannot see very well.
3. If someone is in poor health, they are ill.
poppy (poppies) *noun*
A poppy is a plant with a large flower. Wild poppies are bright red.
popular *adjective*
1. Someone who is popular is liked by most of the people in a particular group.

2. Something that is popular is liked by a lot of people.
>**popularly** *adverb*
population (populations) *noun*
1. The population of a country or area is all the people who live in it.
2. The population of a place is also the number of people who live there.
porch (porches) *noun*
A porch is a sheltered place at the entrance to a building. Porches have a roof and sometimes walls.
porcupine (porcupines) *noun*
A porcupine is an animal that has many long, strong, pointed hairs called quills on its back. The quills protect it if it is attacked.
pore (pores) *noun*
1. Pores are the small holes in the skin of people and animals, and on the surface of plants.
2. Pores are also tiny gaps or cracks in rocks or soil.
>**pore over** *phrase*
If you pore over something, like writing, maps or charts, you look at it and study it carefully.
pork *noun*
Pork is meat from a pig.
porpoise (porpoises) *noun*
A porpoise is a sea animal which looks like a dolphin or a small whale.
porridge *noun*
Porridge is a thick, sticky food made from oats cooked in water or milk. Porridge is eaten hot, usually for breakfast.
port (ports) *noun*
A port is a town which has a harbour.
porter (porters) *noun*
1. A porter is a person whose job is to look after a building, such as a block of flats.
2. A porter is also someone whose job is to carry things; for example, people's luggage at a railway station.
porthole (portholes) *noun*
A porthole is a small, round window in the side of a ship.
portion (portions) *noun*
A portion of food is the amount that is given to one person at a meal.
portrait (portraits) *noun*
A portrait is a picture of a particular person.
position (positions) *noun*
1. The position of someone or something is the place where they are at a particular moment.
2. Someone's position can also be the way they are sitting or standing: *Try to stay in that position while I draw you.*
positive *adjective*
If you are positive about something, you are very sure about it.
>**positively** *adverb*
possess (possesses, possessing, possessed) *verb*
If you possess something, you have it or own it.
possession (possessions) *noun*
Your possessions are the things that you own or have with you at a particular time.
possible *adjective*
1. Something that is possible can be done.
2. You can also use possible to talk about something that may happen but is not certain: *It's possible we might go abroad next year.*
>**possibly** *adverb*
post (posts) *noun*
1. Post is letters or parcels delivered by the post office.
2. A post is a strong piece of wood or metal fixed upright in the ground.
post (posts, posting, posted) *verb*
If you post a letter, you send it to someone by putting it in a postbox.
postbox (postboxes) *noun*
A postbox is a metal box with a slot in it. You can post letters in a postbox to be collected by a postman.
postcard (postcards) *noun*
A postcard is a piece of thin card which you can write on and post to someone without using an envelope. Postcards often have pictures on one side.
postcode (postcodes) *noun*
A postcode is the letters and numbers at the end of an address.

poster (posters) *noun*
A poster is a large notice that is put on a wall or notice board, which tells people about something. Posters often have pictures on them.
postman (postmen) *noun*
A postman is a man whose job is to collect and deliver letters and parcels sent by post.
post office (post offices) *noun*
A post office is a place you can go to buy stamps, and to post letters and parcels.
postwoman (postwomen) *noun*
A postwoman is a woman whose job is to collect and deliver letters and parcels sent by post.
pot (pots) *noun*
1. A pot is a deep, round container, used for cooking.
2. A pot is also a container for paint, jam or any other thick liquid.
3. A flower pot is a container made of clay or plastic, used for growing plants in.
potato (potatoes) *noun*
A potato is a round vegetable that grows under the ground. Potatoes can be boiled, baked or fried. They can also be made into chips or crisps.
pottery *noun*
Pottery is articles, such as dishes and ornaments, that are made from clay.
pouch (pouches) *noun*
1. A pouch is a small bag for keeping things in.
2. A pouch can also be a pocket of skin on an animal. Female kangaroos and other marsupials have a pouch on their stomach. Their babies grow in this pouch. Hamsters have pouches in their cheeks, for storing food.
pounce (pounces, pouncing, pounced) *verb*
When an animal pounces on something, it leaps on it and grabs it.
pound (pounds) *noun*
1. A pound is a unit of money used in Britain. One pound is divided up into 100 pence.
2. A pound is also a measure of weight. One pound equals 0.454 kilograms.
pour (pours, pouring, poured) *verb*
If you pour a liquid, you tip it out of a container.
powder *noun*
Powder is something which has been ground into very tiny pieces.
power *noun*
1. If someone has power, they have control over other people.
2. The power of something, such as the wind or the sea, is the strength that it has.
3. Power is energy that can be used to make things work. For example, cars need power to make them go along the road. They get their power from fuel, such as petrol.
powerful *adjective*
1. A person or an organization that is powerful is able to affect or control events or other people's behaviour.
2. A person, animal, or part of a body that is powerful is physically strong.
>**powerfully** *adverb*
practical *adjective*
1. If you are practical, you are sensible and can deal with problems calmly.
2. Practical people are good at doing jobs with their hands.
3. Practical ideas are ones that are likely to work.
>**practically** *adverb*
practice *noun*
Practice is regular training or exercise that you do to improve your skill at something: *With a bit more practice you'll do very well.*
practise (practises, practising, practised) *verb*
If you practise, you do exercises in something, such as a sport or playing music, to improve your skill at it: *She has been practising this piece of music for months.*
praise (praises, praising, praised) *verb*
If someone praises you for something you have done, they say how well you have done it.
pram (prams) *noun*
A pram is a small carriage that a baby can be pushed around in.

prawn (prawns) *noun*
A prawn is a small shellfish like a large shrimp.

pray (prays, praying, prayed) *verb*
When someone prays, they speak to the god that they believe in, to give thanks or to ask for help.

prayer (prayers) *noun*
A prayer is the words someone says when they are praying.

precaution (precautions) *noun*
A precaution is an action that you take to try to stop something dangerous or unpleasant from happening: *They took an umbrella with them as a precaution.*

precious *adjective*
1. Something that is precious is worth a lot of money.
2. You also say something is precious if it is very important to you.

precipice (precipices) *noun*
A precipice is a very steep side on a mountain or rock.

precisely *adverb*
Precisely means accurately and exactly.

precision *noun*
If something is done with precision, it is exact and accurate.

predict (predicts, predicting, predicted) *verb*
If you predict something, you say that you believe it will happen, or that it will happen in a particular way.

preen (preens, preening, preened) *verb*
1. When birds preen, they clean their feathers and arrange them using their beak.
2. If you preen yourself, you spend a lot of time making yourself look neat and tidy.

prefer (prefers, preferring, preferred) *verb*
If you prefer someone or something, you like that person or thing better than another: *You could have an apple - or would you prefer a banana?*

prehistoric *adjective*
Something that is prehistoric belongs to the time before history was written down.

premises *noun*
The premises of an organization, such as a business or a school, are all the buildings and land that it occupies.

preparation (preparations) *noun*
1. Preparation is getting something ready: *They're clearing the hall in preparation for the school play.*
2. Preparations are all the things that have to be done before an event: *My family are thinking about nothing but the preparations for my sister's wedding.*

prepare (prepares, preparing, prepared) *verb*
1. If you prepare for something that is going to happen, you get ready for it.
2. If you prepare someone or something, you get them ready for something that is going to happen.

preposition (prepositions) *noun*
In grammar, a preposition is a word such as 'by', 'for' or 'with', that goes in front of a noun group. For example, in the sentence 'She fell into the pond', 'into' is a preposition and 'the pond' is a noun group.

present *adjective*
If someone is present somewhere, they are there: *Both her parents were present when she was given the prize.*

present (presents) *noun*
1. A present is something nice you give to someone, for example on their birthday.
2. The present is the period of time that is taking place now.

presentation (presentations) *noun*
A presentation is an event or ceremony in which someone is given something, such as a prize or a reward.

presently *adverb*
If you say something will happen presently, you mean it will happen soon.

preserve (preserves, preserving, preserved) *verb*
1. If you preserve something, you do something to keep it the way it is.
2. To preserve food means to stop it from going bad. There are several ways of preserving food. It can be frozen, dried, pickled, tinned or bottled.

president (presidents) *noun*
The president of a country or an organization is the head of it.
press (presses, pressing, pressed) *verb*
1. If you press something against something else, you hold it there firmly: *He pressed the phone against his ear.*
2. If someone presses clothes, they iron them.
pressure *noun*
1. Pressure is the force that you produce when you press hard on something.
2. Pressure is also the force that a quantity of gas or liquid has on any surface that it touches: *I'd better check the tyre pressure.*
pretend (pretends, pretending, pretended) *verb*
If you pretend to be someone or pretend to be doing something, you act as though it were real although it is not: *Let's pretend to be doctors and nurses.*
pretty (prettier, prettiest) *adjective*
Someone who is pretty is nice to look at.
>**prettily** *adverb*
prevent (prevents, preventing, prevented) *verb*
If you prevent someone from doing something, you stop them doing it.
prey *noun*
The prey of an animal is the creatures that it hunts for food.
price (prices) *noun*
The price of something is the amount of money that you must pay to buy it.
prick (pricks, pricking, pricked) *verb*
If something sharp, such as a pin, pricks you, it makes a tiny hole in your skin.
prickle (prickles) *noun*
A prickle is a small, sharp point that sticks out from a leaf or from the stem of a plant.
pride (prides) *noun*
1. Pride is a good feeling of happiness that you have when you have done something good or when you own something you think is good.
2. A pride of lions is a group of lions that live together.
prime minister (prime ministers) *noun*
The prime minister of a country is the leader of that country's government.
primrose (primroses) *noun*
A primrose is a small, wild plant, which has pale yellow flowers in spring.
prince (princes) *noun*
A prince is the son of a king or queen.
princess (princesses) *noun*
A princess is the daughter of a king or queen, or the wife of a prince.
print (prints) *noun*
1. A print is one of the photographs from a film.
2. A print is also a footprint or a fingerprint.
print (prints, printing, printed) *verb*
1. When someone prints something such as a poster or a newspaper, they use a machine to make lots of copies of it.
2. If you print words, you write in letters that are not joined together.
printout (printouts) *noun*
A printout is printed information that you can get from a computer.
prison (prisons) *noun*
A prison is a building where people are kept when they have done something very bad.
prisoner (prisoners) *noun*
1. A prisoner is someone who is kept in prison as a punishment.
2. A prisoner is also someone who has been captured by an enemy, for example in war.
private *adjective*
1. If something is private, it is for one person or group only: *All the rooms have a private bath.*
2. Private talks are those that are held between a few people. The things that are said are kept secret from everyone else.
>**privately** *adverb*
>**in private** *phrase*
If you do something in private, you do it without other people being there. This is usually because it is something you want to keep secret.
prize (prizes) *noun*
A prize is something that is given to someone as a reward.
probably *adverb*
You say probably when you think something

might be true, but you are not sure: *We shall probably be home before four o'clock.*
problem (problems) *noun*
1. A problem is something that is difficult.
2. A problem is also something, like a puzzle, that you have to work out.
process (processes) *noun*
1. A process is a series of actions which are carried out to get a particular result.
2. A process is also a series of developments which happen naturally and result in a change of some sort.
procession (processions) *noun*
A procession is a line of people walking or riding through the streets on a special occasion.
produce (produces, producing, produced) *verb*
1. To produce things means to make them.
2. When animals produce offspring, or plants produce things like leaves or flowers, these things form as a result of a natural process.
3. When something produces energy, such as heat or sound, the energy comes from it or is made by it.
4. If you produce an object from somewhere, such as a pocket, you bring it out into the open so that it can be seen.
5. Someone who produces a play, film or television programme organizes its preparation and gets it ready to show to the public.
professor (professors) *noun*
A professor in a British university has the highest rank of the teachers in a department.
profit (profits) *noun*
A profit is an amount of money that is gained in business, for example when the cost of making something is less than the amount it is sold for.
program (programs) *noun*
A program is a set of instructions that a computer uses in order to do particular things.
program (programs, programming, programmed) *verb*
When someone programs a computer, they write a set of instructions that a computer can use in order to do particular things.
programme (programmes) *noun*
1. A programme is a plan of things that will take place.
2. A radio or television programme is the thing, such as a play or talk, that is being broadcast.
progress *noun*
1. Progress is gradually getting nearer to achieving something or finishing something.
2. The progress of something is the way it changes and develops over a period of time.
project (projects) *noun*
A project is a study of something: *We're doing a project on the environment at school.*
promise (promises, promising, promised) *verb*
If you promise that you will do something, you mean you really will do it.
prong (prongs) *noun*
The prongs of a fork are the long, pointed parts. A fork usually has three or four prongs.
pronounce (pronounces, pronouncing, pronounced) *verb*
To pronounce a word means to say it in a particular way.
proof *noun*
Proof of something is evidence or facts that show that it is true or that it exists.
prop (props) *noun*
1. A prop is an object that you use to hold something else up. For example, you can use a long stick as a prop to hold up a washing line.
2. A prop is also an object or piece of furniture that is used for a play on the stage.
propeller (propellers) *noun*
A propeller is the blades that turn to drive an aircraft or ship.
proper *adjective*
1. Proper means right: *Put those things back in the proper place.*

2. You can also use proper to mean real: *You need a proper screwdriver for that job.*
>**properly** *adverb*
property (properties) *noun*
1. Someone's property is the things that belong to them.
2. A property is a piece of land that belongs to a person or an organization, and the buildings on it.
prophecy (prophecies) *noun*
A prophecy is when someone says that something will happen or become true in the future.
proportion (proportions) *noun*
If you talk about a proportion of a whole thing, you mean a part of it, especially when compared in size with the whole thing.
protect (protects, protecting, protected) *verb*
To protect someone or something means to keep them safe from harm or damage.
protection *noun*
If something gives protection against something unpleasant, it keeps people or things safe from it: *This cream will give you some protection against the harmful rays of the sun.*
proud (prouder, proudest) *adjective*
If you feel proud, you feel glad about something you have done, or something you own, that you think is good.
>**proudly** *adverb*
prove (proves, proving, proved) *verb*
To prove that something is true means to show definitely that it is true.
proverb (proverbs) *noun*
A proverb is a short sentence that people often say. Proverbs give advice about life. For example, the proverb 'Look before you leap' means that you should think carefully before you do something.
provide (provides, providing, provided) *verb*
If you provide something for someone, you give it to them so that they have it when they need it.
prune (prunes) *noun*
A prune is a dark purple plum that has been dried.
prune (prunes, pruning, pruned) *verb*
When someone prunes a tree, they cut off some of the branches so that it will grow better.
public *adjective*
Something which is public can be used by anyone. For example, anyone can pay to travel on public transport, such as trains and buses.
>**publicly** *adverb*
pudding (puddings) *noun*
A pudding is a cooked sweet food which is usually eaten after the main part of a meal.
puddle (puddles) *noun*
A puddle is a small pool of liquid on the ground or floor. You can see puddles of water on the ground when it has been raining.
pull (pulls, pulling, pulled) *verb*
1. When you pull something, you hold it firmly and move it towards you.
2. When an animal or vehicle pulls something, such as a cart or trailer, it is fixed to them so that it moves along behind them.
3. When you pull a curtain, you move it across a window.
4. If someone pulls down a building, they destroy it completely.
5. When a train pulls in at a station, it arrives at a station and stops.
6. When a vehicle pulls off the road, it turns into somewhere such as a parking space.
7. When a vehicle pulls out, it moves out on to the road.
8. When a train pulls out, it leaves the station.
9. When a vehicle pulls up, it slows down and stops.
pulley (pulleys) *noun*
A pulley is made up of a chain or piece of rope stretched over the rim of a wheel. You can use a pulley to lift heavy loads.
pullover (pullovers) *noun*
A pullover is a knitted woollen garment that covers the top part of your body. You put it on by pulling it over your head.

pulse *noun*
Your pulse is the regular beating of blood through your body. You can feel your pulse when you touch particular parts of your body, especially your wrist.
pump (pumps) *noun*
1. A pump is a machine that is used to force gas or liquid to move the way it is wanted.
2. A pump is also an object which can be used to put air into tyres on cycles or other vehicles.
pumpkin (pumpkins) *noun*
A pumpkin is a very large, orange-coloured fruit with a thick skin. It is soft inside, with a lot of pips. Pumpkins grow on plants which trail across the ground.
punch (punches, punching, punched) *verb*
If you punch someone or something, you hit them hard with your fist.
punctual *adjective*
Someone who is punctual arrives somewhere or does something at exactly the right time.
>**punctually** *adverb*
punctuation *noun*
Punctuation is the marks such as full stops and commas, that you use in writing.
puncture (punctures) *noun*
A puncture is a small hole in a tyre. When a tyre has a puncture, the air inside escapes and the tyre goes flat.
punish (punishes, punishing, punished) *verb*
To punish someone means to make them suffer in some way because they have done something wrong.
pupil (pupils) *noun*
1. The pupils of a school are the children who go there to learn.
2. The pupil in your eye is the small round black hole in the centre. The size of your pupils changes with the light. When it is bright, your pupils are very small. When the light is low, your pupils grow larger.
puppet (puppets) *noun*
A puppet is a kind of doll that you can move. Some puppets have strings fixed to them which you can pull. Others are made so that you can put your hand inside.
puppy (puppies) *noun*
A puppy is a young dog.
purchase (purchases) *noun*
A purchase is something that you buy.
purchase (purchases, purchasing, purchased) *verb*
When you purchase something, you buy it.
pure (purer, purest) *adjective*
1. Something that is pure is not mixed with anything else.
2. Pure also means clean, healthy, and free from anything that might harm you.
purple *adjective*
Something that is purple is of a reddish-blue colour.
purpose (purposes) *noun*
If something is made for a particular purpose, it is made to be used in that way: *I use this as a hammer but it wasn't made for that purpose.*
>**on purpose** *phrase*
If you do something on purpose, you mean to do it. It does not happen by accident.
purr (purrs, purring, purred) *verb*
When a cat purrs, it keeps making a low sound that shows it is happy.
purse (purses) *noun*
A purse is a small bag that people keep their money in.
push (pushes, pushing, pushed) *verb*
When you push something, you press it hard.
puzzle (puzzles) *noun*
1. A puzzle is something that is hard to understand.
2. A puzzle can also be a game or toy that you have to think about carefully; for example, a crossword puzzle.
pyjamas *noun*
A pair of pyjamas is a loose jacket and trousers that a person can wear in bed.
pyramid (pyramids) *noun*
1. A pyramid is a solid shape with a flat base and flat sides the shape of triangles. The sides slope upwards and inwards to a point.
2. A pyramid is also an ancient building made of stone, in the shape of a pyramid. There are pyramids in Egypt and Mexico.

Q

quack (quacks) *noun*
A quack is a sound that a duck makes.
quality *noun*
The quality of something is how good or bad it is, compared with other things of the same kind.
quantity (quantities) *noun*
A quantity is an amount that you can measure or count: *We shall need a large quantity of food for the weekend.*
quarantine *noun*
Quarantine is the period of time during which a person or animal that may have a disease is kept apart from others so that the disease does not have a chance to spread.
quarrel (quarrels, quarrelling, quarrelled) *verb*
If people quarrel, they have an angry argument.
quarry (quarries) *noun*
1. A quarry is an animal that is being hunted.
2. A quarry is also a deep hole that has been dug in a piece of land. Quarries are dug to provide materials such as stone for building and other work.
quarter (quarters) *noun*
A quarter is one of four equal parts of something.
queen (queens) *noun*
1. A queen is a woman who rules a country. Queens are not chosen by the people. They are born into a royal family.
2. The wife of a king is also called a queen.
3. In the insect world, a queen is a large female bee, ant or wasp which can lay eggs. There is usually only one queen in each group of insects.
question (questions) *noun*
A question is words you say or write when you want to ask something.
question mark (question marks) *noun*
A question mark is the punctuation mark (?) which you use in writing at the end of a question.
queue (queues) *noun*
A queue is a line of people waiting for their turn. People sometimes stand in a queue in shops or at bus stops. A line of vehicles can also be called a queue, if they are waiting to move.
quick (quicker, quickest) *adjective*
1. Someone or something that is quick moves with great speed.
2. Something that is quick lasts only a short time: *I'll have a quick look at it.*
>**quickly** *adverb*
quiet (quieter, quietest) *adjective*
1. Someone or something that is quiet makes only a small amount of noise.
2. If a place is quiet, there is very little noise there.
3. If someone tells you to be quiet, they do not want you to say anything at all.
4. A quiet person always behaves in a calm and gentle way.
>**quietly** *adverb*
quite *adverb*
1. Quite means rather: *I think he's quite nice.*
2. Quite can also mean completely: *The work is now quite finished.*
quiz (quizzes) *noun*
A quiz is a game or test. Someone tries to find out how much you know by asking you questions.

R

rabbit (rabbits) *noun*
A rabbit is a small, furry animal with long ears. Rabbits are often kept as pets. Wild rabbits live in holes in the ground called burrows. A group of burrows is called a warren.
race (races) *noun*
1. A race is a competition to see who is the fastest; for example, in running or swimming.
2. A race is also a large group of people who look alike in some way. Different races

have, for example, different skin colour, or differently shaped eyes.

rack (racks) *noun*
1. A rack is a frame that is used for holding things or for hanging things on. Racks are usually made with something such as hooks, pegs or bars.
2. A rack is also a shelf over the seats in a bus, plane or train. Passengers can put bags and other pieces of luggage on the rack.

racket (rackets) *noun*
1. If someone is making a racket, they are making a loud, unpleasant noise.
2. A racket is also a bat with an oval frame and strings across and down it. You hold a racket in your hand when you are playing tennis, squash or badminton, and use it to hit the ball or shuttlecock.

radar *noun*
Radar is a way of showing the position and speed of ships and aircraft when they cannot be seen. Radio signals give the information on a screen.

radiator (radiators) *noun*
1. A radiator is a hollow metal object that can be filled with liquid in order to heat a room. Radiators are usually connected by pipes to a boiler.
2. In a car, the radiator holds the water that is used to cool the engine.

radio (radios) *noun*
A radio is a piece of equipment which receives sounds through the air. You can use a radio to listen to programmes that are broadcast.

raft (rafts) *noun*
A raft is a floating platform. Rafts are often made of large pieces of wood fixed together.

rag (rags) *noun*
1. A rag is a piece of old cloth that you can use to clean or wipe things.
2. Rags are old, torn clothes.

rage *noun*
Someone who is in a rage is very, very angry.

ragged *adjective*
1. Clothes that are ragged are old and torn, and rather dirty.
2. An edge that is ragged is uneven and rough.

raid (raids) *noun*
A raid is a sudden attack against an enemy.

rail (rails) *noun*
1. A rail is a horizontal bar that is firmly fixed to posts. Rails are used as fences, or for people to lean on.
2. Rails are the heavy metal bars that trains run on.

railing (railings) *noun*
A railing is a kind of fence made from metal bars.

railway (railways) *noun*
A railway is a way of travelling and carrying things from one place to another. A locomotive pulls carriages or trucks along rails which are fixed to the ground.

rain *noun*
Rain is water that falls from the clouds in small drops.

rainbow (rainbows) *noun*
A rainbow is an arch of different colours that can sometimes be seen in the sky after it has been raining.

raincoat (raincoats) *noun*
A raincoat is a waterproof coat that you wear when it is raining.

raindrop (raindrops) *noun*
A raindrop is a single drop of rain.

rainforest (rainforests) *noun*
A rainforest is a forest with lots of tall trees in an area of the world that is very hot and has a lot of rain.

raise (raises, raising, raised) *verb*
1. If you raise something, you move it so that it is higher.
2. If you raise your voice, you speak more loudly.
3. Someone who raises children looks after them until they are grown up.

raisin (raisins) *noun*
A raisin is a dried grape. Raisins can be eaten raw, or used in cakes or puddings.

rake (rakes) *noun*
A rake is a garden tool. It has a row of metal teeth, like a comb, fixed to a long handle.

ram (rams) *noun*
A ram is an adult male sheep.
ramp (ramps) *noun*
1. A ramp is a sloping surface between two places that are at different levels; for example, one that has been built so that it can be used by cars or wheelchairs.
2. A ramp is also a small hump that is built on a road to make cars slow down when they drive over it.
ranch (ranches) *noun*
In the United States, a ranch is a large farm for raising cattle, sheep or horses.
range (ranges) *noun*
1. The range of something is the area or distance over which it can be used.
2. A range is a row of hills or mountains.
rank (ranks) *noun*
A rank is a position that a person holds in an organization. The higher the rank, the more important they are.
rapid *adjective*
Something that is rapid is very quick.
>rapidly *adverb*
rapids *noun*
Rapids are parts of a river where the water moves very fast, often over rocks.
rare (rarer, rarest) *adjective*
Something that is rare is not very often seen, or does not happen very often.
>rarely *adverb*
rash (rashes) *noun*
A rash is a lot of spots that appear on your skin if you have certain illnesses.
rash *adjective*
Someone who is rash does or says things that are foolish, because they act without thinking carefully first.
>rashly *adverb*
rasher (rashers) *noun*
A rasher is a thin slice of bacon.
raspberry (raspberries) *noun*
A raspberry is a small, red fruit, which is soft and juicy, with a lot of small seeds called pips. Raspberries grow on bushes.
rat (rats) *noun*
A rat is a small animal with a long scaly tail. It looks rather like a large mouse. Rats have very sharp teeth.
rather *adverb*
1. Rather means slightly: *I'm rather angry about that.*
2. You can say rather if there is something else you want to do: *I don't want to go out. I'd rather watch television.*
rattle (rattles) *noun*
A rattle is a baby's toy that makes a noise when it is shaken.
rattle (rattles, rattling, rattled) *verb*
When something rattles, it makes short, rapid, knocking sounds: *Can you stop that window rattling?*
raven (ravens) *noun*
A raven is a large bird that belongs to the crow family. Ravens have shiny black feathers and a harsh call.
ravine (ravines) *noun*
A ravine is a very deep, narrow valley with steep sides. Ravines are made by streams flowing through them, wearing away the stone.
raw *adjective*
Food that is raw is not cooked.
ray (rays) *noun*
A ray is a line of light.
razor (razors) *noun*
A razor is a tool that people use to remove hair from their face or another part of their body.
reach (reaches, reaching, reached) *verb*
1. When you reach a place, you arrive there.
2. If you reach somewhere, you stretch out your hand: *I reached across the table for the salt.*
reaction (reactions) *noun*
A reaction is something that you feel or do because of something that has happened: *When he fell over, his first reaction was to laugh.*
read (reads, reading, read) *verb*
1. When you read, you look at words or symbols and understand what they mean.
2. When you read aloud, you say the words that are written.

reading *noun*
Reading is looking at words or symbols and understanding them.
ready *adjective*
If someone or something is ready, they are properly prepared for doing something.
real *adjective*
1. Something that is real is true. It is not imaginary: *I've seen a real princess.*
2. You also say real when you mean the thing itself and not a copy: *I've got a lovely pony made of velvet. But Jenny's got a real pony.*
realize/realise (realizes, realizing, realized) *verb*
If you realize something, you work it out or notice it: *I've just realized you must be Alex's sister.*
really *adverb*
You can use really to make something you are saying stronger: *I really don't like that boy.*
rear *noun*
The rear of something, such as a vehicle or a building is the part that is at the back of it.
rear (rears, rearing, reared) *verb*
1. If a person or animal rears young animals, they look after them until they are able to look after themselves.
2. If an animal like a horse rears, it stands on its back legs and lifts its front legs high in the air.
reason (reasons) *noun*
The reason for something is why it happens: *I'm sorry I'm late. There is a good reason.*
reasonable *adjective*
1. People who are reasonable behave in a fair and sensible way.
2. A price that is reasonable seems fair. It is not too high.
>**reasonably** *adverb*
rebel (rebels) *noun*
A rebel is someone who fights against people who are in charge.
rebellious *adjective*
Someone who is rebellious refuses to do what people want them to do.
>**rebelliously** *adverb*
receive (receives, receiving, received) *verb*
When you receive something, you get it after it has been given or sent to you.
recent *adjective*
Something that is recent happened or appeared only a short time ago.
>**recently** *adverb*
recipe (recipes) *noun*
A recipe tells you how to make something to eat or drink. It gives you a list of the things you need, and tells you how to mix and cook them.
recite (recites, reciting, recited) *verb*
When you recite something, such as a poem, you say it aloud from memory.
reckon (reckons, reckoning, reckoned) *verb*
1. If you reckon that something is true, you think it is true.
2. If you had not reckoned with something, you had not expected it and so were not prepared for it.
recognize/recognise (recognizes, recognizing, recognized) *verb*
If you recognize someone, you know who they are when you see them, because you have seen them before.
recommend (recommends, recommending, recommended) *verb*
If you recommend someone, you praise them and suggest that they would be suitable for a particular job.
record (records) *noun*
1. A record is a round, flat piece of plastic. When it is played, you can hear sounds such as music.
2. A record is also the very best performance of something: *He set a new record in that race.*
record (records, recording, recorded) *verb*
If someone records something that happens, they write it down or put it onto tape or film so that other people will know about it.
recorder (recorders) *noun*
A recorder is a musical instrument, which you play by blowing into one end and putting your fingers over the holes. As you cover different holes, you make a different sound.

recover (recovers, recovering, recovered) *verb*
1. When you recover from something such as an illness, you become well again.
2. If you recover from something such as an unpleasant experience, you stop being affected by it.
rectangle (rectangles) *noun*
A rectangle is a shape with four straight sides and square corners. It has two equal long sides and two equal short sides.
recycle (recycles, recycling, recycled) *verb*
If something, such as paper, is recycled, it has been used once already and then has been treated in some way so that it can be used again.
red (redder, reddest) *adjective*
Something that is red is the colour of a ripe tomato.
reed (reeds) *noun*
A reed is a plant with a tall, hollow stem. Reeds grow in large groups in or near water.
reef (reefs) *noun*
A reef is a long line of rocks or sand that is just below the surface of the sea.
reel (reels) *noun*
A reel is an object shaped like a cylinder. It is used to hold long, thin material, such as thread or wire.
referee (referees) *noun*
A referee is a person whose job is to control a sports match. Referees make sure the players follow the rules properly.
refill (refills) *noun*
A refill is a full container that replaces an empty one inside a permanent container: *Have you got a refill to fit this ballpoint?*
refill (refills, refilling, refilled) *verb*
If you refill something, you fill it again after it has been emptied.
reflect (reflects, reflecting, reflected) *verb*
1. When a surface reflects rays of something, like light or heat, the rays bounce back from the surface.
2. When a mirror reflects a person or thing, it shows what they look like.

reflection (reflections) *noun*
A reflection is what you see when you look in a mirror or other shiny surface.
refract (refracts, refracting, refracted) *verb*
If a ray of light is refracted, it is bent; for example, when it passes from air into water.
refreshing *adjective*
Something that is refreshing makes you feel energetic or cool again after you have been tired or hot.
>refreshingly *adverb*
refrigerator (refrigerators) *noun*
A refrigerator is a large metal container which is kept cool inside so that the food and drink in it keeps fresh longer. A refrigerator is often called a fridge for short.
refuse *noun*
Refuse is things that are not wanted and have been thrown away.
refuse (refuses, refusing, refused) *verb*
If you refuse to do something, you say you will not do it.
register (registers) *noun*
A register is a list of names or things that have happened.
register (registers, registering, registered) *verb*
When you register, you put your name on a list.
regular *adjective*
Something that is regular does not change its pattern. For example, a regular heartbeat does not get faster or slower.
>regularly *adverb*
reign (reigns) *noun*
The reign of a king or queen is the period during which they rule.
rein (reins) *noun*
1. A rein is one of the leather straps that are used to control a horse.
2. Reins are thin straps that are used to control a small child who has just learned to walk.
reindeer *noun*
A reindeer is a large deer that lives in the cold northern parts of the world.

related *adjective*
People who are related belong to the same family.
relation (relations) *noun*
If someone is your relation, they belong to the same family as you.
relationship (relationships) *noun*
1. Your relationship with someone is the way in which you are related to them.
2. The relationship between two things is the way in which they are connected or linked.
relative (relatives) *noun*
If someone is your relative, they belong to the same family as you.
relax (relaxes, relaxing, relaxed) *verb*
When you relax, you stop worrying and feel more calm.
release (releases, releasing, released) *verb*
1. If someone releases a person or animal that has been trapped or held in some way, they set them free.
2. If someone releases a new record or video, people can buy it.
reliable *adjective*
If something or someone is reliable, you can depend on them.
>**reliably** *adverb*
relief *noun*
Relief is being glad that something unpleasant has not happened or is no longer happening.
relieved *adjective*
If you are relieved, you are glad because something unpleasant has not happened or is no longer happening.
religion (religions) *noun*
A religion is a set of beliefs about a god, or about several gods.
reluctant *adjective*
If you are reluctant to do something, you do not want to do it. You hesitate, or do it slowly and without enthusiasm.
>**reluctantly** *adverb*
rely (relies, relying, relied) *verb*
If you rely on something or someone, you need them and depend on them.
remain (remains, remaining, remained) *verb*
If you remain in a place, you stay there and do not go away.
remainder *noun*
1. The remainder of something is the part of it that remains after the other parts have gone or been dealt with.
2. The remainder in arithmetic is the amount left over when one number cannot be exactly divided by another number.
remark (remarks) *noun*
A remark is something that you say: *The others keep making remarks about my haircut.*
remarkable *adjective*
Someone or something that is remarkable is unusual in some way that causes people to notice them and feel surprised.
>**remarkably** *adverb*
remember (remembers, remembering, remembered) *verb*
1. If you can remember something, you can bring it back into your mind.
2. If you remember to do something, you do it when you said you would: *I must remember to go to the post office.*
remind (reminds, reminding, reminded) *verb*
1. If someone reminds you of something you already know about, they do or say something which makes you think about it.
2. If something reminds you to do something, they make you remember a task you should be dealing with.
3. If someone reminds you of someone else, something about them makes you think of the other person.
removal (removals) *noun*
1. The removal of something is the act of taking it away or getting rid of it.
2. A removal company takes furniture from one building to another when people move house.
remove (removes, removing, removed) *verb*
1. If you remove something from somewhere, you take it away.
2. When you remove your clothing, you take it off.

rent *noun*
Rent is the money that a person pays so that they will be allowed to use something that belongs to someone else. People often pay rent so that they can live in a house that is owned by someone else.
repair (repairs, repairing, repaired) *verb*
If you repair something that has been damaged or is not working properly, you mend it.
repeat (repeats, repeating, repeated) *verb*
If you repeat something, you say it or do it again.
repeatedly *adverb*
If you do something repeatedly, you keep doing it.
replace (replaces, replacing, replaced) *verb*
1. If something replaces something else, it takes its place.
2. If you replace something, you put it back where it was before.
3. If you replace something that is lost or is no longer any use, you get a new one.
reply (replies, replying, replied) *verb*
When you reply, you answer someone.
report (reports) *noun*
1. A report is something that is said or written about something that has happened.
2. A school report is a piece of paper written by a teacher to say how well a pupil has worked during the term.
reporter (reporters) *noun*
A reporter is someone who works for a newspaper, radio or television. Their job is to find out what is happening in the world so that their report can be printed or broadcast.
reptile (reptiles) *noun*
A reptile is a cold-blooded animal with a scaly skin. Female reptiles lay eggs. Tortoises, snakes and crocodiles are all reptiles.
request (requests) *noun*
1. A request is a very polite demand for something.
2. A request is also something which has been asked for, especially a piece of music played on the radio.
rescue (rescues, rescuing, rescued) *verb*
If a person rescues someone, they help them get away from danger.
resent (resents, resenting, resented) *verb*
If you resent something, you feel indignant about it.
reserve (reserves, reserving, reserved) *verb*
If you reserve something, like a table in a restaurant or a seat in a theatre, you arrange for it to be kept for you.
>in reserve *phrase*
If you have something in reserve, you have it ready to use if it is needed.
reservoir (reservoirs) *noun*
A reservoir is a lake that is used for storing drinking water for a city or other area.
resign (resigns, resigning, resigned) *verb*
1. If someone resigns from a job, they say they do not want to go on doing it, and they leave.
2. If you resign yourself to something unpleasant, you accept it without complaining, because you realize that you cannot change it.
resist (resists, resisting, resisted) *verb*
1. If you resist someone, you fight against them to avoid being defeated.
2. If you resist doing something, or resist the temptation to do something, you stop yourself although you would like to do it.
respect (respects, respecting, respected) *verb*
If you respect someone, you look up to them and think their opinions are important.
rest (rests) *noun*
1. A rest is a period of time when you do not work.
2. The rest is all the things in a group that are left: *I've done some of the washing-up. I'll do the rest tomorrow.*
rest (rests, resting, rested) *verb*
When you rest, you sit or lie down. You do not do anything active for a while.
restaurant (restaurants) *noun*
A restaurant is a place where meals are served.
restful *adjective*
Something that is restful helps you to feel calm and relaxed.

result (results) *noun*
A result is something that happens because of something else: *The milk boiled over and the result was a real mess.*
retire (retires, retiring, retired) *verb*
When someone retires, they stop doing their job, usually because they have reached an age when they can get a pension.
retreat (retreats, retreating, retreated) *verb*
When an army retreats, it moves away from the enemy.
return (returns) *noun*
A return is a ticket that allows you to travel to a particular place and back again, on something such as a train.
return (returns, returning, returned) *verb*
1. When you return to a place, you go back there after you have been away.
2. If you return something to someone, you give it back to them.
reveal (reveals, revealing, revealed) *verb*
1. If you reveal something that has been secret, you tell people about it.
2. If you reveal something that has been out of sight, you uncover it so that people can see it.
revenge *noun*
Revenge is something a person does to hurt someone who has hurt them.
reverse (reverses, reversing, reversed) *verb*
If a car reverses, it goes backwards.
revise (revises, revising, revised) *verb*
When you revise, you read something again so that you can learn it and answer questions on it in an exam.
revision *noun*
Revision is reading something again so that you can answer questions on it in an exam.
revive (revives, reviving, revived) *verb*
When someone revives, they become conscious again after they have been unconscious.
revolver (revolvers) *noun*
A revolver is a hand gun which can fire several bullets before it needs reloading.
reward (rewards) *noun*
A reward is something you are given for doing well.
rhinoceros (rhinoceroses) *noun*
A rhinoceros is a big animal with a very thick skin and one or two horns on its nose. Rhinoceroses live in Africa and Asia and eat plants, especially grass. They are often called rhinos for short.
rhyme (rhymes, rhyming, rhymed) *verb*
If two words rhyme, they have a similar sound. People often use words that rhyme at the ends of lines in poems: *I need a word to rhyme with 'dog'. - How about 'fog'?*
rhythm (rhythms) *noun*
Rhythm is a regular pattern of sound or movement. Music and dancing have rhythm.
rib (ribs) *noun*
Your ribs are the curved bones that go from your backbone to your chest. People and animals have 12 ribs on either side of their bodies. They protect the heart and other organs.
ribbon (ribbons) *noun*
A ribbon is a long, narrow piece of fine cloth. It is used for tying things together, or as a decoration.
rice *noun*
Rice is white or pale brown grains which are boiled and eaten. In many countries rice is the main food.
rich (richer, richest) *adjective*
Someone who is rich has a lot of money or valuable things.
>**get rid of** *phrase*
When you get rid of something that you do not want, you remove it or throw it away.
riddle (riddles) *noun*
A riddle is a kind of puzzle. You ask a question which has a funny answer.
ride (rides, riding, rode, ridden) *verb*
1. When a person rides a horse or a bicycle, they sit on it and control its movements.
2. When you ride in a vehicle such as a car, you travel in it.
ridiculous *adjective*
If you say something is ridiculous, you mean it is very foolish.
>**ridiculously** *adverb*

right *adjective*
1. If something is right, it is correct.
2. Someone's right hand is the hand most people write with.

rigid *adjective*
Something that is rigid is very stiff and does not bend, stretch or twist easily.
>**rigidly** *adverb*

rim (rims) *noun*
1. The rim of a container, such as a cup, is the edge that goes all the way round the top.
2. The rim of a circular object, such as a wheel, is the outside edge of it.

rind (rinds) *noun*
The rind of a fruit such as an orange or a lemon is its thick outer skin.

ring (rings) *noun*
1. A ring is an ornament that people wear on a finger.
2. Anything in the shape of circle can be called a ring.
3. A ring is also the sound made by a bell.

ring (rings, ringing, rang, rung) *verb*
If you ring someone, you call them on the telephone.

rip (rips, ripping, ripped) *verb*
If someone rips something, they tear it violently with their hands or a knife: *She ripped open the envelope to see who the letter was from.*

ripe (riper, ripest) *adjective*
When fruit or grain is ripe, it is ready to be harvested or eaten.

ripple (ripples) *noun*
A ripple is a little wave on the surface of water.

rise (rises, rising, rose, risen) *verb*
1. If something rises, it moves upwards.
2. When the sun or the moon rises, it appears above the horizon.

risk (risks) *noun*
A risk is a danger that something bad might happen.
>**take a risk** *phrase*
If someone takes a risk, they do something knowing that it could be dangerous.

rival (rivals) *noun*
Your rival is someone who is competing for the same things as you are.

river (rivers) *noun*
A river is a large amount of fresh water flowing in a long, curving line across the land. Rivers flow into the sea, a lake, or another river.

road (roads) *noun*
A road is a long, smooth, hard piece of ground. Roads are made so that vehicles can travel from place to place.

roar (roars) *noun*
A roar is a very loud noise. For example, the noise made by wild animals such as lions is called a roar. You can also describe the noise made by traffic as a roar.

roast (roasts, roasting, roasted) *verb*
When someone roasts food, such as meat, they cook it in an oven or over an open fire.

robber (robbers) *noun*
A robber is a person who steals.

robin (robins) *noun*
A robin is a small, brown bird with a red neck and breast.

robot (robots) *noun*
A robot is a machine which is programmed to do a number of things. Robots are sometimes used in factories.

rock (rocks) *noun*
1. Rock is the very hard material that is in the earth. Cliffs and mountains are made of rock.
2. Rock is also a kind of popular music.
3. There is a kind of sweet made in long sticks which is called rock.

rock (rocks, rocking, rocked) *verb*
When something rocks, it moves slowly backwards and forwards, or from side to side.

rocket (rockets) *noun*
A rocket is a missile that drives itself into space.

rocky (rockier, rockiest) *adjective*
A place that is rocky is covered with rocks.

rod (rods) *noun*
A rod is a long, thin, straight bar of something such as wood or metal.

rodent (rodents) *noun*
A rodent is a small mammal with sharp front

teeth. Rats, mice, rabbits and squirrels are all rodents.

roll (rolls) *noun*
1. A roll of something, such as paper or tape, is a long piece of it wrapped round several times.
2. A roll is a very small loaf of bread for one person.

roll (rolls, rolling, rolled) *verb*
When a round object, such as a ball, rolls, it moves along turning over and over.

roller (rollers) *noun*
1. A roller is a large, heavy wheel. Some rollers have handles and can be used in the garden. Larger rollers are fixed to vehicles. They are used to make roads flat.
2. Rollers are hollow tubes used for curling hair.

roller skate (roller skates) *noun*
A roller skate is a type of shoe with four small wheels on the bottom. People wear roller skates for pleasure, when they want to move quickly and smoothly over flat surfaces.

roof (roofs) *noun*
A roof is the covering on top of a building or vehicle.

rook (rooks) *noun*
A rook is a large, black bird of the crow family. It has a harsh, loud cry.

room (rooms) *noun*
1. A room is one of the parts of a house or other building. It has its own walls and door. Halls and landings are not called rooms.
2. Room is space to move about in and to put things in: *We can't have the party here. There wouldn't be enough room for everybody.*

roost (roosts, roosting, roosted) *verb*
When birds roost, they settle in a particular place for the night.

root (roots) *noun*
1. A root is the part of a plant that grows underground.
2. The root of a hair, tooth or nail is the part that you cannot see because it is covered with skin.

rope (ropes) *noun*
A rope is a piece of very thick, strong string.

rose (roses) *noun*
A rose is a flower. There are many different kinds of rose. Most of them grow on very thorny stems. Some roses have a very pleasant smell.

rot (rots, rotting, rotted) *verb*
1. When vegetables and other foods rot, they go bad.
2. When something such as wood rots, it goes soft and can be easily pulled to pieces.

rotten *adjective*
1. Food that is rotten has gone bad.
2. Rotten wood has been badly damaged by something such as damp or insects.

rough (rougher, roughest) *adjective*
1. If something is rough, the surface is uneven and not smooth.
2. If the sea is rough, there are big waves.
3. Something that is rough is not made very well.

>**roughly** *adverb*

round *adjective*
Something that is round is shaped like a ball or a circle.

round *preposition*
If something is round something else, it is on all sides of it: *There was a wall round the garden.*

roundabout (roundabouts) *noun*
1. A roundabout is a large machine at a fair, with large toy animals or cars on it. Children can sit on the toys and go round and round.
2. A roundabout is also an island in the middle of the road at a place where several roads meet.

route (routes) *noun*
1. A route is a way from one place to another.
2. A route is also the particular path that is planned in advance for a public event such as a march or procession.

row (rows) *noun*
A row is a number of people or things arranged in a line.

row (rows, rowing, rowed) *verb*
When someone rows a boat, they make it move through the water by using oars.

royal *adjective*
1. Someone who is royal belongs to the family of a king or queen.
2. Something that is royal is connected with a royal family.
rub (rubs, rubbing, rubbed) *verb*
When you rub something, you wipe it hard. You can rub it with your hand alone, or you can use a cloth.
rubber (rubbers) *noun*
1. Rubber is a strong, stretchy material that is made from the sap of a tropical tree.
2. A rubber is a small piece of rubber that you use to get rid of pencil marks on paper.
rubbish *noun*
1. Rubbish is also waste material, such as used paper or empty tins.
2. If someone says that something is rubbish, they mean they think it is of very poor quality: *There is so much rubbish on television.*
rudder (rudders) *noun*
1. A rudder is a vertical piece of wood or metal at the back of a boat. It is used to steer the boat.
2. A rudder is also a vertical piece of metal at the back of an aeroplane. It is used to make it turn.
rude (ruder, rudest) *adjective*
If someone is rude, they behave badly and are not polite: *It's rude to stare at people.*
>rudely *adverb*
rug (rugs) *noun*
A rug is a piece of thick material like a small carpet.
rugby *noun*
Rugby is a game played with an oval ball. Two teams try to score points by carrying the ball across a line, or by kicking the ball over a bar.
ruin (ruins) *noun*
The ruins of a building are the parts of it that are left after it has been badly damaged or spoiled.
ruin (ruins, ruining, ruined) *verb*
To ruin something means to damage it very badly or spoil it.
rule (rules) *noun*
Rules are directions that tell you what you are allowed to do and what you are not allowed to do. Rules are used in games, and in some places such as schools.
rule (rules, ruling, ruled) *verb*
To rule a country means to be in charge of the way a country works.
ruler (rulers) *noun*
1. A ruler is a person, such as a king, queen, or prime minister, who is the leader of a country.
2. A ruler is also a long, flat piece of something, such as wood or plastic, with straight edges. It is used for measuring things.
rumour (rumours) *noun*
A rumour is a story or piece of information which may or may not be true, but which people are talking about.
run (runs, running, ran, run) *verb*
1. When you run, you move on your feet faster than when you walk.
2. When a vehicle such as a train or bus runs somewhere, it travels at set times: *The bus runs every 20 minutes.*
3. If you run water, you make it flow from something such as a tap.
4. If you run out of something, you have no more of it left.
rung (rungs) *noun*
A rung is a wooden or metal bar that forms a step on a ladder.
runway (runways) *noun*
A runway is a long, narrow strip of ground with a hard, level surface. Runways are used by aeroplanes when they are taking off or landing.
rush (rushes) *noun*
1. A rush of air or water is the sound or feeling of it moving quickly.
2. Rushes are plants that grow near water.
rush (rushes, rushing, rushed) *verb*
If you rush somewhere, you go there quickly.
rust *noun*
Rust is a reddish-brown coating that forms on metal such as iron and steel if it is left in a damp place. Rust gradually destroys metal.

rustle *noun*
A rustle is a soft sound made by things, such as papers or leaves moving gently together.
rusty (rustier, rustiest) *adjective*
Something that is rusty is affected by rust.
rut (ruts) *noun*
A rut is a deep, narrow mark made in the ground by the wheels of vehicles.

S

sack (sacks) *noun*
A sack is a large, strong bag made of cloth or plastic. Sacks are used to carry or store things, such as potatoes or coal.
sad (sadder, saddest) *adjective*
If you are sad, you are unhappy because something has happened that you do not like.
>sadly *adverb*
saddle (saddles) *noun*
A saddle is a seat for a rider on a horse or bicycle.
safari (safaris) *noun*
A safari is a journey to hunt or see wild animals.
safari park (safari parks) *noun*
A safari park is a large, fenced area of land where wild animals live and move around freely.
safe (safer, safest) *adjective*
1. If you are safe, you are not in any danger.
2. If something is safe, it cannot cause harm: *Is this soap powder safe for wool?*
3. If something is in a safe place, it cannot be lost or stolen.
>safely *adverb*
safe (safes) *noun*
A safe is a strong, metal cupboard with special locks. People keep money or valuable things in a safe.
safety *noun*
Safety is being safe.
sail (sails) *noun*
1. A sail is a large piece of material fixed to the mast of a ship or boat. The wind blows against the sail and pushes the ship or boat along.
2. A sail is also one of the flat pieces of wood on the top of a windmill. The wind drives the sails of a windmill.
sail (sails, sailing, sailed) *verb*
1. To sail a boat means to make it move across water using its sails.
2. When a ship sails, it moves across water.
sailing *noun*
Sailing is the sport of sailing boats.
sailor (sailors) *noun*
A sailor is a person who works on a ship as a member of the crew.
salad (salads) *noun*
A salad is a mixture of raw vegetables; for example, lettuce, cucumber and tomatoes. Salads are usually eaten with other foods such as cold meat or cheese.
sale (sales) *noun*
1. The sale of anything is the selling of it for money.
2. A sale is a period during which a shop sells things at less than their usual price.
>for sale *phrase*
Something that is for sale is there for people to buy: *Is that parrot for sale?*
>on sale *phrase*
Things that are on sale are in the shops ready to be bought: *This new computer will be on sale early next year.*
salmon *noun*
A salmon is a large, silvery fish which is good to eat. Salmon live in the sea, but they swim up rivers to lay their eggs.
salt *noun*
Salt is a white powder or crystal with a bitter taste. Salt is found in the earth and in sea water. It is used to flavour or preserve food.
salute (salutes) *noun*
A salute is a sign of greeting or respect used especially in the armed forces. Soldiers give a salute by raising their right hand and touching their forehead with their fingers. At some important occasions, guns are fired into the air as a salute.

same *adjective*
If two things are the same, they are exactly like each other in some way: *Look! Your dress is the same as mine.*
sample (samples) *noun*
A sample of something is an example or a small quantity of it that gives you an idea of what the whole of it is like.
sample (samples, sampling, sampled) *verb*
If you sample food or drink, you taste a small amount of it to see if you like it.
sand *noun*
Sand is very small grains of rock, shells and other material. Most deserts and beaches are made of sand.
sandal (sandals) *noun*
Sandals are light shoes for warm weather. The soles are held on by straps which go over your foot.
sandpaper *noun*
Sandpaper is strong paper that has a coating of sand, which is used for rubbing wood or metal surfaces to make them smoother.
sandpit (sandpits) *noun*
A sandpit is a shallow box in the ground with sand in it, where small children can play.
sandwich (sandwiches) *noun*
A sandwich is two slices of bread with a layer of food, such as meat, cheese or jam, in between.
sap *noun*
Sap is the liquid that carries food through plants and trees.
sardine (sardines) *noun*
A sardine is a small sea fish of the herring family which is eaten as food. Sardines are often preserved and sold in tins.
satellite (satellites) *noun*
1. A satellite is a natural object in space that moves around a larger object. For example, the moon is a satellite of the earth.
2. A satellite is also an object that is sent into space. It travels round the earth or another planet.
satisfy (satisfies, satisfying, satisfied) *verb*
1. Someone or something that satisfies you gives you enough of what you want to make you contented.
2. To satisfy someone also means to convince them that something is true, especially if they have doubted it.
Saturday *noun*
Saturday is one of the seven days of the week. It comes after Friday and before Sunday.
sauce (sauces) *noun*
A sauce is a thick liquid, often made from vegetables or fruit. It is served with other food to add to the taste.
saucepan (saucepans) *noun*
A saucepan is a deep, metal cooking pot, usually with a long handle. Most saucepans have lids.
saucer (saucers) *noun*
A saucer is a small, curved plate for putting a cup on.
sausage (sausages) *noun*
A sausage is a finely minced meat mixture put into a skin.
savage *adjective*
1. A savage animal is wild and fierce.
2. Someone who is savage is cruel and violent.
>**savagely** *adverb*
save (saves, saving, saved) *verb*
1. If you save someone or something, you help them to escape from harm or danger: *He fell in the river and his father dived in to save him.*
2. If you save money, you gradually collect it by not spending it as soon as you get it.
savings *noun*
Your savings are the money that you have saved, especially in something like a bank.
saw (saws) *noun*
A saw is a tool for cutting wood and other materials. It has a blade with sharp teeth along one edge.
sawdust *noun*
Sawdust is dust and very small pieces of wood that are made when wood is sawn.
say (says, saying, said) *verb*
When you say something, you speak words.
scald (scalds, scalding, scalded) *verb*
If you scald yourself, you burn yourself with very hot liquid or steam.

scale (scales) *noun*
1. A scale is a series of musical notes that are played or sung in order.
2. A scale is also one of the small, flat pieces of skin that cover the body of fish, snakes and other reptiles.
scales *noun*
Scales are a machine used to weigh people or things.
scamper (scampers, scampering, scampered) *verb*
When people or small animals scamper, they move with small, quick, bouncing steps.
scar (scars) *noun*
A scar is a mark that is left on the skin after a wound has healed.
scare (scares, scaring, scared) *verb*
Someone or something that scares you makes you feel frightened.
scarecrow (scarecrows) *noun*
A scarecrow is an object in the shape of a person that is put in a field where crops are growing, to frighten birds away. It is usually made by hanging old clothes on sticks.
scarf (scarves) *noun*
A scarf is a piece of cloth that you wear round your neck to keep you warm. Scarves are often long and narrow.
scatter (scatters, scattering, scattered) *verb*
If you scatter things, you throw or drop a lot of them all over an area.
scene (scenes) *noun*
1. The scene of something is the place where it happened: *The police went to the scene of the crime.*
2. The scene around you is everything that you can see.
3. If you make a scene, you shout and sound very cross.
scenery *noun*
1. Scenery is the way a place looks, especially a part of the countryside with beautiful views and natural features.
2. Scenery is also all the cloths and boards that are used as the background for the stage in a theatre.
scent (scents) *noun*
1. A scent is a pleasant smell.
2. Scent is a liquid that some people put on their skin to make them smell nice.
scheme (schemes) *noun*
1. A scheme is a plan produced by someone as a way of achieving something.
2. A scheme can also be a plan produced by a government or another organization: *My brother is going on one of the new training schemes.*
school (schools) *noun*
A school is a place for teaching and learning.
science *noun*
Science is the study of natural things. We learn about these things by looking and testing very carefully.
scientist (scientists) *noun*
A scientist is a person who finds out why things happen by doing tests and by careful study.
scissors *noun*
A pair of scissors is a small tool that is used for cutting paper and cloth. It has two sharp blades, and two rings for your thumb and fingers.
scone (scones) *noun*
A scone is a small cake made from flour and fat. Scones are usually eaten at teatime with butter.
scoop (scoops) *noun*
1. A scoop is a tool with a handle and a hollow part like a spoon which is used for holding or serving food such as flour, sugar or ice cream.
2. A scoop is also a large bucket on a machine that is used to move earth.
3. A scoop can be an exciting news story which is reported in one newspaper or magazine before it appears anywhere else.
scoop (scoops, scooping, scooped) *verb*
If you scoop something up, you pick it up with a scoop, or by putting your hands under it and lifting it quickly: *She scooped up the kitten and ran as fast as she could.*

scooter (scooters) *noun*
1. A scooter is a small, light motorcycle with a low seat.
2. Another kind of scooter is a toy. It has two wheels joined by a footboard. A child steers the scooter with a long handle attached to the front wheel, and moves it forward by putting one foot on the board and pushing against the ground with the other.
score (scores) *noun*
The score in a game is the total number of points made by the two teams or players.
score (scores, scoring, scored) *verb*
If someone scores, they get a goal or other point in a game.
scornful *adjective*
Someone who is scornful is filled with great contempt for someone or something.
>**scornfully** *adverb*
scramble (scrambles, scrambling, scrambled) *verb*
If you scramble over rough or difficult ground, you move over it quickly, using your hands to help you.
scrap (scraps) *noun*
A scrap of something, such as cloth or paper, is a small piece of it.
scrape (scrapes, scraping, scraped) *verb*
If you scrape something, you take off its surface by dragging a knife across it.
scratch (scratches) *noun*
A scratch is a small cut on your body.
scratch (scratches, scratching, scratched) *verb*
1. If you scratch part of your body, you rub your fingernails against your skin.
2. If you scratch something, you damage it by making small cuts on it: *I fell into the hedge and scratched my bike.*
scrawny (scrawnier, scrawniest) *adjective*
A scrawny person or animal is unpleasantly thin and bony.
scream (screams, screaming, screamed) *verb*
When someone screams, they make a very loud, high cry. People usually scream if they are very frightened or are in a lot of pain.
screen (screens) *noun*
A screen is a flat, vertical surface on which a picture is shown. Television sets and computers have screens.
screw (screws) *noun*
A screw is a small, sharp piece of metal rather like a nail. It has a groove going round it, and a slot in the head. Screws are used to fix pieces of wood together.
screw (screws, screwing, screwed) *verb*
If you screw something up, you twist it or squeeze it so that it gets very creased: *He screwed up the paper and threw it in the bin.*
screwdriver (screwdrivers) *noun*
A screwdriver is a tool used for turning screws. It has a handle, and a long, metal rod with a thin, flattened end which fits into the slot in the head of a screw.
scribble (scribbles, scribbling, scribbled) *verb*
If you scribble words, you write them quickly and roughly.
scrub (scrubs, scrubbing, scrubbed) *verb*
If you scrub something, you rub it clean, usually with a stiff brush and water.
sculptor (sculptors) *noun*
A sculptor is someone who shapes or carves material such as stone, wood or clay.
sculpture (sculptures) *noun*
A sculpture is an object that has been made by an artist. Sculptures are often made by carving stone or by modelling clay.
sea (seas) *noun*
The sea is the salty water that covers about three quarters of the earth's surface.
seagull (seagulls) *noun*
A seagull is a big bird that lives near the sea.
seal (seals) *noun*
A seal is a large animal that lives partly on land and partly in the sea.
seal (seals, sealing, sealed) *verb*
If you seal an envelope, you stick it down so that people cannot see what is inside.
search (searches, searching, searched) *verb*
If you search for something, you try to find it by looking very carefully.
seaside *noun*
The seaside is a place by the sea, especially

one where people go for their holidays.
season (seasons) *noun*
1. A season is one of the main periods of a year. Most parts of the world have four seasons: spring, summer, autumn and winter.
2. A season is also the period of a year that is the proper time for something: *The football season starts next week.*
seat (seats) *noun*
A seat is a place where you can sit; for example, a chair or a stool.
seat belt (seat belts) *noun*
A seat belt is a strap attached to a car seat or aeroplane seat which you fasten across your body to prevent yourself being thrown out of the seat.
seaweed *noun*
Seaweed is a plant that grows in the sea. There are many kinds of seaweed.
second (seconds) *noun*
A second is a very short period of time. There are 60 seconds in one minute.
secret (secrets) *noun*
A secret is something that is known about by only a small number of people.
section (sections) *noun*
A section of something is one of the separate parts it is divided into.
secure *adjective*
1. If you feel secure, you feel safe and not worried about life.
2. If something is secure, it is fixed firmly in position.
>securely *adverb*
secure (secures, securing, secured) *verb*
If you secure something, you make it safe from attack, harm or loss.
see (sees, seeing, saw, seen) *verb*
1. When you see, you use your eyes to look at something.
2. If someone says they see what you mean, they understand what you are saying.
seed (seeds) *noun*
A seed is the small, hard part of a plant from which a new plant grows.
seek (seeks, seeking, sought) *verb*
1. When someone seeks something such as a job or a place to live, they try to find one.
2. If you seek someone's help or advice, you go to them and ask for it.
seem (seems, seeming, seemed) *verb*
1. If you say that someone seems, for example, to be happy or sad, you mean that is the way they look: *Tim seems to be a bit upset today.*
2. If you say something seems a certain way, you mean that is the way it feels to you: *I only had to wait for ten minutes, but it seemed like hours.*
seesaw (seesaws) *noun*
A seesaw is a long board which is balanced on a fixed part in the middle. If you sit on one end, the other end goes up in the air.
seize (seizes, seizing, seized) *verb*
1. If you seize something, you take hold of it quickly and firmly.
2. If an engine seizes up, it suddenly stops working.
seldom *adverb*
If something seldom happens, it does not happen very often.
select (selects, selecting, selected) *verb*
When you select someone or something, you choose them.
selfish *adjective*
People who are selfish only think about themselves. They do not care about other people.
>selfishly *adverb*
sell (sells, selling, sold) *verb*
When someone sells something, they give it in exchange for money.
semicolon (semicolons) *noun*
A semicolon is the punctuation mark (;) which is used in writing to separate different parts of a sentence or list, or to show a pause.
send (sends, sending, sent) *verb*
1. When you send something to someone, you arrange for it to be delivered to them. People often send things through the post.
2. If someone sends someone somewhere, they tell them to go there: *She was sent home from school because she was ill.*
3. If someone sends for you, you get a message to go and see them.

senior *adjective*
The senior people in an organization are the people who have the highest and most important jobs in it.

sensation (sensations) *noun*
A sensation is a physical feeling.

sense (senses) *noun*
1. Your senses are the powers you have to find out about the things around you. Most people have five senses. They are the senses of sight, smell, hearing, touch and taste.
2. Sense is knowing the right thing to do: *Why did you do that? You should have had more sense.*

>make sense *phrase*
If something makes sense, you can understand it.

sensible *adjective*
People who are sensible are good at deciding what to do. They do not do anything silly.

>sensibly *adverb*

sensitive *adjective*
1. If you are sensitive to things such as other people's feelings, you show a deep understanding of them.
2. If you are sensitive about something, you are easily offended about it: *He is very sensitive about his big ears.*
3. Something that is sensitive is easily affected by certain things: *I have a sensitive skin and mustn't stay out in the sun too long.*
4. A sensitive piece of scientific equipment can measure very small changes.

>sensitively *adverb*

sentence (sentences) *noun*
A sentence is a group of words that mean something. If a sentence is written down, it begins with a capital letter and ends with a full stop.

separate *adjective*
If one thing is separate from another, the two things are apart from each other. They are not joined together.

>separately *adverb*

September *noun*
September is the ninth month of the year. It has 30 days.

sequence (sequences) *noun*
1. A sequence is a number of things which come one after the other in a fixed order.
2. A film sequence is part of a film that shows one event or set of actions.

series *noun*
1. A series of things is a number of things of the same kind that follow each other.
2. A radio or television series is a set of programmes about the same thing.

serious *adjective*
1. Things that are serious are important. They must be thought about carefully.
2. Serious people are usually quiet and do not laugh very much.
3. When people are serious, they mean what they say. They are not joking.

>seriously *adverb*

serve (serves, serving, served) *verb*
1. If someone serves something such as a company or a country, they work for it.
2. If someone serves food and drink, they give it to people; for example, in a restaurant or at a meal.
3. If someone serves people in a shop, they help them to buy what they want.

service (services) *noun*
1. A service is an organization or system that provides something that the public needs, such as transport or communications.
2. A service is also a job that a person or an organization can do for you if you need it: *We provide a 24-hour service.*

set (sets) *noun*
1. A set is a number of things of the same kind that belong together.
2. In maths, a set is a collection of numbers that are treated as a group.
3. A set is also a television or a radio.

set (sets, setting, set) *verb*
1. When the sun sets, it goes down behind the horizon.
2. When something such as jelly or concrete sets, it becomes firm or hard.

settee (settees) *noun*
A settee is a long, comfortable seat for two or more people.

settle (settles, settling, settled) *verb*
1. If you settle, you sit or make yourself comfortable.
2. If something such as dust or snow settles, it sinks slowly and becomes still.
3. If someone settles an argument, they end it by deciding who is right.
4. When people settle, they start living or working in one place, instead of moving around a lot.
5. When things such as birds or insects settle on something, they land on it from above.

severe (severer, severest) *adjective*
1. Severe is used to describe something bad or undesirable that is very great: *The storm caused severe damage.*
2. Someone who is severe treats people harshly and does not easily forgive them if they do something wrong.
>**severely** *adverb*

sew (sews, sewing, sewed, sewn) *verb*
When someone sews, they join pieces of cloth together by using a needle and thread.

sewer (sewers) *noun*
A sewer is a large, underground pipe that carries away waste matter from homes and factories, as well as rain water that drains from roads and buildings.

sewing machine (sewing machines) *noun*
A sewing machine is a machine that you use for sewing, with a needle that is driven by an electric motor or by movements of your hand or foot.

sex (sexes) *noun*
The two sexes are the two groups that people and other living things are divided into. One sex is male and the other sex is female. Only animals of the female sex are able to have babies.

shabby (shabbier, shabbiest) *adjective*
1. Something that is shabby looks old and nearly worn out.
2. Someone who looks shabby is wearing old, worn clothes.
>**shabbily** *adverb*

shade (shades) *noun*
1. Shade is the darkness that is caused when something stops sunlight reaching a place: *It was hot in the garden, so she sat in the shade of an apple tree.*
2. A shade is something that partly covers a light to stop it shining in your eyes.

shadow (shadows) *noun*
A shadow is a dark shape that is made when something stands between a light and a surface.

shake (shakes, shaking, shook, shaken) *verb*
1. If you shake something, you move it quickly up and down or backwards and forwards.
2. If something shakes, it moves quickly from side to side or up and down: *When the lorry went by outside, the table shook.*

shaky (shakier, shakiest) *adjective*
If you are shaky, you are shaking or feeling weak because you are frightened or ill.
>**shakily** *adverb*

shallow (shallower, shallowest) *adjective*
Something, such as a hole or a container, that is shallow measures only a short distance from top to bottom.

shame *noun*
Shame is an unhappy feeling that people have when they have done something wrong.

shampoo *noun*
Shampoo is a soapy liquid that you use for washing your hair.

shape (shapes) *noun*
1. The shape of something is the way its outside edges look; for example, whether they are straight or curved.
2. A shape is something that has its outside edges joining in a particular way. For example, circles and squares are shapes.

share (shares, sharing, shared) *verb*
1. If you share something with another person, you both have the use of it: *She went up to the bedroom she shared with her sister.*
2. If you share something between a group of people, you divide it so that everyone gets some.

shark (sharks) *noun*
A shark is a very large fish that has sharp teeth and lives in the sea. Some sharks attack people.

sharp (sharper, sharpest) *adjective*
1. A sharp object has a very thin edge that is good for cutting things.
2. Sharp can also mean finely pointed. For example, pins and needles are sharp.
3. A sharp bend or turn is one that changes direction suddenly.
4. A sharp pain affects you suddenly in a way that hurts.
5. A sharp sound is very short and sudden and quite loud.

sharpen (sharpens, sharpening, sharpened) *verb*
When someone sharpens something, they make it sharp, or sharper than it was.

shave (shaves, shaving, shaved) *verb*
When a man shaves, he cuts hair from his face. He uses a razor or shaver so that he can get very close to his skin.

shear (shears, shearing, sheared, shorn) *verb*
To shear a sheep means to cut its wool off.

shears *noun*
Shears are a tool like a very large pair of scissors, used especially for cutting hedges.

shed (sheds) *noun*
A shed is a small building, often made of wood. It is used for storing things such as garden tools.

sheep *noun*
A sheep is a farm animal with a thick, woolly coat. Sheep are usually kept for their wool or their meat.

sheer *adjective*
1. Sheer means complete and not mixed with anything else: *I fell asleep from sheer boredom.*
2. A sheer cliff or drop is so steep it is almost vertical.

sheet (sheets) *noun*
1. A sheet is a large piece of thin cloth, such as cotton, which is put on the bed.
2. A sheet of something, such as paper or glass, is a rectangular piece of it.

shelf (shelves) *noun*
A shelf is something flat which is fixed to a wall or inside a cupboard.

shell (shells) *noun*
1. The shell of an egg or nut is the hard covering round it.
2. The shell of an animal such as a tortoise or snail is the hard covering that it has on its back.

shellfish *noun*
A shellfish is any small sea creature that has a shell. Prawns and crabs are shellfish.

shelter (shelters) *noun*
A shelter is a small building or covered place where people or animals can be safe from bad weather or danger.

shield (shields) *noun*
A shield is a large piece of metal or leather which soldiers used to carry. They used the shields to protect themselves from injury when they were fighting.

shield (shields, shielding, shielded) *verb*
If someone or something shields a person or thing from a particular danger or damage, they protect them from it: *He put up a hand to shield his eyes against the sun.*

shift (shifts) *noun*
A shift is a period of time during the day or night during which people work, and then are replaced by other people who continue the work: *My father's on night shift this week.*

shift (shifts, shifting, shifted) *verb*
If you shift something, you move it slightly from one place to another.

shimmer (shimmers, shimmering, shimmered) *verb*
If something shimmers, it shines with a faint, flickering light, for example, as the moon does on water.

shin (shins) *noun*
Your shin is the front part of your leg, between your knee and your ankle.

shine (shines, shining, shone) *verb*
1. When something shines, it gives out bright light.
2. If you make an object shine, you make it bright by rubbing or polishing it.

shiny (shinier, shiniest) *adjective*
Something that is shiny is bright and looks as if it has been polished.

ship (ships) *noun*
A ship is a large boat which sails on the sea.

shirt (shirts) *noun*
A shirt is a piece of clothing worn on the top part of your body.
shiver (shivers, shivering, shivered) *verb*
When you shiver, your body shakes slightly, usually because you are cold or frightened.
shock (shocks) *noun*
A shock is a sudden, nasty surprise.
shoe (shoes) *noun*
Shoes are objects that you wear to cover your feet.
shoelace (shoelaces) *noun*
A shoelace is a long, narrow piece of material like a piece of string that is used to fasten a shoe.
shoot (shoots, shooting, shot) *verb*
1. To shoot means to fire a bullet from a gun, or to fire an arrow from a bow.
2. If someone shoots in a game such as football, they try to score a goal.
shoot (shoots) *noun*
A shoot is a new part growing from a plant or tree.
shop (shops) *noun*
A shop is a building or part of a building where things are sold.
shopkeeper (shopkeepers) *noun*
A shopkeeper is a person who owns or looks after a small shop.
shopping *noun*
1. Shopping is going to shops and buying things.
2. Your shopping is the things that you have bought from shops, especially food and groceries.
shore (shores) *noun*
The shore of a sea or lake is the land along the edge of it.
short (shorter, shortest) *adjective*
1. If something lasts for a short time, it does not last very long.
2. Someone who is short is not as tall as most other people.
3. Something that is short is not very long.
>**is short for** *phrase*
If a name is short for another name, it is a quick way of saying it: *Phone is short for telephone.*
shorts *noun*
Shorts are short trousers.
shoulder (shoulders) *noun*
Your shoulder is the place where your arm joins on to your body.
shout (shouts) *noun*
A shout is a loud call or cry.
shout (shouts, shouting, shouted) *verb*
If you shout, you say words as loudly as you can.
shove (shoves, shoving, shoved) *verb*
If someone shoves you, they push you roughly.
shovel (shovels) *noun*
A shovel is a tool like a spade, with a rounded blade on a long handle. Shovels are used for moving things like earth or coal.
show (shows) *noun*
1. A show is a kind of entertainment at the theatre or on television.
2. A show is also a kind of competition. There are shows for things such as flowers, dogs and cattle.
show (shows, showing, showed, shown) *verb*
1. If you show someone something, you let them see it.
2. If you show someone how to do something, you do it yourself so that they can watch you.
3. If something shows, people can see it: *Do you think that mark will show?*
shower (showers) *noun*
1. A shower is a short period of light rain.
2. A shower is also a piece of equipment in the bathroom. It gives out a fine spray of water so that you can wash yourself.
shred (shreds) *noun*
1. A shred of material is a small, narrow piece which is torn or cut from a larger piece: *He tore the paper into shreds.*
2. A shred of something is a very small amount of it: *There's not a shred of truth in any of his stories.*
shred (shreds, shredding, shredded) *verb*
If you shred something, such as food or paper, you cut or tear it into very small pieces.

shriek (shrieks, shrieking, shrieked) *verb*
If you shriek, you give a sudden, sharp cry. This is usually because you are excited or in pain.

shrill (shriller, shrillest) *adjective*
A shrill sound is high-pitched, piercing and unpleasant to listen to.
>**shrilly** *adverb*

shrimp (shrimps) *noun*
A shrimp is a small, grey shellfish with a long tail and a pair of pincers. It turns pink when it is cooked.

shrink (shrinks, shrinking, shrank, shrunk) *verb*
If a piece of clothing shrinks, it becomes smaller. This is usually because it has been washed.

shrivel (shrivels, shrivelling, shrivelled) *verb*
When something shrivels, it becomes dry and wrinkled, usually because it loses moisture in the heat.

shrug (shrugs, shrugging, shrugged) *verb*
If you shrug, you raise your shoulders to show that you are not interested in something, or that you do not know or care about it.

shudder (shudders, shuddering, shuddered) *verb*
If you shudder, you tremble with fear or disgust.

shuffle (shuffles, shuffling, shuffled) *verb*
1. If you shuffle, you walk without lifting your feet properly off the ground.
2. To shuffle can also mean to move your feet about while standing, or to move your bottom about while sitting, usually because you feel uncomfortable or embarrassed.

shut (shuts, shutting, shut) *verb*
1. If you shut something such as a door, you move it so that it fills a gap.
2. If you shut your eyes, you lower your lids so that you cannot see.
3. If you shut your mouth, you put your lips together.
4. If a place such as a shop shuts, it is closed. You cannot go in until it is open again.

shy (shyer, shyest) *adjective*
A shy person is someone who is afraid to meet or speak to anyone they do not know.
>**shyly** *adverb*

sick (sicker, sickest) *adjective*
If you are sick, you are not well.

side (sides) *noun*
1. The side of something is to the left or right of it: *He parted his hair on the left side.*
2. The side of something can be the edge of it: *There is a fence on three sides of the garden.*
3. The sides of a river or lake are its banks.
4. The sides of a hill are the sloping parts between the top and bottom.
5. The sides of a piece of paper are its front and back: *What does it say on the other side?*
6. The two sides in a game are the teams playing against each other.

sideboard (sideboards) *noun*
A sideboard is a large piece of dining-room furniture. Sideboards have cupboards and drawers to hold things such as plates and knives and forks.

sideways *adverb*
Sideways means moving or facing towards one side: *The gap in the fence was narrow and she had to squeeze in sideways.*

sigh (sighs, sighing, sighed) *verb*
When you sigh, you breathe out heavily. People usually sigh when they are tired or bored.

sight *noun*
Sight is being able to see.

sightseer (sightseers) *noun*
A sightseer is someone who is travelling around to visit places of interest.

sign (signs) *noun*
1. A sign is a mark or shape that means something; for example, a plus sign.
2. A sign is also a piece of something, such as wood or metal, with words or pictures on it. Signs can tell you something such as the name of a town. They can also tell you what to do, or what you are not allowed to do: *At the end of the road there was a sign which said 'Stop'.*

3. You can make a sign with your body that means something to other people. For example, if you shake your head it is a sign that you mean 'No'.
4. Something can be a sign of something else. For example, a dark cloud is a sign of rain.
sign (signs, signing, signed) *verb*
If you sign something, you write your name on it.
signal (signals) *noun*
A signal is a message that is given by signs. For example, a flashing light is a signal that a driver is turning left or right.
silence *noun*
If there is silence, it is quiet because nobody is speaking.
silent *adjective*
1. If you are silent, you are not speaking.
2. Something that is silent makes no sound at all.
3. A silent letter is one that is written but not pronounced: *The 'g' is silent in the word 'gnat'.*
>**silently** *adverb*
silhouette (silhouettes) *noun*
A silhouette is the outline of a dark shape with a bright light or a pale background behind it.
silk *noun*
Silk is a thread spun by silkworms which is made into fine, smooth cloth.
silkworm (silkworms) *noun*
A silkworm is a type of caterpillar that produces silk.
silly (sillier, silliest) *adjective*
If someone says you are silly, they mean you are behaving in a foolish or childish way.
silver *noun*
Silver is a valuable greyish-white metal used for making jewellery and ornaments.
similar *adjective*
If something is similar to something else, the two things are rather alike.
simmer (simmers, simmering, simmered) *verb*
When you simmer food, you cook it by boiling it very gently.
simple (simpler, simplest) *adjective*
If something is simple, it is easy to do or understand.
>**simply** *adverb*
sincere *adjective*
Sincere people say things that they really mean or believe.
>**sincerely** *adverb*
sing (sings, singing, sang, sung) *verb*
1. If you sing a song, you make music with your voice. Usually people sing words that fit the music.
2. When birds sing, the sounds they make are like music.
single *adjective*
Single means one of something: *We can't park here. It's a single yellow line.*
singular *noun*
In grammar, the singular of a word is the one you use when you are talking about one person or thing and not more.
sink (sinks) *noun*
A sink is a large basin in a kitchen. Sinks have water taps and a drain.
sink (sinks, sinking, sank, sunk) *verb*
If something sinks, it moves slowly downwards and disappears from sight, especially below the surface of water.
sip (sips, sipping, sipped) *verb*
If you sip a drink, you drink it a little at a time.
siren (sirens) *noun*
A siren is something that makes a loud, wailing noise as a warning. Fire engines, police cars and ambulances have sirens.
sister (sisters) *noun*
Someone's sister is a girl or woman who has the same parents as they have.
sit (sits, sitting, sat) *verb*
1. When you sit, you seat yourself on something such as a chair or the floor.
2. When a bird sits on its eggs, it covers them with its body to hatch them.
site (sites) *noun*
A site is a piece of ground that is used or will be used for a particular purpose: *They stopped as soon as they saw a caravan site.*

situation (situations) *noun*
You can use the word situation to talk generally about what is happening in a particular place at a particular time: *The situation was getting serious and they couldn't think what to do.*
size (sizes) *noun*
The size of something is how big or small it is.
sizzle (sizzles, sizzling, sizzled) *verb*
If something sizzles, it makes a hissing sound like the noise made by frying food.
skate (skates) *noun*
1. Skates are special boots that you wear to ice-skate or roller-skate.
2. A skate is also a very flat sea fish. It has two large fins like wings.
skateboard (skateboards) *noun*
A skateboard is a narrow board with four wheels. You can stand on it and ride about.
skeleton (skeletons) *noun*
The skeleton of a person or animal is all the bones that support the body.
skewer (skewers) *noun*
A skewer is a long, metal or wooden pin that is used to hold pieces of meat or other food together during cooking.
ski (skis) *noun*
Skis are long, flat, narrow pieces of wood, metal or plastic. They can be fixed to boots so that the person wearing them can move easily on snow.
skid (skids, skidding, skidded) *verb*
If a vehicle skids, it slides sideways while it is moving along. This is usually because the road is slippery.
skilful *adjective*
Someone who is skilful at something does it very well.
>**skilfully** *adverb*
skill *noun*
Skill is the ability to do something very well.
skim (skims, skimming, skimmed) *verb*
1. If you skim something from the surface of a liquid, you remove it.
2. If something skims a surface, it moves fast just above it.
3. If you skim flat stones, you throw them across water so that they touch the surface and bounce off it several times.
skin (skins) *noun*
1. Your skin is the natural covering of your body.
2. The skin of a fruit or vegetable is its outer layer or covering.
skinny (skinnier, skinniest) *adjective*
Someone who is skinny is very thin.
skip (skips, skipping, skipped) *verb*
1. When you skip, you move along almost as though you were dancing, with little jumps.
2. If you skip with a rope, you swing the rope over your head and under your feet while jumping.
skip (skips) *noun*
A skip is a large, metal container for holding things, like rubbish and bricks, that need to be taken away.
skipper (skippers) *noun*
A skipper is the captain of a ship or boat.
skirt (skirts) *noun*
A skirt is a piece of clothing worn by women and girls. It hangs from the waist.
skull (skulls) *noun*
Your skull is the bony part of your head. It has your brain inside it.
sky *noun*
The sky is the space around the earth which you can see when you stand outside and look upwards.
skyscraper (skyscrapers) *noun*
A skyscraper is a very tall building.
slab (slabs) *noun*
A slab of material, such as stone, wood or meat, is a thick, flat piece of it, which is usually square or oblong in shape.
slack (slacker, slackest) *adjective*
1. Something that is slack is loose, and not firmly stretched or tightly in position.
2. A slack period of business is one in which there is not much work being done.
slam (slams, slamming, slammed) *verb*
If you slam a door, you shut it hard so that it makes a loud noise.
slant (slants, slanting, slanted) *verb*
If something slants, it lies along a line that is

neither horizontal nor vertical.
slap (slaps, slapping, slapped) *verb*
1. If you slap someone, you hit them with the palm of your hand.
2. If you slap something on to a surface, you put it there quickly or carelessly: *If we slap a bit of paint on, it will cheer the room up.*
slate *noun*
Slate is a dark grey rock that splits easily into thin layers. It is often used for roofs.
sledge (sledges) *noun*
A sledge is a vehicle for travelling on snow.
sleek (sleeker, sleekest) *adjective*
Hair or fur that is sleek is smooth and shiny.
sleep (sleeps, sleeping, slept) *verb*
When you sleep, you close your eyes and your whole body rests.
sleet *noun*
Sleet is rain that is partly frozen as it falls.
sleeve (sleeves) *noun*
The sleeves of a coat or other piece of clothing are the parts that cover your arms.
slice (slices) *noun*
A slice is a piece of food that has been cut from a larger piece.
slide (slides) *noun*
1. A slide is a picture on a small piece of film with a frame around it. Slides can be shown on a screen.
2. A slide is also a piece of playground equipment for sliding down.
slide (slides, sliding, slid) *verb*
When something slides, it moves smoothly over a surface.
slight (slighter, slightest) *adjective*
Something that is slight is very small: *She has a slight cut.*
>**slightly** *adverb*
slim (slimmer, slimmest) *adjective*
Someone who is slim has an attractively thin body.
slime *noun*
1. Slime is a thick, sticky substance which comes from the bodies of slugs and snails.
2. Slime is also any thick, slippery substance which covers a surface and which looks and smells unpleasant.
slimy (slimier, slimiest) *adjective*
Something that is slimy is covered in slime.
sling (slings) *noun*
1. A sling is a piece of cloth which you hang from your neck to support a broken or injured arm.
2. A sling is also something which people use for carrying babies in.
sling (slings, slinging, slung) *verb*
1. If you sling something somewhere, you throw it carelessly and with a lot of force.
2. If you sling something over your shoulder, you hang it there loosely so that you can carry it.
slip (slips, slipping, slipped) *verb*
If you slip, you accidentally slide and lose your balance.
slip (slips) *noun*
A slip is a small mistake.
slipper (slippers) *noun*
Slippers are loose, soft shoes that people wear in the house.
slippery *adjective*
Something that is slippery is smooth, wet or greasy, and is difficult to keep hold of or walk on without sliding.
slit (slits) *noun*
1. A slit is a long, narrow cut.
2. A slit is also a long, narrow opening in something.
slit (slits, slitting, slit) *verb*
If you slit something, you make a long, narrow cut in it.
slope (slopes) *noun*
A slope is ground that goes up or down.
slot (slots) *noun*
A slot is a narrow opening in a machine or container. For example, public telephones have slots to put money or cards in.
slow (slower, slowest) *adjective*
1. Something that is slow moves along without much speed..
2. If a watch or clock is slow, it shows a time that is earlier than the correct time.
>**slowly** *adverb*
slug (slugs) *noun*
A slug is a small, slow-moving creature with a long slimy body, like a snail but without a shell.

sly (slyer, slyest) *adjective*
1. If someone gives a sly look or makes a sly remark, they show that they know something that other people present might not know.
2. Someone who is sly is rather secretive and good at deceiving people.
>**slyly** *adverb*
smack (smacks, smacking, smacked) *verb*
If a person smacks someone, they hit them with an open hand.
small (smaller, smallest) *adjective*
1. Something that is small is not as large as other things of the same kind.
2. A small group has only a few people or things in it.
smart (smarter, smartest) *adjective*
Someone who is smart looks neat and clean.
>**smartly** *adverb*
smash (smashes, smashing, smashed) *verb*
1. If something smashes, it falls and hits the ground. It makes a loud noise and breaks into lots of pieces.
2. If someone or something smashes an object, they drop it or hit it so that it breaks into lots of pieces: *The falling tree smashed the window.*
smell (smells, smelling, smelled/smelt) *verb*
1. When you smell something, you notice it with your nose.
2. If something smells nice or nasty, people's noses tell them about it.
smile (smiles, smiling, smiled) *verb*
When you smile, the corners of your mouth move upwards and you look happy.
smoke *noun*
Smoke is made up of clouds of gas and small bits of solid material. Smoke goes into the air when something is burning.
smooth (smoother, smoothest) *adjective*
1. A smooth surface has no roughness, lumps or holes.
2. A smooth liquid or mixture does not have any lumps in it.
3. A smooth ride is one that is comfortable because there are no bumps or jerks.
>**smoothly** *adverb*
smother (smothers, smothering, smothered) *verb*
1. If you smother a fire, you cover it with something in order to put it out.
2. If a lot of things smother something, they cover it all over: *The grass was smothered in daisies.*
smudge (smudges) *noun*
A smudge is a dirty mark, often made by rubbing your hand over something wet or dirty.
smug (smugger, smuggest) *adjective*
Someone who is smug is too pleased with how good or clever they are.
>**smugly** *adverb*
smuggle (smuggles, smuggling, smuggled) *verb*
1. To smuggle means to take goods or people into or out of a country against the law.
2. If you smuggle someone or something to a place where they should not be, you take them there secretly.
snack (snacks) *noun*
A snack is a small, quick meal. For example, a sandwich is a snack.
snag (snags) *noun*
A snag is a small difficulty or problem.
snail (snails) *noun*
A snail is a small, slow-moving creature with a shell on its back.
snake (snakes) *noun*
A snake is a long, thin reptile with scales on its skin and no legs.
snap (snaps) *noun*
1. A snap is a photograph.
2. Snap is a card game played by children.
snap (snaps, snapping, snapped) *verb*
1. If something snaps, it breaks suddenly. It usually makes a sharp, cracking noise.
2. If a dog or other animal snaps, it closes its jaws suddenly.
3. If someone snaps at you, they speak crossly.
snarl (snarls, snarling, snarled) *verb*
1. When an animal snarls, it makes a fierce, rough sound in its throat while showing its teeth.
2. If someone snarls something, they say it in a fierce, angry way.

snatch (snatches, snatching, snatched) *verb*
If you snatch something, you take it quickly and suddenly.
sneak (sneaks, sneaking, sneaked) *verb*
If you sneak somewhere, you go there very quietly on foot, trying to be careful that other people do not see you or hear you.
sneer (sneers, sneering, sneered) *verb*
If a person sneers at something, they show contempt for it.
sneeze (sneezes, sneezing, sneezed) *verb*
When you sneeze, you take in your breath and blow it down your nose suddenly.
sniff (sniffs, sniffing, sniffed) *verb*
If you sniff, you breathe in through your nose hard enough to make a sound.
snore (snores, snoring, snored) *verb*
When people snore, they breathe very noisily while they are sleeping.
snorkel (snorkels) *noun*
A snorkel is an air tube that swimmers sometimes use. One end stays above the water so that a person swimming under water can breathe.
snow *noun*
Snow is frozen water that falls from the sky as snowflakes in cold weather.
snowball (snowballs) *noun*
A snowball is a ball made from snow pressed together. Children often make snowballs to throw at each other.
snowdrift (snowdrifts) *noun*
A snowdrift is a deep pile of snow, which is made by the wind blowing a lot of snow into one place.
snowdrop (snowdrops) *noun*
A snowdrop is a small, white flower which appears in January.
snowflake (snowflakes) *noun*
A snowflake is one of the soft, white bits of frozen water that fall as snow.
snowman (snowmen) *noun*
A snowman is a pile of snow that is made to look like a person.
snowstorm (snowstorms) *noun*
A snowstorm is a very heavy fall of snow, with a strong wind.
snug (snugger, snuggest) *adjective*
If you feel snug, you are very warm and comfortable, especially when you are protected from the cold weather.
>**snugly** *adverb*
soak (soaks, soaking, soaked) *verb*
When liquid soaks something, it makes it very wet.
soap *noun*
Soap is a solid, liquid or powder that you use with water for washing.
soar (soars, soaring, soared) *verb*
If something soars into the air, it goes quickly up into it.
sob (sobs, sobbing, sobbed) *verb*
When someone sobs, they cry in a noisy way, breathing in short breaths.
soccer *noun*
Soccer is football played with a round ball.
society (societies) *noun*
1. Society is people in general.
2. A society is an organization for people who have the same interests or aims.
sock (socks) *noun*
A sock is a soft piece of clothing which covers your foot and ankle.
socket (sockets) *noun*
1. A socket is a place on the wall that you can put an electric plug into.
2. A socket is also any hollow part or opening in a structure that another part fits into: *She looked as though her eyes might pop out of their sockets.*
sofa (sofas) *noun*
A sofa is a long, comfortable seat for more than one person. Sofas have a back, and usually arms.
soft (softer, softest) *adjective*
1. Something that is soft changes shape easily when you touch it.
2. A soft sound or voice is quiet and gentle.
3. A soft light or colour is pleasant and restful because it is not too bright.
>**softly** *adverb*
software *noun*
Software is computer programs.

soggy (soggier, soggiest) *adjective*
Something that is soggy is unpleasantly wet or full of water.
soil *noun*
Soil is the top layer of earth, which plants can grow in.
soil (soils, soiling, soiled) *verb*
If you soil something, you make it dirty.
solar *adjective*
1. Solar is used to describe something that is to do with the sun.
2. Solar heating or energy uses the sun's light and heat to provide energy.
soldier (soldiers) *noun*
A soldier is a person in an army.
sole (soles) *noun*
1. The sole of your foot is the underneath surface of it.
2. A sole is the underneath of a shoe or sock.
3. A sole is also a flat sea fish.
solemn *adjective*
Someone or something that is solemn is very serious, rather than cheerful.
>**solemnly** *adverb*
solid *adjective*
Something that is solid stays the same shape whether it is in a container or not. Things that are solid are also firm or hard. Metal, wood and rock are all solid.
solid (solids) *noun*
1. A solid is a substance that stays the same shape whether it is in a container or not.
2. A solid is also a three-dimensional shape like a cylinder or a cone.
solution (solutions) *noun*
1. A solution is the answer to a problem.
2. A solution can also be a liquid in which a substance, such as a powder, has been dissolved.
solve (solves, solving, solved) *verb*
If you solve a problem, you find an answer to it.
somersault (somersaults) *noun*
If you somersault, you put your head on the ground, curl up and roll forward, so that the rest of your body goes over your head. Some people can somersault in mid-air.
son (sons) *noun*
A boy is the son of his parents.
song (songs) *noun*
A song is a piece of music with words.
soon (sooner, soonest) *adverb*
Soon means in the very near future.
soot *noun*
Soot is black powder which comes from burning coal or wood.
sore (sorer, sorest) *adjective*
If part of your body is sore, it is painful: *Her throat was so sore she couldn't talk.*
sorry (sorrier, sorriest) *adjective*
1. If you feel sorry about something that has happened, you feel disappointed or sad: *I was sorry to leave all my friends.*
2. If you feel sorry for someone, you feel sad for them.
sort (sorts) *noun*
Sort means kind or type.
>**all sorts** *phrase*
All sorts of things means lots of different things.
sort (sorts, sorting, sorted) *verb*
If you sort things, you put them into groups: *Can you sort your socks into pairs?*
sound (sounds) *noun*
A sound is something that you hear.
soup *noun*
Soup is a liquid food. It is made by boiling things such as meat or vegetables in water.
sour *adjective*
1. Something that is sour tastes sharp.
2. If milk is sour, it is no longer fresh.
south *noun*
South is one of the four main points of the compass. If you face the point where the sun rises, south is on your right.
sow (sows, sowing, sowed, sown) *verb*
If you sow seeds, you plant them in the ground so that they will grow.
space (spaces) *noun*
1. Space is the amount of the area in something such as a building or container that is empty: *There is just enough space for a bed and a chair in my room.*
2. Space is also the place far above the earth where there is no air.

3. A space is a gap or empty place.
spaceship (spaceships) *noun*
A spaceship is a vehicle that carries people through space.
spacesuit (spacesuits) *noun*
A spacesuit is a special suit that is worn by an astronaut, which covers the whole body.
spade (spades) *noun*
A spade is a tool used for digging. It has a flat, metal blade and a long handle.
spaghetti *noun*
Spaghetti is a type of food made from pasta, which looks like long pieces of string. Spaghetti is usually served with a sauce.
span (spans) *noun*
A span is the distance right across something, especially if it is stretched out. For example, when a bird stretches its wings, the distance from wing tip to wing tip is called its wing span.
span (spans, spanning, spanned) *verb*
A bridge that spans something, such as a river, stretches right across it.
spanner (spanners) *noun*
A spanner is a tool with a specially shaped end that fits round a metal nut so that it can be loosened or tightened.
spare *adjective*
You use spare to describe something that can be used when it is needed: *We had a puncture and had to put the spare tyre on.*
spark (sparks) *noun*
1. A spark is a tiny piece of very bright, burning material. A spark can fly up from something burning, or it can be caused by two hard things hitting against each other.
2. A spark is also a flash of light caused by electricity.
sparkle (sparkles, sparkling, sparkled) *verb*
If something sparkles, it gives off little flashes of light.
sparrow (sparrows) *noun*
A sparrow is a small, brown bird. It is very common in Britain and many other countries.
speak (speaks, speaking, spoke, spoken) *verb*
1. When you speak, you use your voice to say words.
2. If you speak a foreign language, you know the language: *Can you speak French?*
spear (spears) *noun*
A spear is a weapon which is made from a long pole, with a sharp metal point at one end.
special *adjective*
1. Something that is special is more important or better than other things of its kind.
2. Special can also mean something that is made for a particular use: *You need a special tool to do this job.*
>**specially** *adverb*
speck (specks) *noun*
A speck is a tiny piece of something: *There wasn't a speck of dust anywhere.*
spectacles *noun*
Someone's spectacles are their glasses.
spectator (spectators) *noun*
A spectator is someone who watches something, especially a sporting event.
speech (speeches) *noun*
1. Speech is the ability to speak.
2. A speech is a talk that someone gives when something special is happening. For example, the bride's father usually makes a speech at a wedding.
speechless *adjective*
If you are speechless, you are unable to speak for a little while, usually because something you have heard or seen has amazed you.
speed (speeds) *noun*
1. The speed of something is how fast or slowly it travels: *At what speed does a snail travel?*
2. Speed can be used to talk about how fast or slowly something happens: *My two children are growing at different speeds.*
3. Speed is also very fast movement.
spell (spells) *noun*
In fairy stories, a spell is words that have a magic power.
spell (spells, spelling, spelled/spelt) *verb*
When you spell a word, you write or say the letters in the right order.

spellbound *adjective*
If you are spellbound, you are so fascinated by something that you cannot think about anything else.
spelling *noun*
Spelling is the way that words are spelled.
spend (spends, spending, spent) *verb*
1. When you spend money, you pay out the money for things that you want.
2. If you spend time doing something, you use that amount of time doing it: *I spend hours playing football.*
sphere (spheres) *noun*
A sphere is an object or shape that is like a ball.
spice (spices) *noun*
A spice is the powder or seeds from a particular plant which people put in food when they are cooking to give it flavour.
spider (spiders) *noun*
A spider is a small creature with eight legs. Most kinds of spider make webs which they use to catch insects for food.
spike (spikes) *noun*
A spike is a long piece of metal with a sharp point at one end.
spill (spills, spilling, spilled/spilt) *verb*
If you spill a liquid, it accidentally flows over the edge of a container.
spin (spins, spinning, spun) *verb*
1. If something spins, it turns round and round quickly.
2. When someone spins thread, they pull out threads of cotton or wool and twist them together very quickly.
3. When a spider spins a web, it makes it from a silklike thread that comes out of its body.
spine (spines) *noun*
1. Your spine is the row of bones down your back that holds your body up.
2. Spines are long, sharp points on the bodies of some animals; for example, hedgehogs. Some plants such as cactuses also have spines.
spiral (spirals) *noun*
A spiral is a curved shape which winds round and round, with each curve above or outside the one before.
spire (spires) *noun*
A spire is a tall, cone-shaped structure on top of a building such as a church.
spite *noun*
Spite is a feeling that makes a person behave in a nasty way towards someone else.
spiteful *adjective*
Someone who is spiteful says or does nasty things to people they dislike.
>**spitefully** *adverb*
splash (splashes) *noun*
A splash is the sound that is made when something hits some water.
splash (splashes, splashing, splashed) *verb*
If you splash, you throw water about.
splendid *adjective*
Something that is splendid is excellent and of very good quality.
>**splendidly** *adverb*
splinter (splinters) *noun*
A splinter is a very thin, sharp piece of something, like wood, glass or metal, that has been broken off a larger piece.
split (splits, splitting, split) *verb*
If something, such as wood or a piece of clothing, splits, a long crack or tear appears in it.
spoil (spoils, spoiling, spoiled/spoilt) *verb*
1. If you spoil something, you make it less enjoyable than it would have been.
2. If someone spoils an object, they damage it.
3. If someone spoils a child, they give it all its own way.
spoke (spokes) *noun*
Spokes are the bars that join the rim of a wheel to its centre.
sponge (sponges) *noun*
1. A sponge is a sea creature with a soft round body. The skeleton of a sponge is full of holes and can hold a lot of water. This is called natural sponge. There is a similar man-made material which is also called sponge.
2. A sponge is also a light cake or pudding.
spoon (spoons) *noun*
A spoon is a tool shaped like a small shallow

bowl with a long handle. It is used for eating, mixing and serving food.

sport (sports) *noun*
Sports are games such as football and cricket which need energy and skill. In most sports, the players are organized in teams, and each team tries to win.

spot (spots) *noun*
1. A spot is a round area on a surface. Some fabrics have patterns of spots.
2. A spot can be a particular place: *This would be a nice spot for a picnic.*
3. A spot can also be a small, raised mark on a person's skin.

spotless *adjective*
Something that is spotless is perfectly clean.
>spotlessly *adverb*

spout (spouts) *noun*
A spout is a specially shaped opening or tube in a container which allows liquids to be poured easily.

sprawl (sprawls, sprawling, sprawled) *verb*
If you sprawl somewhere, you sit or lie down and spread your legs and arms out in a careless way.

spray *noun*
Spray is a lot of small drops of water or other liquid.

spread (spreads, spreading, spread) *verb*
1. If you spread something, you arrange it over a surface: *They spread their wet clothes out to dry.*
2. If you spread something such as butter, you put a thin layer of it on to something.
3. If you spread parts of your body, such as your arms, you stretch them out until they are far apart.

spring (springs) *noun*
1. Spring is the season between winter and summer. Plants begin to grow in the spring.
2. A spring is a curled piece of wire.
3. A spring is also a pool that forms where water comes up through the ground.

sprinkle (sprinkles, sprinkling, sprinkled) *verb*
If you sprinkle something, like water or sugar, you scatter it in small drops or pieces over something.

sprint (sprints) *noun*
A sprint is a short, fast race.

sprint (sprints, sprinting, sprinted) *verb*
If you sprint, you run as fast as you can over a short distance.

sprout (sprouts) *noun*
Sprouts are small, green vegetables which look like very small cabbages.

sprout (sprouts, sprouting, sprouted) *verb*
When plants sprout, they put out new leaves or shoots.

spur (spurs, spurring, spurred) *verb*
If someone or something spurs you on, they encourage you to do something.
>on the spur of the moment *phrase*
If you do something on the spur of the moment, you do it suddenly and without any preparation.

spurt (spurts, spurting, spurted) *verb*
When a liquid or flame spurts out of something, it comes out quickly and suddenly in a thin, powerful stream.

spy (spies) *noun*
A spy is a person whose job is to find out secret information about another country or organization.

square (squares) *noun*
1. A square is a shape which has four straight sides all the same length.
2. A square is also a flat, open place in a town or city.

squash (squashes, squashing, squashed) *verb*
If you squash something, you press it so that it goes flat: *She put her bag on the tomatoes and squashed them.*

squash *noun*
1. Squash is a game in which two people use rackets to hit a small ball against the walls of a court.
2. Squash is also a fruit drink.

squat (squats, squatting, squatted) *verb*
If you squat, or squat down, you sit close to the ground, balancing on your feet with your legs bent under your body.

squeak (squeaks, squeaking, squeaked) *verb*
If a person, animal or thing squeaks, they make a short, high sound.
squeal (squeals, squealing, squealed) *verb*
If a person, animal or thing squeals, they make a long, high sound.
squeeze (squeezes, squeezing, squeezed) *verb*
When you squeeze something, you press it firmly on all sides.
squelch (squelches, squelching, squelched) *verb*
To squelch means to make a wet, sucking sound like someone walking on soft, muddy ground.
squirrel (squirrels) *noun*
A squirrel is a small, furry animal with a long, bushy tail. It eats things such as nuts and seeds. Squirrels usually live in trees. A squirrel's nest is called a drey.
squirt (squirts, squirting, squirted) *verb*
If a liquid squirts, it comes out of a narrow opening in a thin, fast stream.
stable (stables) *noun*
A stable is a building in which horses are kept.
stack (stacks) *noun*
A stack is a number of things, such as books, arranged in a neat pile.
staff *noun*
The staff of an organization are the people who work for it.
stag (stags) *noun*
A stag is an adult male deer.
stage (stages) *noun*
1. A stage is a particular step or period of development: *Our baby's at the stage where he wants to walk everywhere.*
2. A stage is a raised platform in a theatre or hall. Stages are often used for plays or other entertainment.
stagecoach (stagecoaches) *noun*
A stagecoach was a large carriage pulled by horses. Stagecoaches were used in the past to carry passengers and mail.
stagger (staggers, staggering, staggered) *verb*
If you stagger, you walk or stand as if you are about to fall.
stain (stains) *noun*
A stain is a dirty mark which is difficult to remove.
stair (stairs) *noun*
Stairs are a set of steps, usually inside a building. You use them to walk up or down to a different level.
staircase (staircases) *noun*
A staircase is a set of stairs inside a building, usually with a rail that you can hold on to.
stake (stakes) *noun*
A stake is a pointed piece of wood or metal that is pushed into the ground. Stakes are often used to support young trees, or as part of a fence.
stale (staler, stalest) *adjective*
Something which is stale is no longer fresh.
stalk (stalks) *noun*
1. A stalk is the main stem of a plant.
2. A stalk is also the part of a plant that joins the flowers, fruit and leaves to the main stem.
stalk (stalks, stalking, stalked) *verb*
If you stalk a wild animal, you follow it slowly and quietly.
stammer (stammers, stammering, stammered) *verb*
If you stammer, you speak with difficulty, hesitating and repeating words or sounds. People sometimes stammer when they are nervous or afraid.
stamp (stamps) *noun*
A stamp is a small piece of gummed paper, usually with a picture on it. You have to stick a stamp on to a letter or parcel before you post it.
stamp (stamps, stamping, stamped) *verb*
If you stamp your foot, you lift your foot and suddenly put it down very hard. Some children stamp their foot if they are cross.
stampede (stampedes, stampeding, stampeded) *verb*
When animals in a herd stampede, they rush away suddenly and wildly in a large group, usually because they are frightened.
stand (stands, standing, stood) *verb*

When you stand, your body is upright and you are on your feet.
stand (stands) *noun*
A stand is an open building at a sports ground. People can sit or stand there in rows to watch what is happening.
standard (standards) *noun*
A standard is a measure of how good or bad something is: *Your work is of a very high standard.*
standard *adjective*
Something which is standard is usual, and not special or extra: *Power-assisted steering is now a standard feature on this car.*
star (stars) *noun*
1. A star is a large natural object in space. Stars can be seen as tiny points of light in the sky at night.
2. A star is also a shape with a number of sharp points.
3. A star can also be a very well-known person in entertainment or sport.
stare (stares, staring, stared) *verb*
If you stare, you look at someone or something for a long time with wide-open eyes.
starfish *noun*
A starfish is a flat star-shaped creature with five arms. Starfish live in the sea.
starling (starlings) *noun*
A starling is a very common European bird with greenish-black feathers. Starlings live and fly in large groups.
start (starts, starting, started) *verb*
1. When you start to do something, you begin doing it.
2. If someone starts an engine, they make it begin to work.
start *noun*
The start of something is the first part of it.
startle (startles, startling, startled) *verb*
If something startles you, it frightens you by making a sudden movement or noise.
starve (starves, starving, starved) *verb*
When people or animals starve, they suffer greatly from lack of food and sometimes die.
state (states) *noun*
1. The state of someone or something is how they are: *Have you seen the state of the garden? It's waist-high in nettles.*
2. A state is a country.
station (stations) *noun*
1. A station is a building where trains or buses stop for passengers.
2. A station is also a building which is used by people such as the police or the fire brigade.
stationery *noun*
Stationery is paper, envelopes, pens and other equipment used for writing.
statue (statues) *noun*
A statue is a large sculpture of a person or animal.
stay (stays, staying, stayed) *verb*
If you stay in a place, you do not move away.
steady (steadier, steadiest) *adjective*
1. If something such as a ladder is steady, it is firm and does not shake or move about.
2. If you look at someone in a steady way, you look at them in a calm and controlled way which shows that you are not nervous.
>steadily *adverb*
steak (steaks) *noun*
A steak is a thick slice of beef or fish.
steal (steals, stealing, stole, stolen) *verb*
If someone steals something, they take away something that belongs to someone else, without permission.
stealthy (stealthier, stealthiest) *adjective*
Stealthy actions and movements are quiet and secretive.
>stealthily *adverb*
steam *noun*
Steam is the hot mist that water turns into when it boils.
steel *noun*
Steel is a very strong metal made mostly from iron.
steep (steeper, steepest) *adjective*
Something, such as a road or hill, that is steep slopes very sharply.
>steeply *adverb*
steeple (steeples) *noun*
A steeple is a church tower with a high, pointed top.

steeplejack (steeplejacks) *noun*
A steeplejack is a person who climbs and repairs things like steeples and tall chimneys.
steer (steers, steering, steered) *verb*
When someone steers something, like a car or cycle, they make it go in the direction they want.
stem (stems) *noun*
1. The stem of a plant is the long, thin centre part.
2. A stem is also one of the smaller parts of a plant which hold leaves, flowers or fruit.
stencil (stencils) *noun*
A stencil is a piece of something like paper or plastic which has a design cut out of it. You print the design on to a surface by rolling or pressing ink or paint across the stencil so that it comes through the holes on to the surface below.
step (steps) *noun*
1. A step is the movement you make when you lift your foot and put it down in a different place.
2. A step is also a raised, flat surface like a block. There are often two or more steps together, which you walk on to get up or down to a different level.
3. Steps are a sort of ladder that will stand up on its own.
stereo *adjective*
Stereo is used to describe a system of playing music in which the sound comes through two different speakers.
stern (sterner, sternest) *adjective*
Someone who is stern is very serious and expects to be obeyed.
>sternly *adverb*
stew (stews) *noun*
A stew is a meal which you make by simmering meat, fish or vegetables for a long time.
stick (sticks) *noun*
1. A stick is a long, thin piece of wood.
2. A stick of something is a long, thin piece of it: *I need a few sticks of rhubarb.*
stick (sticks, sticking, stuck) *verb*
1. If you stick a pointed object, such as a drawing pin, into something, you push it in.
2. If you stick two things together, you fix them with something like glue or tape.
3. If something like a drawer sticks, it cannot be moved.
sticker (stickers) *noun*
A sticker is a small piece of paper or plastic that you can stick on to a surface. It has writing or a picture on one side.
sticky (stickier, stickiest) *adjective*
1. Something that is sticky is covered with a substance that can stick to other things and leave unpleasant marks.
2. Something such as a label or tape that is sticky has glue on one side so that you can stick it to surfaces.
stiff (stiffer, stiffest) *adjective*
1. Something that is stiff is quite hard or firm. It will not bend very much if it is pressed: *Use a stiff broom to sweep up the leaves.*
2. A stiff mixture is hard to stir.
3. If a person is stiff, their muscles or joints hurt when they move.
>stiffly *adverb*
stile (stiles) *noun*
A stile is a kind of fixed gate with a step on each side. It is made so that people can get into a field without letting animals out.
still *adverb*
You say still when something is the same as it was before: *Are you feeling better? – No, I've still got a headache.*
still (stiller, stillest) *adjective*
1. If you sit or stand still, you stay in the same position and do not move.
2. Something that is still is quiet: *After the storm, everything was still.*
stilt (stilts) *noun*
1. Stilts are two long pieces of wood with small ledges high up on the sides. People, such as clowns, stand on the ledges, hold onto the stilts, and walk with them high up above the ground.
2. Stilts are also long pieces of wood or metal which are sunk upright in the ground to support buildings above wet or boggy ground.

sting (stings) *noun*
The sting of an insect or plant is the part that can prick someone's skin and leave poison behind.
stink (stinks, stinking, stank, stunk) *verb*
Something that stinks smells extremely unpleasant.
stir (stirs, stirring, stirred) *verb*
If you stir a liquid, you mix it inside a container, moving something such as a spoon round and round in it.
stitch (stitches, stitching, stitched) *verb*
If you stitch fabric, you push a needle and thread in and out through it.
stocking (stockings) *noun*
Stockings are two pieces of clothing worn by women to cover their feet and legs.
stomach (stomachs) *noun*
Your stomach is the part of your body that holds food when you have eaten it.
stone (stones) *noun*
1. Stone is a hard, dry material that is dug out of the ground. It is often used for building houses and walls.
2. A stone is a small piece of rock which you find on the surface of the ground.
3. A jewel is sometimes called a stone.
4. A stone is also a large, hard seed which grows in the middle of some kinds of fruit. For example, peaches and plums have stones in them.
stony (stonier, stoniest) *adjective*
1. Stony ground is rough and contains a lot of stones.
2. A stony voice or face shows no sympathy or friendliness.
>**stonily** *adverb*
stool (stools) *noun*
A stool is a seat with legs but no back.
stoop (stoops, stooping, stooped) *verb*
1. If you stoop, you stand or walk with your back and shoulders bent forward and downwards.
2. To stoop also means to bend your body down from the waist or from the knees, usually so that you can pick something up from the ground, or avoid a low ceiling.
stop (stops, stopping, stopped) *verb*
1. If you stop what you are doing, you no longer do it.
2. If you stop somewhere, you stay there for a short while.
stopper (stoppers) *noun*
The stopper of a bottle or jar is the thing that fits into the top of it to prevent the contents from spilling.
store (stores) *noun*
A store is a large shop which sells a lot of different things.
store (stores, storing, stored) *verb*
When you store things, you put them away and keep them until they are wanted.
stork (storks) *noun*
A stork is a large bird with a long beak and long legs. Storks usually live near water.
storm (storms) *noun*
A storm is very bad weather with heavy rain and strong winds. Often there is thunder and lightning.
story (stories) *noun*
A story is a tale about something that has happened. It can be about something real or something made up.
stout (stouter, stoutest) *adjective*
1. Someone who is stout is rather fat.
2. Things such as branches and sticks that are stout are thick and strong.
stove (stoves) *noun*
A stove is something which provides heat, for cooking or heating a room.
straight (straighter, straightest) *adjective*
Something, such as a line, which is straight does not bend or curve.
straighten (straightens, straightening, straightened) *verb*
When you straighten something, you arrange it in its proper position, or make it neat and tidy.
strain *noun*
Strain is a force that pushes, pulls or stretches something tightly, often causing it to break or move out of place.
strain (strains, straining, strained) *verb*
If you strain something such as food, you remove the liquid from it.

strand (strands, stranding, stranded) *verb*
1. If a ship or a whale is stranded, it goes out of the sea on to the shore and cannot get back to the sea.
2. If someone is stranded somewhere, they are left helpless and cannot get away, often because they have no money.
strange (stranger, strangest) *adjective*
1. Something that is strange is odd or unexpected.
2. A strange place is one you have never been to before.
>strangely *adverb*
stranger (strangers) *noun*
A stranger is a person you do not know.
strap (straps) *noun*
A strap is a strip of something like leather which is used to carry or fasten things.
straw (straws) *noun*
1. Straw is dried stalks of cereal such as wheat. It can be used to make mats and baskets, or for animals to sleep on.
2. A straw is a thin tube made of paper or plastic, which you can use to suck drink into your mouth.
strawberry (strawberries) *noun*
A strawberry is a small, red fruit. It is soft and juicy, and has tiny yellow seeds on its skin.
stray *adjective*
A stray pet or farm animal is one that has wandered away from home and is lost.
stray (strays, straying, strayed) *verb*
1. If something strays, it wanders away from where it is supposed to be.
2. If your thoughts stray, you do not concentrate on one particular thought but start thinking about something else.
stream (streams) *noun*
1. A stream is a small river.
2. A stream is also a steady flow of water or other fluid.
3. A stream of things, such as people or cars, is a long line of them going in one direction.
street (streets) *noun*
A street is a road in a town or village. It has buildings along it, often with a pavement on each side.
strength *noun*
1. Your strength is your ability to move or lift things.
2. The strength of a wind or a water current is its force and the speed at which it moves.
stretch (stretches) *noun*
A stretch of land or water is an area or distance of land or water, usually one that is fairly large.
stretch (stretches, stretching, stretched) *verb*
1. If you stretch, you pull your arms or legs stiffly away from your body.
2. If you stretch something soft or elastic, you pull it until it becomes tight or firm.
strict (stricter, strictest) *adjective*
1. Someone who is strict is very firm and will not put up with bad behaviour.
2. A strict rule or law is one that must be obeyed.
>strictly *adverb*
stride (strides) *noun*
A stride is a long step which you take when you are walking or running.
strike (strikes) *noun*
A strike is a refusal by workers to go on working. This is usually because they are not happy with their pay or working conditions.
strike (strikes, striking, struck) *verb*
1. If you strike something, you hit it.
2. When a clock strikes, its bells make a sound to show what the time is.
3. If someone strikes a match, they make a flame or sparks with the match.
string (strings) *noun*
1. String is thin cord made of twisted threads, used for tying things together.
2. On a musical instrument, a string is a thin length of something such as wire or nylon that is stretched tightly. Instruments like violins and guitars have strings.
strip (strips) *noun*
A strip of paper, cloth or other material is a long, narrow piece of it.
stripe (stripes) *noun*
A stripe is a long line which is usually a different colour from the parts which are next to it.

stroke (strokes, stroking, stroked) *verb*
If you stroke something, such as an animal, you move your hand gently over it.
strong (stronger, strongest) *adjective*
1. People or animals that are strong can work hard and carry heavy things.
2. Objects or materials that are strong will not break easily.
3. Wind or water currents that are strong move very fast or with great force.
4. Smells and tastes that are strong are easily noticed.
5. Strong colours are very bright.
>**strongly** *adverb*
structure (structures) *noun*
A structure is something that has been built or made, especially a large building.
struggle (struggles, struggling, struggled) *verb*
1. If you struggle to do something, you try very hard to do it although it is difficult for you.
2. If you struggle when you are being held by something or someone, you twist, kick and move violently to try to get free.
stubborn *adjective*
Someone who is stubborn is determined to do what they want.
>**stubbornly** *adverb*
student (students) *noun*
A student is a person who is studying or training at a university or college.
studio (studios) *noun*
1. A studio is a room where an artist works.
2. A studio is also a room where radio or television programmes are recorded, records are produced, or films are made.
study (studies) *noun*
A study is a room which is used for reading and writing in.
study (studies, studying, studied) *verb*
1. If you study something, you spend time learning about it.
2. If you study an object, such as a map or a picture, you look at it very carefully.
stuff (stuffs, stuffing, stuffed) *verb*
1. If you stuff something somewhere, you push it quickly and roughly into something: *He stuffed a tissue into his pocket.*
2. If you stuff something like a toy or a cushion, you fill it with material until it is full and solid.
3. If you stuff something like a chicken or turkey, you put a mixture of food inside it before cooking it.
stuffing *noun*
1. Stuffing is a mixture of food that is put inside something like a chicken or turkey before cooking it.
2. Stuffing is also material that is put inside something like a toy or a cushion to make it firm and solid.
stuffy (stuffier, stuffiest) *adjective*
If it is stuffy in a room, there is not enough fresh air in it.
stumble (stumbles, stumbling, stumbled) *verb*
If you stumble when you are walking, you trip and almost fall.
stump (stumps) *noun*
A stump is the small part of something, such as a tree, that remains when most of it has been removed.
stun (stuns, stunning, stunned) *verb*
1. If you are stunned by something, you are shocked or astonished by it.
2. If a blow on the head stuns someone, it makes them unconscious or confused about where they are.
stupid (stupider, stupidest) *adjective*
Someone who is stupid does things that are not at all sensible.
>**stupidly** *adverb*
sturdy (sturdier, sturdiest) *adjective*
1. Someone who is sturdy looks strong and is unlikely to be easily tired or injured.
2. Something that is sturdy looks strong and is unlikely to be easily damaged or knocked over.
>**sturdily** *adverb*
sty (sties) *noun*
A sty is a hut with a yard where pigs are kept.
style (styles) *noun*
The style of something is the general way in which it is done, or how it looks.

subject (subjects) *noun*
A subject is a particular thing that people study at school or college; for example, science or drawing.
>**change the subject** *phrase*
If you change the subject when you are talking to someone, you suddenly talk about something different.
submarine (submarines) *noun*
A submarine is a ship that can travel under water.
substance (substances) *noun*
A substance is any material, such as a solid or liquid, that behaves in a particular way.
subtract (subtracts, subtracting, subtracted) *verb*
If you subtract one number from another, you take it away. For example, if you subtract two from four, you are left with two.
suburb (suburbs) *noun*
A suburb is an area of a town or city which is not close to the centre. People who work in the town or city often live in the suburbs.
subway (subways) *noun*
A subway is a tunnel under a road. People can use it to get to the other side of a road safely.
succeed (succeeds, succeeding, succeeded) *verb*
If you succeed, you manage to do what you set out to do.
success *noun*
Success is managing to do something that you set out to do.
successful *adjective*
Something that is successful achieves what it was intended to achieve.
>**successfully** *adverb*
suck (sucks, sucking, sucked) *verb*
If you suck something, you draw liquid from it into your mouth.
suction *noun*
Suction is the way in which liquids, gases or other substances are drawn from one space to another, in the way that a drink is sucked through a straw.
sudden *adjective*
Something that is sudden happens quickly and unexpectedly.
>**suddenly** *adverb*
suffer (suffers, suffering, suffered) *verb*
If you suffer, you feel pain. This is usually because you are ill or have been injured. People also suffer when something has made them very unhappy.
sugar *noun*
Sugar is a sweet food which you usually buy in crystal form. It is used to sweeten other foods and drinks. Sugar comes from sugar beet or sugar cane.
suggest (suggests, suggesting, suggested) *verb*
If you suggest something to someone, you put forward a plan or an idea for them to think about.
suit (suits) *noun*
A suit is a set of clothes made from the same material. A suit usually has a jacket and trousers.
suit (suits, suiting, suited) *verb*
If a piece of clothing suits you, you look nice in it.
suitable *adjective*
Something that is suitable for a particular purpose is right for it: *You can't wear those shoes for running. They're not suitable.*
>**suitably** *adverb*
suitcase (suitcases) *noun*
A suitcase is a case with a handle that you can carry your clothes in when you are travelling.
sultana (sultanas) *noun*
A sultana is a dried, white grape.
sum (sums) *noun*
1. A sum is an amount of money.
2. A sum is also a problem in arithmetic.
summer (summers) *noun*
Summer is the season between spring and autumn. In the summer, the weather is usually warmer and drier than it is during other seasons.
sun *noun*
The sun is the ball of fire in the sky that the earth goes round. It gives us light and heat.

sunbeam (sunbeams) *noun*
A sunbeam is a ray of light from the sun.
sunburn *noun*
If someone has sunburn, they have sore, red patches on their skin. This is because they have spent too much time in hot sunshine.
Sunday *noun*
Sunday is one of the seven days of the week. It comes after Saturday and before Monday.
sunflower (sunflowers) *noun*
A sunflower is a very tall plant. It has a large, flat flower with yellow petals and a brown centre.
sunlight *noun*
Sunlight is the light that comes from the sun during the day.
sunny (sunnier, sunniest) *adjective*
When the weather is sunny, the sun is shining brightly.
sunrise *noun*
Sunrise is the time of the morning when the sun is first seen in the sky.
sunset *noun*
Sunset is the time of the evening when the sun disappears from the sky.
sunshine *noun*
Sunshine is the light and heat that reaches us from the sun.
supermarket (supermarkets) *noun*
A supermarket is a large shop which sells all kinds of food and things for the house.
supersonic *adjective*
Supersonic speeds are greater than the speed of sound.
supper *noun*
Supper is an evening meal.
suppertime *noun*
Suppertime is the time in the evening when people usually have supper.
supply (supplies, supplying, supplied) *verb*
If someone supplies you with something, they provide you with it.
supply (supplies) *noun*
1. A supply of something is the amount of it which someone has.
2. Supplies are food, equipment and other things needed by a group of people, for example by an army, or by people going on an expedition.
>**in short supply** *phrase*
If something is in short supply, there is very little of it.
support (supports, supporting, supported) *verb*
1. If something supports an object, it holds it up firmly.
2. If you support a sports team, you go regularly to their games and hope that they will win.
suppose (supposes, supposing, supposed) *verb*
If you suppose something is true, you think that it is likely to be true.
sure (surer, surest) *adjective*
If you are sure something is true, you believe it is true.
>**surely** *adverb*
surf *noun*
Surf is the large waves that break on the sea shore.
surface (surfaces) *noun*
The surface of something is the outside or top part of it.
surgery (surgeries) *noun*
1. A surgery is the place where a doctor or dentist sees their patients.
2. Surgery is the cutting and repairing of parts of the body that are not healthy.
surprise (surprises) *noun*
A surprise is something unexpected.
surrender (surrenders, surrendering, surrendered) *verb*
If someone surrenders, they stop fighting and agree that they have lost.
surround (surrounds, surrounding, surrounded) *verb*
If something surrounds something else, it is all round it or covers it completely.
survive (survives, surviving, survived) *verb*
If someone survives, they continue to live after being close to death.

suspect (suspects, suspecting, suspected) *verb*
1. If you suspect something, you think that it is probably true.
2. If you suspect someone of something, such as a crime, you have a feeling that they are guilty of it.
suspense *noun*
Suspense is excitement or worry about something that is going to happen very soon; for example, when you are waiting for some news.
suspicious *adjective*
1. If you are suspicious of someone, you feel or show that you do not trust them.
2. If something is suspicious, it causes people to feel that something is wrong in some way, so that they are not sure what to believe.
>**suspiciously** *adverb*
swallow (swallows, swallowing, swallowed) *verb*
When you swallow food or drink, it goes down your throat into your stomach.
swallow (swallows) *noun*
A swallow is a small, dark blue and white bird. Swallows catch insects as they fly.
swamp (swamps) *noun*
A swamp is an area of very wet land.
swan (swans) *noun*
A swan is a large bird with a long neck which lives on rivers and lakes. Swans are usually white.
swap (swaps, swapping, swapped) *verb*
If you swap something for something else, you give it to someone and receive something else in exchange for it.
swarm (swarms) *noun*
A swarm is a large group of bees or other insects flying together.
sway (sways, swaying, swayed) *verb*
When people or things sway, they lean or swing slowly first to one side and then to the other, usually several times.
sweat *noun*
Sweat is the salty liquid which comes from your skin when you are hot.
sweater (sweaters) *noun*
A sweater is a warm, knitted garment. You put on a sweater by pulling it over your head.
sweep (sweeps, sweeping, swept) *verb*
If you sweep a floor or a path, you clean it by pushing a broom over it.
sweep (sweeps) *noun*
A sweep is someone who cleans chimneys.
sweet (sweeter, sweetest) *adjective*
1. Food or drink that is sweet has sugar in it, or tastes as though it has sugar in it.
2. If you say something small is sweet, you mean it is pretty and delightful.
>**sweetly** *adverb*
sweet (sweets) *noun*
1. Sweets are things such as chocolates and toffees.
2. A sweet can be something such as yoghurt or fruit salad that is eaten after the main part of a meal.
swell (swells, swelling, swelled, swelled/swollen) *verb*
If something swells, it becomes larger and rounder than usual.
swerve (swerves, swerving, swerved) *verb*
If something that is moving swerves, it suddenly changes direction.
swift (swifter, swiftest) *adjective*
Something that is swift can move very quickly.
>**swiftly** *adverb*
swift (swifts) *noun*
A swift is a small blackish-brown bird with curved wings and a forked tail. Swifts make a loud noise like a scream. They fly very quickly and catch insects while they are flying.
swim (swims, swimming, swam, swum) *verb*
When you swim, you move through water by making movements with your arms and legs.
swimming pool (swimming pools) *noun*
A swimming pool is a place built for people to swim in.
swing (swings) *noun*
A swing is a seat that hangs from two ropes or chains. A child can sit on the seat and move backwards and forward.

switch (switches) *noun*
A switch is a small control for a piece of electrical equipment such as a light or radio.
swivel (swivels, swivelling, swivelled) *verb*
If something swivels, it turns on a central point so that it is facing in a different direction.
swoop (swoops, swooping, swooped) *verb*
When a bird or an aeroplane swoops, it suddenly moves downwards through the air in a smooth curve.
sword (swords) *noun*
A sword is a weapon with a long blade, and a handle at one end.
symbol (symbols) *noun*
A symbol is a shape or pattern that means something. For example, + is a symbol. It means you have to add two numbers together.
sympathy *noun*
If you feel or show sympathy for someone who is unhappy, you are sorry for them and show it in the way you behave towards them.
synagogue (synagogues) *noun*
A synagogue is a building where Jews pray.
syrup *noun*
1. Syrup is a sweet, fairly thick liquid made by cooking sugar with water.
2. Syrup is also a very sweet, sticky liquid food; for example, golden syrup.
system (systems) *noun*
1. A system is a way of working, organizing or doing something in which you follow a fixed plan or set of rules: *I've worked out a new system to get me to school on time.*
2. A system is also a particular set of rules, especially one in mathematics or science.
3. A system can be a set of roads, railways and canals that are linked together so that people and vehicles can travel from one place to another: *My friend says the transport system in his country is excellent.*
4. A system can also be a set of equipment or parts that are used to supply water or heat, or provide electrical power: *We really need a whole new central heating system.*

T

table (tables) *noun*
A table is a piece of furniture with a flat top for putting things on.
tablet (tablets) *noun*
1. A tablet is a small, hard piece of medicine which you swallow.
2. A tablet is also a flat piece of something, like clay or stone, which people used to write on before paper was invented.
table tennis *noun*
Table tennis is a game played indoors by two or four people. They stand at each end of a long table which has a low net across its middle and hit a small, light ball to each other.
tackle (tackles, tackling, tackled) *verb*
1. If you tackle a difficult task or problem, you deal with it in a determined way.
2. If you tackle someone in a game, such as football or hockey, you try to take the ball away from them.
3. If you tackle a person or animal, you attack and fight them, especially when they are bigger than you.
4. If you tackle someone about something, you speak to them about it, especially to tell them off or to try to persuade them to change their mind.
tact *noun*
Tact is the ability to avoid upsetting or offending people by being careful not to say or do things that would hurt their feelings.
tadpole (tadpoles) *noun*
Tadpoles are small water creatures that grow into frogs or toads. They have long tails and round, black heads.
tail (tails) *noun*
1. A tail is the part of an animal, bird or fish that grows out of the end of its body.
2. A tail is also a long part of something, such as a kite, that sticks out from the end.
3. The back part of an aeroplane is called the tail.

tale (tales) *noun*
A tale is a story, especially one about adventure or magic.
talent (talents) *noun*
A talent is the natural ability that a person has to do something well.
talk (talks, talking, talked) *verb*
When you talk, you use words so that people will understand you.
talkative *adjective*
Someone who is talkative talks a lot.
tall (taller, tallest) *adjective*
1. Someone who is tall is higher than a lot of other people.
2. Something that is tall is higher than other things of the same kind: *At the end of the street there is a tall building.*
3. You use tall when you are talking about how high somebody or something is: *My little brother is only one metre tall.*
tame (tamer, tamest) *adjective*
A tame animal or bird is one which is not afraid of humans and will not hurt them.
tan *noun*
If someone has a tan, their skin has become darker than it usually is because they have spent a lot of time in the sun.
tangle (tangles) *noun*
A tangle is a mass of things such as string, wire or hair, that are twisted together in an untidy way so that they are difficult to smooth out.
tangle (tangles, tangling, tangled) *verb*
1. If something tangles or you tangle it, it becomes twisted together in an untidy way so that it is difficult to smooth out.
2. If you are tangled in something, such as a mass of wires or ropes, you are caught in them so that it is difficult to get free.
tank (tanks) *noun*
1. A tank is a large container for liquid or gas.
2. A tank is also a vehicle for soldiers. Tanks are covered with strong metal armour, and have guns or rockets.
tanker (tankers) *noun*
A tanker is a ship, truck or railway vehicle for carrying gas or liquid.
tap (taps) *noun*
A tap is a handle fixed to a pipe or container, which controls the flow of gas or liquid.
tap (taps, tapping, tapped) *verb*
If you tap something, you hit it gently.
tape (tapes) *noun*
1. A tape is a long, thin, magnetic strip that you can record sounds or pictures on.
2. Tape is also a long, narrow strip of cloth. Tapes are used to tie things together, or to put names on clothes.
3. Some tape is made from thin paper or plastic with one sticky side. You can use it to stick things such as pieces of paper together.
tape measure (tape measures) *noun*
A tape measure is a long, narrow strip of plastic or cloth that has centimetres or inches marked on it. You can use it for measuring things such as the size of your body.
tape recorder (tape recorders) *noun*
A tape recorder is a machine that records and plays music, speech or other sounds on tape.
tar *noun*
Tar is a thick, black liquid that goes hard when it is cold. Tar is used mainly for making roads.
target (targets) *noun*
A target is an object that people aim at when they are shooting. It is usually a board with circles marked on it.
tart (tarts) *noun*
A tart is a piece of pastry filled with jam or fruit.
task (tasks) *noun*
A task is a piece of work which has to be done.
tassel (tassels) *noun*
A tassel is a bunch of short pieces of wool or other material tied together at one end and attached as a decoration to something, such as a piece of clothing or a rug.
taste *noun*
Taste is one of the five senses that people and animals have. It is your sense of taste that lets you know what you are eating or drinking.

tasty (tastier, tastiest) *adjective*
Something that is tasty has a fairly strong and pleasant flavour.
taxi (taxis) *noun*
A taxi is a car that people pay to be driven somewhere in.
tea *noun*
1. Tea is a drink made by pouring boiling water on to the dried leaves of the tea plant.
2. Tea is also a meal in the afternoon or early evening.
teabag (teabags) *noun*
A teabag is a small, thin, paper bag which has tea leaves inside it. Teabags can be used to make tea in a cup or in a teapot.
teach (teaches, teaching, taught) *verb*
If someone teaches you something, they help you to learn about it, or show you how to do it.
teacher (teachers) *noun*
A teacher is a person whose job is to help people learn.
team (teams) *noun*
A team is a number of people or animals working or playing together.
teapot (teapots) *noun*
A teapot is a container for making and serving tea. It has a lid, a handle and a spout.
tear (tears, tearing, tore, torn) *verb*
If someone tears something, such as paper or fabric, they pull it apart.
tear (tears) *noun*
Tears are the drops of salty liquid that come out of your eyes when you cry.
tease (teases, teasing, teased) *verb*
If someone teases you, they make fun of you.
teatime *noun*
Teatime is the time in the afternoon when people usually have tea.
technology *noun*
Technology is the practical use of science in areas such as industry, farming or medicine.
teddy bear (teddy bears) *noun*
A teddy bear is a child's soft toy which looks like a friendly bear.
teenager (teenagers) *noun*
A teenager is someone between 13 and 19 years of age.
tee-shirt (tee-shirts) *noun*
A tee-shirt is a piece of clothing that you wear on the top half of your body. It has short sleeves, no collar and no buttons down the front.
telephone (telephones) *noun*
A telephone is an instrument for talking to someone else who is in another place. A telephone is often called a phone for short.
telescope (telescopes) *noun*
A telescope is an instrument for making objects that are far away look nearer and larger.
television (televisions) *noun*
A television is a piece of electrical equipment. On a television, people can watch programmes of pictures and sounds that have come through the air.
tell (tells, telling, told) *verb*
1. If you tell someone something, you give them information about it.
2. If someone tells you to do something, they say you must do it.
3. If you can tell the time, you can find out what the time is by looking at a clock or watch.
temper *noun*
Someone's temper is how cheerful or how angry they are feeling at a particular time.
>lose your temper *phrase*
If you lose your temper, you become so angry that you cannot think clearly about what you are saying or doing.
temperate *adjective*
A temperate place has weather that is never extremely hot or extremely cold.
temperature (temperatures) *noun*
1. The temperature is the amount of heat there is in a place. In hot countries, the temperature is very high. Temperatures can be measured.
2. Your temperature is the temperature of your blood. It usually stays about the same unless you are ill.

tempt (tempts, tempting, tempted) *verb*
If something tempts you, it attracts you and makes you want it, often when it is something which you know you should avoid.
tender (tenderer, tenderest) *adjective*
1. Meat or other food which is tender is very soft and easy to cut or chew.
2. Someone or something that is tender shows gentle and caring feelings.
>**tenderly** *adverb*
tennis *noun*
Tennis is a game for two or four players. The players use a soft ball and rackets. They hit the ball backwards and forwards over a net. Tennis is played on an area called a tennis court.
tent (tents) *noun*
A tent is a shelter made of canvas or nylon which is held up by poles and ropes. People sleep in a tent when they are camping.
tentacle (tentacles) *noun*
The tentacles of an animal such as an octopus are its long, thin arms.
term (terms) *noun*
A term is one of the periods that schools and colleges divide the year into. In Britain, there are usually three terms in a year.
terrace (terraces) *noun*
1. A terrace is a row of similar houses joined together by their side walls.
2. A terrace is also a flat area of stone or grass next to a house where people can sit.
3. The terraces at a football ground are wide steps that people can stand on when they are watching a game.
terrible *adjective*
You say something is terrible when you think it is very bad or unpleasant.
>**terribly** *adverb*
terrify (terrifies, terrifying, terrified) *verb*
If something terrifies you, it makes you feel very frightened.
territory (territories) *noun*
1. Territory is land which is controlled by a particular country or ruler.
2. An animal's territory is an area which it considers its own and which it defends when other animals try to enter it.
terror *noun*
Terror is very great fear.
test (tests) *noun*
A test is something you have to do to show how much you know.
test (tests, testing, tested) *verb*
If someone tests something, they try to find out whether it works properly.
test tube (test tubes) *noun*
A test tube is a small, tube-shaped, glass container that scientists use when they are doing experiments.
textbook (textbooks) *noun*
A textbook is a book about a particular subject, that is used in schools or colleges by people studying that subject.
thank (thanks, thanking, thanked) *verb*
You thank people when you are grateful for something they have done or said.
thaw (thaws, thawing, thawed) *verb*
When something that is frozen thaws, it melts.
theatre (theatres) *noun*
A theatre is a building with a stage in it. People go to the theatre to watch plays and other entertainments.
thermometer (thermometers) *noun*
A thermometer is an instrument for measuring how hot or cold something is.
thick (thicker, thickest) *adjective*
1. An object that is thick is deeper through than other things of the same kind: *I should like a thick slice of bread, please.*
2. Something that is thick is made up of a lot of things growing closely together: *She found herself in a thick forest.*
3. Liquids that are thick do not flow easily.
4. Something, such as smoke or fog, that is thick is difficult to see through.
thief (thieves) *noun*
A thief is a person who steals something.
thigh (thighs) *noun*
Your thighs are the top parts of your legs, between your knees and your hips.
thimble (thimbles) *noun*
A thimble is a small, metal or plastic object that you put on your finger when you are sewing. The thimble helps you push the

needle through the cloth.
thin (thinner, thinnest) *adjective*
1. Something that is thin is much narrower than it is long: *The witch's nose was long and thin.*
2. A person who is thin weighs less than most other people.
3. Something, such as paper or cloth, that is thin has only a very small distance between front and back.
4. Liquids that are thin are watery.
thing (things) *noun*
1. You can use thing or things to talk about objects, actions, ideas, or events in a general way: *We shall need all sorts of things for this holiday.*
2. Things are objects or equipment that are used for a particular purpose: *Can you clear away the breakfast things?*
think (thinks, thinking, thought) *verb*
1. If you say you think something is true, you mean you believe it is true but you are not sure.
2. If you are thinking about something, you have words or ideas in your mind.
thirsty (thirstier, thirstiest) *adjective*
If you are thirsty, you feel that you need to drink something.
>**thirstily** *adverb*
thistle (thistles) *noun*
A thistle is a wild plant that has prickly leaves and purple flowers.
thorn (thorns) *noun*
A thorn is one of the sharp points on the stem of a plant such as a rose.
thorough *adjective*
1. Someone who is thorough is always very careful in their work.
2. A thorough action is one that is done very carefully so that nothing is forgotten: *The doctor gave the little boy a thorough examination.*
>**thoroughly** *adverb*
thought (thoughts) *noun*
1. A thought is an idea that you have in your mind.
2. Thought is the action of thinking carefully about something.
3. A person's thoughts are all the ideas in their mind when they are concentrating on one particular thing.
thoughtful *adjective*
1. If you are thoughtful, you are quiet and serious because you are thinking about something.
2. A thoughtful person remembers what other people want or feel, and tries not to upset them.
>**thoughtfully** *adverb*
thread (threads) *noun*
A thread is a long, very thin piece of material, such as cotton, wool, silk or nylon. Thread can be woven into cloth or used for sewing fabrics together.
thread (threads, threading, threaded) *verb*
When you thread a needle, you put a piece of thread through a hole in the top of it.
threat (threats) *noun*
A threat is a warning of something unpleasant.
threaten (threatens, threatening, threatened) *verb*
1. If someone threatens you, they warn you that something unpleasant may happen if you do not do what they want.
2. If something unpleasant threatens, it seems likely to happen: *The river threatens to burst its banks.*
three-dimensional *adjective*
A three-dimensional object is solid rather than flat.
thrill (thrills) *noun*
A thrill is a sudden feeling of great excitement or pleasure.
throat (throats) *noun*
Your throat is the back of your mouth and inside your neck. It contains the tubes for breathing and for swallowing food.
throne (thrones) *noun*
A throne is a special chair used by people such as kings and queens on important official occasions.
throw (throws, throwing, threw, thrown) *verb*
If you throw an object that you are holding, you send the object through the air.

thrush (thrushes) *noun*
A thrush is a songbird with a brown back and a pale, spotted chest.
thrust (thrusts, thrusting, thrust) *verb*
If you thrust something somewhere, you push it or move it there quickly using a lot of force.
thud (thuds) *noun*
A thud is a dull sound, such as a heavy object makes when it falls on to a carpet.
thumb (thumbs) *noun*
Your thumb is one of the five fingers on your hand. It is the finger which is nearest to your wrist.
thump (thumps, thumping, thumped) *verb*
If you thump someone or something, you hit them hard, usually with your fist: *He shouted and thumped the table.*
thunder *noun*
Thunder is the loud noise that you hear after a flash of lightning in a storm.
thunderstorm (thunderstorms) *noun*
A thunderstorm is a storm in which there is thunder and lightning and a lot of heavy rain.
Thursday *noun*
Thursday is one of the seven days of the week. It is the day after Wednesday and before Friday.
tick (ticks) *noun*
A tick is a sign to show that something is correct.
ticket (tickets) *noun*
A ticket is a small piece of card or paper which shows that you have paid for something such as a train ride.
tickle (tickles) *noun*
A tickle is an unpleasant and annoying feeling somewhere on your body. If you have a tickle in your throat, it makes you want to cough.
tickle (tickles, tickling, tickled) *verb*
If you tickle someone, you move your fingers gently on part of their body to make them laugh.
tide (tides) *noun*
The tide is the regular change in the level of the sea on the shore. There are two high tides and two low tides every day.
tidy (tidier, tidiest) *adjective*
Something that is tidy is neat, with things in their proper place.
>**tidily** *adverb*
tie (ties) *noun*
1. A tie is a long, narrow piece of cloth that is worn round the neck.
2. A tie is also a result in a race or competition when two people do as well as each other.
tie (ties, tying, tied) *verb*
1. If you tie an object to something else, you fasten it with something, such as string.
2. If you tie something, such as shoelaces, you fasten the ends together in a bow.
tiger (tigers) *noun*
A tiger is a large, fierce animal that belongs to the cat family. Tigers live in Asia. Their fur is usually orange with black stripes.
tight (tighter, tightest) *adjective*
1. Clothes that are tight fit closely to your body. Tight clothes are often uncomfortable.
2. Something that is tight is firmly fastened and is difficult to move.
>**tightly** *adverb*
tight *adverb*
1. If you hold something tight, you hold it very firmly.
2. Something that is shut tight is shut very firmly.
tights *noun*
Tights are a piece of clothing made of thin, stretchy material, which women and girls wear on their legs and bottom. Dancers and acrobats also wear tights.
tile (tiles) *noun*
1. A tile is a flat square piece of something like clay, carpet or cork. Tiles are put together edge to edge to cover floors or walls.
2. A tile is also a flat square or rectangular piece of clay which is used for covering roofs.
tilt (tilts, tilting, tilted) *verb*
1. If you tilt something, it moves into a sloping position with one end higher than the other.

2. If you tilt your head, you move it slightly upwards or to one side.
timber *noun*
Timber is wood that is used for things such as building and making furniture.
time (times) *noun*
1. Time is what we measure in units such as hours, days and years.
2. Time also means a particular moment: *What's the time now? - It's half past three.*
3. You use times in arithmetic to talk about numbers that are multiplied together: *Three times two equals six.*
time (times, timing, timed) *verb*
If you time something, you measure how long it takes.
>**in time** *phrase*
If you are in time for something, you are not late.
>**keep time** *phrase*
If a clock or watch keeps good time, it does not run fast or slow.
tin (tins) *noun*
1. Tin is a silvery-white metal.
2. A tin is a metal container which is filled with food and sealed. This preserves the food for long periods.
3. A tin is also a metal container with a lid, for storing things, such as biscuits.
tingle (tingles, tingling, tingled) *verb*
When part of your body tingles, you feel a slight prickling or stinging.
tinned *adjective*
Tinned food is food that has been preserved by being sealed in a tin.
tin opener (tin openers) *noun*
A tin opener is something you use for opening tins of food.
tiny (tinier, tiniest) *adjective*
Something that is tiny is very small.
tip (tips) *noun*
The tip of something long and narrow is the end of it: *The cat caught the tip of its tail in the door.*
tip (tips, tipping, tipped) *verb*
1. If you tip an object, you move it so that it is no longer straight: *She tipped her chair back and almost fell over.*
2. If you tip something somewhere, you pour it quickly.
tiptoe (tiptoes, tiptoeing, tiptoed) *verb*
If you tiptoe somewhere, you walk there very quietly on your toes.
tired *adjective*
If you are tired, you feel that you want to rest or sleep.
tiresome *adjective*
A person or thing that is tiresome makes you feel annoyed, irritated or bored.
>**tiresomely** *adverb*
tiring *adjective*
Something that is tiring makes you tired so that you want to rest or sleep.
tissue (tissues) *noun*
1. Tissue is thin paper that is used especially for wrapping things, such as objects made of glass or china.
2. A tissue is a piece of soft paper that you can use as a handkerchief. It can be thrown away after use.
title (titles) *noun*
1. The title of something such as a book is the name given to it by the person who wrote it.
2. Someone's title is a name such as Mr, Mrs, Lady, or Professor, that goes in front of their own name.
toad (toads) *noun*
A toad is a creature which is similar to a frog. It has drier skin than a frog, and does not spend so much time in the water. Toads walk. They do not leap as frogs do.
toadstool (toadstools) *noun*
A toadstool is a poisonous plant that looks like a mushroom.
toast *noun*
Toast is bread which has been cut into slices and made brown and crisp by heating.
toboggan (toboggans) *noun*
A toboggan is a vehicle for travelling on snow. It has a flat seat attached to two long narrow pieces of wood or metal that slide easily over the snow.
today *adverb*
Today is the day that is happening now.

toddler (toddlers) *noun*
A toddler is a small child who has only just learned to walk.
toe (toes) *noun*
Your toes are the five movable parts at the end of your foot.
toffee *noun*
Toffee is a sticky, chewy sweet made from butter and sugar.
together *adverb*
1. If two people do something together, they both do it.
2. If two things happen together, they happen at the same time.
3. If things are fixed, joined or mixed together, they are put with each other.
toilet (toilets) *noun*
1. A toilet is a bowl connected to a drain and fitted with a seat. It is used to get rid of waste matter from the body.
2. A toilet is also a room where the toilet is. Sometimes there is a washbasin in the room as well.
tomato (tomatoes) *noun*
A tomato is a soft, small, red fruit. Tomatoes can be cooked or eaten raw in salads.
tomorrow *adverb*
Tomorrow is the day after today.
tongue (tongues) *noun*
1. Your tongue is the soft, moving part inside your mouth. You use your tongue for tasting, eating and speaking.
2. The tongue of a shoe or boot is the piece of material underneath the laces.
tonic (tonics) *noun*
1. A tonic is a medicine that makes you feel stronger, healthier and less tired.
2. A tonic is also anything that makes you feel stronger or more cheerful.
tonight *adverb*
Tonight is the evening of today or the night that follows today.
tonne (tonnes) *noun*
A tonne is a measure of weight that is equal to 1000 kilograms.
tool (tools) *noun*
A tool is any instrument or piece of equipment that you hold in your hands to help you do something. For example, knives and forks, hammers and screwdrivers are all tools.
tooth (teeth) *noun*
1. A tooth is one of the hard, white objects which grow in your mouth. You use your teeth for biting and chewing food.
2. The teeth of objects such as combs, saws and zips are the parts that stick out in a row on their edge.
toothbrush (toothbrushes) *noun*
A toothbrush is a small brush with a long handle which you use for cleaning your teeth.
toothpaste *noun*
Toothpaste is a thick paste which you put on your toothbrush to clean your teeth.
top (tops) *noun*
1. The top of something is its highest point.
2. The top of something such as a bottle or tube is the lid or cap that fits on to the end of it.
torch (torches) *noun*
A torch is a small lamp which you carry in your hand. It gets its power from batteries inside it.
torpedo (torpedoes) *noun*
A torpedo is a weapon shaped like a long, narrow cylinder, which is fired from ships, submarines or aircraft. It travels underwater and explodes when it hits its target.
tortoise (tortoises) *noun*
A tortoise is a slow-moving animal with a hard, thick shell. It can pull its legs and head inside the shell to protect itself.
toss (tosses, tossing, tossed) *verb*
1. If you toss something, you throw it lightly, often in a rather careless way.
2. If you toss and turn in bed, you keep moving from side to side.
total *adjective*
Total means complete: *The picnic was a total failure.*
>totally *adverb*
total (totals) *noun*
A total is a number of things added together.

touch (touches, touching, touched) *verb*
1. If you touch something, you feel it with your hand.
2. If two things are touching, there is no space between them.
tough (tougher, toughest) *adjective*
1. Someone who is tough is very strong, and is not afraid of pain.
2. Material that is tough is strong and difficult to cut, tear or break.
tour (tours) *noun*
1. A tour is a journey during which you visit several places of interest.
2. A tour is also a short trip you make round a place so that you can look at it.
tourist (tourists) *noun*
A tourist is a person who visits places for pleasure and interest.
tow (tows, towing, towed) *verb*
If a vehicle tows another vehicle, it pulls it along behind.
towards *preposition*
1. If you move towards something or someone, you go in that direction: *As soon as she saw her friend, she ran towards her.*
2. If you give money towards something, you help pay for it.
towel (towels) *noun*
A towel is a piece of thick, soft cloth that you use to dry yourself with.
tower (towers) *noun*
A tower is a tall, narrow building or part of a building. Many churches and castles have towers.
town (towns) *noun*
A town is a place with a lot of streets and buildings where people live and work. Towns are larger than villages and smaller than cities.
toy (toys) *noun*
A toy is an object that children play with; for example, a doll or a model car.
trace (traces) *noun*
A trace is a sign that tells you that someone or something has been present in a particular place.
>**without trace** *phrase*
If someone or something disappears without trace, they disappear without leaving any signs of where they have gone.
trace (traces, tracing, traced) *verb*
1. If you trace the cause of something, you find out what it is after looking for it.
2. If you trace something that has disappeared, you find it by looking in all the places where you think that it could be.
3. If you trace something such as a map, you copy it by covering it with a piece of transparent paper and drawing over the lines underneath.
track (tracks) *noun*
1. A track is a rough, narrow road or path. Some tracks are made by people or animals walking along them.
2. A track is also a special road or path that is used for racing.
3. A railway track is a long, narrow strip of ground with rails on either side, which trains travel along.
tractor (tractors) *noun*
A tractor is a vehicle with large rear wheels. Tractors are used on farms for pulling or lifting things.
trade *noun*
Trade is the buying, selling or exchanging of goods or services. Trade can be between people, companies or countries.
trade (trades, trading, traded) *verb*
When people trade, they buy, sell or exchange goods between themselves.
tradition (traditions) *noun*
A tradition is something that the people in a particular group have done or believed in for a long time: *It is an American tradition to have turkey on Thanksgiving Day.*
traditional *adjective*
Something, like dress or customs, that is traditional has existed in a place for a long time without changing: *In Britain, it is traditional for a bride to wear white.*
>**traditionally** *adverb*
traffic *noun*
Traffic is the movement of vehicles on the road, in the air, or on water.

traffic jam (traffic jams) *noun*
A traffic jam is a long line of vehicles that cannot move because the road is blocked.
traffic light (traffic lights) *noun*
Traffic lights are special signals to control the flow of traffic. Red lights mean stop and green lights mean go.
traffic warden (traffic wardens) *noun*
A traffic warden is a person whose job is to make sure that cars are parked properly.
trail (trails) *noun*
1. A trail is a rough path across open country or through woods.
2. A trail is also the scent, footprints and other signs that people and animals leave when they move along.
trail (trails, trailing, trailed) *verb*
1. If you trail something, it drags along the ground or moves through the air or water behind you: *As the boat moved, he trailed his fingers in the water.*
2. If someone is trailing along behind, they are moving slowly along behind someone else.
trailer (trailers) *noun*
1. A trailer is a vehicle pulled by a car, used for carrying things such as camping equipment.
2. A trailer is also the long rear part of a lorry which is in two sections.
3. A trailer can also be a series of short pieces taken from a film or a television or radio programme in order to advertise it.
train (trains) *noun*
A train is a number of carriages or trucks which are joined together and pulled by an engine along a railway.
train (trains, training, trained) *verb*
1. If someone trains you to do a job, they teach you the skills you need.
2. If you train a dog, you teach it to behave properly.
trainer (trainers) *noun*
1. A trainer is a person who trains animals to do particular things.
2. A trainer is also a person who coaches other people in sports such as boxing.
3. Trainers are special shoes that people wear for running or playing games.
tram (trams) *noun*
A tram is an electric vehicle for carrying people. Trams travel along rails laid in the surface of a street in a town or city.
trampoline (trampolines) *noun*
A trampoline is something that is used to jump and bounce on. It is made of strong cloth held into a frame by springs.
transfer (transfers, transferring, transferred) *verb*
1. If you transfer something, you move it to a different place or position.
2. If someone transfers, they move to a different place or job in the same organization.
translate (translates, translating, translated) *verb*
If you translate something that someone has said or written, you say or write it in a different language.
translucent *adjective*
If something is translucent, light passes through it so that it seems to glow.
transmitter (transmitters) *noun*
A transmitter is something that is used for broadcasting television or radio programmes.
transparent *adjective*
If something is transparent, you can see through it. For example, glass is transparent.
transport *noun*
Transport is the moving of people and things from one place to another by vehicle.
trap (traps) *noun*
A trap is an object that is specially made to catch animals.
trap (traps, trapping, trapped) *verb*
If a person is trapped somewhere, they cannot escape: *The driver was trapped in his car and had to be rescued.*
trapdoor (trapdoors) *noun*
A trapdoor is a small door in a floor or ceiling.
trapeze (trapezes) *noun*
A trapeze is a bar hung from a high place by ropes. People swing from trapezes in circuses.

travel (travels, travelling, travelled) *verb*
1. If you travel, you go from one place to another, especially in foreign countries.
2. If something travels at a particular speed, it moves at that speed.
traveller (travellers) *noun*
A traveller is a person who is making a journey, or who travels a lot.
tray (trays) *noun*
A tray is a flat piece of wood, metal or plastic with raised edges. Trays are used for carrying thing such as food and drinks.
treacherous *adjective*
1. A person who is treacherous cannot be trusted.
2. If something like the sea or the weather is treacherous, it is dangerous because it may change suddenly and unexpectedly.
>**treacherously** *adverb*
treacle *noun*
Treacle is a thick, sweet, sticky liquid made from sugar.
tread (treads, treading, trod, trodden) *verb*
If you tread on something, you step on it or press your foot on it.
tread (treads) *noun*
A tread is the pattern of grooves on the outer surface of a tyre, which helps prevent slipping or skidding.
treasure *noun*
Treasure is a collection of valuable things such as jewels or paintings.
treasure (treasures, treasuring, treasured) *verb*
If you treasure something, it is very important to you.
treat (treats, treating, treated) *verb*
1. If you treat someone in a particular way, you behave that way towards them: *My uncle treats me as though I'm about five.*
2. If someone treats a person who has an illness or injury, they help them to get well again.
treat (treats) *noun*
A treat is something that is especially pleasant or enjoyable.
tree (trees) *noun*
A tree is a large plant with a long trunk made of wood, which usually has leaves and branches. Trees can live for many years.
tremble (trembles, trembling, trembled) *verb*
If you tremble, you shake slightly with small movements that you cannot control. People sometimes tremble if they are excited, frightened or ill.
trespass (trespasses, trespassing, trespassed) *verb*
If you trespass, you go on to someone else's land without their permission.
trial (trials) *noun*
1. In law, a trial is a process to decide whether a person is guilty of a particular crime.
2. A trial is also an experiment in which you test something by using it or doing it for a short time to see how well it works.
triangle (triangles) *noun*
1. A triangle is a shape which has three straight sides and three angles.
2. A triangle is also a musical instrument which is made from a piece of metal shaped like a triangle. You play it by hitting it with a short metal bar.
tribe (tribes) *noun*
A tribe is a group of people of the same race who share the same customs and language and are ruled by one chief.
trick (tricks) *noun*
A trick is a clever or skilful act that someone does to entertain people.
trick (tricks, tricking, tricked) *verb*
If a person tricks someone, they deceive them.
trickle (trickles, trickling, trickled) *verb*
When a liquid trickles, it flows slowly in very small amounts.
tricycle (tricycles) *noun*
A tricycle is a vehicle similar to a bicycle, but with three wheels.
trifle (trifles) *noun*
1. A trifle is something that is not very important: *Don't bother me with trifles!*
2. Trifle is a cold pudding made of layers of sponge, fruit, jelly and custard.

trigger (triggers) *noun*
A trigger is a small lever on a gun, which is pulled to fire the gun.
trim (trimmer, trimmest) *adjective*
Something that is trim is neat, tidy and attractive.
trim (trims, trimming, trimmed) *verb*
If a person trims something, such as a lawn or a hedge, they cut off small amounts of it to make it look neater and tidier.
trip (trips) *noun*
A trip is a journey to a place and back again.
trip (trips, tripping, tripped) *verb*
If you trip, you knock your foot against something when you are walking, and fall or almost fall.
tripper (trippers) *noun*
A tripper is a person who is on a trip.
triumph *noun*
Triumph is a feeling of great pride resulting from success or victory.
triumphant *adjective*
Someone who is triumphant has gained a victory or succeeded in something and feels very happy about it.
>**triumphantly** *adverb*
tropical *adjective*
Tropical means to do with the tropics.
tropics *noun*
The tropics are the hottest part of the world. They lie north and south of the equator.
trot (trots, trotting, trotted) *verb*
1. When an animal such as a horse trots, it moves fairly fast, lifting its feet quite high off the ground.
2. If you trot somewhere, you move at a speed between walking and running, taking small, quick steps.
trouble (troubles) *noun*
1. Troubles are things that cause worry.
2. If you have trouble doing something, you find it hard to do.
trough (troughs) *noun*
1. A trough is a long, narrow container which holds food or drink for farm animals.
2. A trough is also the area between two big waves in the sea.
trousers *noun*
Trousers are a piece of clothing which covers your legs and the lower part of your body.
trout *noun*
A trout is a fairly large fish that lives in rivers or streams. There are several kinds of trout and many of them are good to eat.
trowel (trowels) *noun*
1. A trowel is a garden tool that is rather like a small curved spade with a short handle.
2. A trowel is also a small tool with a flat blade which is used in building for spreading cement mixtures.
truant (truants) *noun*
A truant is a pupil who stays away from school without permission.
truce (truces) *noun*
A truce is an agreement between two people or groups to stop fighting or quarrelling for a short time.
truck (trucks) *noun*
1. A truck is a large motor vehicle which is open at the back. Trucks are used for carrying all sorts of loads.
2. A truck is also an open vehicle used for carrying things on a railway.
trudge (trudges, trudging, trudged) *verb*
If you trudge somewhere, you walk there slowly and with heavy steps, especially because you are tired or unhappy.
true (truer, truest) *adjective*
1. If something is true, it is correct.
2. A true story is about something real that happened.
>**truly** *adverb*
trumpet (trumpets) *noun*
A trumpet is a brass musical instrument which you play by blowing into it.
trunk (trunks) *noun*
1. The trunk of a tree is its large main stem, from which the branches grow.
2. Your trunk is the main part of your body.
3. An elephant's trunk is its very long nose. It uses its trunk to lift food and water and bring them to its mouth.
4. A trunk is also a large case or box with strong sides and a lid.

trust (trusts, trusting, trusted) *verb*
If you trust someone, you believe that they are honest, and that they would not purposely do anything to hurt you.
truth *noun*
The truth is all the real facts about something or someone, rather than things that are imagined or invented.
truthful *adjective*
Someone who is truthful is honest and tells the truth.
>**truthfully** *adverb*
try (tries, trying, tried) *verb*
1. If you try to do something, you do your best to do it.
2. If you try something, you test it to see what it is like.
tub (tubs) *noun*
A tub is a wide, round container of any size, into which a liquid can be poured.
tube (tubes) *noun*
1. A tube is a long, hollow object like a pipe.
2. A tube is also a long, thin container for thick liquids or pastes such as toothpaste. You squeeze the tube to get the paste out of a hole in the end.
tuck (tucks, tucking, tucked) *verb*
1. If you tuck something somewhere, you put it there so that it is safe or comfortable.
2. If you tuck the end of something in, you fold it in tidily.
Tuesday *noun*
Tuesday is one of the seven days of the week. It is the day after Monday and before Wednesday.
tuft (tufts) *noun*
A tuft is a bunch of something, like hair or grass, that grows closely together or that is held together at the bottom.
tug (tugs, tugging, tugged) *verb*
If you tug something, you give it a quick, strong pull.
tulip (tulips) *noun*
A tulip is a brightly coloured garden flower shaped like an upside-down bell. Tulips grow from bulbs in the spring.
tumble (tumbles, tumbling, tumbled) *verb*
If you tumble, you fall over and over.
tuna *noun*
Tuna are large fish that live in warm seas. They are caught for food.
tune (tunes) *noun*
A tune is a series of musical notes that are usually nice to listen to and easy to remember.
tunnel (tunnels) *noun*
A tunnel is a long passage which has been made under the ground or through a hill.
turkey (turkeys) *noun*
A turkey is a large bird that is kept on a farm for its meat.
turn (turns) *noun*
If it is your turn to do something, it is now fair for you to do it: *It's your turn to do the washing-up.*
>**take turns** *phrase*
If people take turns to do something, they do it one after the other, usually because this is fair.
turn (turns, turning, turned) *verb*
1. When you turn, you move so that you are facing a different way.
2. When you turn something, you move it round.
3. If you turn to a page in a book or newspaper, you find that page.
4. When something turns into something else, it becomes something else: *When water is frozen, it turns into ice.*
turnip (turnips) *noun*
A turnip is a vegetable with a white, yellow or reddish skin. Turnips grow under the ground.
turtle (turtles) *noun*
A turtle is a large reptile with a thick shell. It spends most of its time in the sea.
tusk (tusks) *noun*
Tusks are long, pointed teeth that some animals have. For example, elephants and walruses have tusks.
twice *adverb*
Twice means two times.
twig (twigs) *noun*
A twig is a very small, thin branch of a tree or bush.

twilight *noun*
Twilight is the time after sunset when it is just getting dark.
twin (twins) *noun*
If two people or animals are twins, they have the same mother and were born on the same occasion.
twinkle (twinkles, twinkling, twinkled) *verb*
If a star or light twinkles, it keeps changing from bright to dim.
twist (twists, twisting, twisted) *verb*
When you twist something you hold one end and turn the other end round and round.
type (types) *noun*
Type means kind or sort: *What type of plant is it?*
type (types, typing, typed) *verb*
If a person types something, they write it using a machine such as a typewriter.
typewriter (typewriters) *noun*
A typewriter is a machine that prints words when you press keys with letters on them.
typhoon (typhoons) *noun*
A typhoon is a storm with very strong winds.
tyre (tyres) *noun*
A tyre is a strong rubber ring which is either solid or filled with a lot of air. Tyres are fitted on to the wheels of vehicles, such as cars and bicycles.

U

ugly (uglier, ugliest) *adjective*
Someone or something that is ugly is not nice to look at.
umbrella (umbrellas) *noun*
An umbrella is a shelter from the rain. The top is made from thin cloth stretched over a light frame. This is fixed to a stick so that you can hold it over your head. You can close it when you are not using it.
unable *adjective*
If you are unable to do something, you cannot do it.
unbearable *adjective*
You say that something is unbearable when it is so unpleasant, painful or upsetting that you feel unable to deal with it.
>**unbearably** *adverb*
unbreakable *adjective*
Something that is unbreakable has been made so strongly that it cannot be broken.
uncle (uncles) *noun*
Your uncle is the brother of one of your parents, or the husband of your aunt.
uncomfortable *adjective*
1. If you are uncomfortable, you are not happy because you can feel a very slight pain.
2. If things such as clothes are uncomfortable, they do not feel right.
>**uncomfortably** *adverb*
unconscious *adjective*
1. Someone who is unconscious is unable to see, hear or feel anything that is going on. This is usually because they have fainted or have been badly injured.
2. If you are unconscious of something you have said or done, you do not notice it or the effect that it has on other people.
>**unconsciously** *adverb*
undercarriage (undercarriages) *noun*
The undercarriage of an aeroplane is the part with the wheels on it.
underground *adjective*
Something that is underground is below the surface of the ground.
underground *noun*
The underground is a railway that runs in tunnels under some cities.
undergrowth *noun*
Undergrowth is bushes or trees growing together under the trees in a forest or jungle.
underline (underlines, underlining, underlined) *verb*
If you underline something, such as a word or sentence, you draw a line underneath it to make people notice it or to give it more importance.
underneath *adverb/preposition*
If something is underneath something else, it is below it. (adverb): *They couldn't move the car because their cat was underneath.*

(preposition): *They found the missing card underneath the table.*
understand (understands, understanding, understood) *verb*
If you understand something, you know what it means.
underwear *noun*
Your underwear is the clothing, such as a vest or pants, that you wear next to your skin under your other clothes.
undo (undoes, undoing, undid, undone) *verb*
If you undo something that is fastened or tied together, you unfasten it.
undress (undresses, undressing, undressed) *verb*
When you undress, you take off your clothes.
uneasy (uneasier, uneasiest) *adjective*
If you are uneasy, you feel rather worried that something may be wrong or that there may be some danger.
>**uneasily** *adverb*
uneatable *adjective*
1. Food that is uneatable is so bad or tastes so unpleasant that you do not want to eat it.
2. Food is also called uneatable if it cannot be eaten by people.
uneven *adjective*
Something that is uneven does not have a flat, smooth or regular surface.
>**unevenly** *adverb*
unexpected *adjective*
Something that is unexpected surprises you.
>**unexpectedly** *adverb*
unfair *adjective*
If you think that something is unfair, it does not seem right or reasonable to you.
>**unfairly** *adverb*
unfortunate *adjective*
1. If someone is unfortunate, they are unlucky and do not deserve something unpleasant that happened to them.
2. If you say something is unfortunate, you mean you wish it had not happened.
>**unfortunately** *adverb*
unfriendly (unfriendlier, unfriendliest) *adjective*
Someone who is unfriendly is not at all friendly.
unhappy (unhappier, unhappiest) *adjective*
Someone who is unhappy is sad or miserable.
>**unhappily** *adverb*
unhurt *adjective*
If someone is unhurt after something like an attack or an accident, they are not injured.
unicorn (unicorns) *noun*
A unicorn is an imaginary animal which looks like a horse with a horn in the middle of its forehead.
uniform (uniforms) *noun*
A uniform is a special set of clothes that is worn by people to show that they belong to the same group.
unit (units) *noun*
A unit is a fixed measure of something. For example, a second is a unit of time.
universe *noun*
The universe is the whole of space and everything in it. The earth is part of the universe.
university (universities) *noun*
A university is a place where people can carry on their education when they have left school.
unkind *adjective*
Someone who is unkind is rather cruel and unpleasant.
>**unkindly** *adverb*
unknown *adjective*
1. If something is unknown to you, you do not know about it.
2. If a person is unknown to you, you do not know them.
3. An unknown person is not famous: *This was painted by an unknown artist.*
unlike *preposition*
1. If something is unlike something else, the two things have different qualities.
2. If you say that something a person did or said is unlike them, you mean that they do not usually behave in that way.
unload (unloads, unloading, unloaded) *verb*
If people unload something, such as a lorry, they take the load off it.

unlock (unlocks, unlocking, unlocked) *verb*
If you unlock something, such as a door or a container that has a lock, you open it with a key.
>**unlucky** *adjective*
Someone who is unlucky has bad luck.
>**unluckily** *adverb*
unnecessary *adjective*
Something that is unnecessary is not needed.
>**unnecessarily** *adverb*
unpack (unpacks, unpacking, unpacked) *verb*
When you unpack, you take everything out of a suitcase, bag or box.
unpleasant *adjective*
1. Someone who is unpleasant is not helpful or friendly.
2. Something that is unpleasant is rather nasty and not at all enjoyable.
>**unpleasantly** *adverb*
unscrew (unscrews, unscrewing, unscrewed) *verb*
If you unscrew something, such as a lid, you keep turning it until you can remove it.
unselfish *adjective*
People who are unselfish care more about other people than they do about themselves.
>**unselfishly** *adverb*
untidy (untidier, untidiest) *adjective*
1. Someone who is untidy does not care whether things are neat and well arranged.
2. A place or thing that is untidy is messy and not well arranged.
>**untidily** *adverb*
untie (unties, untying, untied) *verb*
If you untie something or someone, you undo the knots in the string or rope that has been tied round them.
unusual *adjective*
Someone or something that is unusual is different from the ordinary.
>**unusually** *adverb*
unwise *adjective*
Something that is unwise is foolish and likely to lead to a bad result.
>**unwisely** *adverb*
uphill *adverb*
If you go uphill, you go up a slope.
upright *adjective*
1. If you are upright, you are sitting or standing with your back straight, rather than bending or lying down.
2. Something that is upright stands vertically and is taller than it is wide.
uproar *noun*
An uproar is a lot of noise and shouting.
upset *adjective*
If you are upset, you are unhappy or disappointed about something.
upset (upsets, upsetting, upset) *verb*
If someone upsets something, they turn it over by accident: *He upset a tin of paint on the carpet.*
upside down *adjective*
Something that is upside down has been turned so that the part that should be at the top is at the bottom.
upstairs *adverb*
1. If you go upstairs in a building, you go up to a higher floor.
2. Someone or something that is upstairs is on a higher floor than you.
urgent *adjective*
Something that is urgent needs to be done at once.
>**urgently** *adverb*
use (uses, using, used) *verb*
If you use something, such as a tool, you do something with it that helps you.
useful *adjective*
If something is useful, it helps you in some way.
>**usefully** *adverb*
useless *adjective*
If something is useless, you cannot use it.
>**uselessly** *adverb*
usual *adjective*
Something that is usual is the thing that happens most often in a particular situation: *She got up earlier than usual.*
>**usually** *adverb*

V

vacuum cleaner (vacuum cleaners) *noun*
A vacuum cleaner is an electric machine which removes dirt from carpets and furniture by sucking it into the machine.

vagina (vaginas) *noun*
The vagina is an opening in a woman's body through which babies pass when they are being born.

vague (vaguer, vaguest) *adjective*
Things that are vague are not definite or clear: *She had a vague feeling she ought to have been doing something.*
>**vaguely** *adverb*

valley (valleys) *noun*
A valley is a low stretch of land between hills. Valleys quite often have rivers flowing through them.

valuable *adjective*
1. Things such as jewellery or paintings that are valuable are worth a lot of money.
2. Help or advice that is valuable is very useful.

value (values) *noun*
The value of something like a house or a painting is the amount of money that it is worth.

value (values, valuing, valued) *verb*
If you value something, you think that it is important.

van (vans) *noun*
A van is a covered truck. Vans are used to carry things from place to place.

vandal (vandals) *noun*
A vandal is someone who damages something useful or beautiful on purpose and for no good reason.

vanish (vanishes, vanishing, vanished) *verb*
If something vanishes, it disappears suddenly, or in a way that cannot be explained.

vapour (vapours) *noun*
Vapour is a mass of tiny drops of water or other liquids in the air, which appear as clouds, mist or fumes.

various *adjective*
You say various to mean several different things of one kind: *There were various questions she wanted to ask.*

vase (vases) *noun*
A vase is a kind of jar, usually made of glass or pottery. Vases are used to hold cut flowers, or as ornaments.

vast (vaster, vastest) *adjective*
Something that is vast is extremely large.
>**vastly** *adverb*

vegetable (vegetables) *noun*
A vegetable is a plant which is eaten raw or cooked. For example, potatoes, cabbages and onions are vegetables.

vehicle (vehicles) *noun*
A vehicle is a machine such as a car or bus that carries people or things from place to place.

vein (veins) *noun*
A vein is a tube in the body of a person or animal which carries blood to the heart.

velvet *noun*
Velvet is a soft material made from cotton, silk or nylon. It has a thick layer of short, cut threads on one side.

verb (verbs) *noun*
In grammar, a verb is a word which says what people and things do, or what happens to them: *'Run', 'sing' and 'fall' are all verbs.*

verdict (verdicts) *noun*
1. A verdict is what is decided at the end of a trial in a law court.
2. A verdict is also an opinion that someone gives after thinking for a while.

verse (verses) *noun*
A verse is one of the parts that a poem or song is divided into.

vertical *adjective*
Something that is vertical stands or points straight up from a flat surface.
>**vertically** *adverb*

vest (vests) *noun*
A vest is a piece of clothing that people wear on the top half of their body underneath their other clothes.

vet (vets) *noun*
A vet is a person who is specially trained to look after the health of animals. Vet is short for veterinary surgeon.
victim (victims) *noun*
1. A victim is someone who has been hurt or killed by someone or something.
2. A victim is also someone who has suffered as a result of someone else's actions, or because of an unpleasant situation.
victory (victories) *noun*
A victory is the winning of a battle or game.
video (videos) *noun*
1. A video is a machine which can be used to play video tapes on a television set, and to record television programmes on to video tape.
2. A video is also a film or television programme recorded on video tape for people to watch on a television set.
video (videos, videoing, videoed) *verb*
If you video something, you record it on video tape, either by using a special camera and recording the actual events, or by using a video to record a television programme.
video tape (video tapes) *noun*
Video tape is magnetic tape that is used to record signals which can be shown as pictures on television.
view (views) *noun*
The view from a window or high place is everything that can be seen from there.
village (villages) *noun*
A village is a small group of houses and other buildings in a country area. A village is smaller than a town.
vine (vines) *noun*
1. A vine is a climbing plant which has grapes as its fruit.
2. A vine is a climbing or trailing plant with long, twisting stems.
vinegar *noun*
Vinegar is a sharp-tasting liquid, usually made from sour wine or malt. Vinegar is used to add taste to some foods, and is also used for pickling.
violent *adjective*
1. Someone who is violent behaves in a way that is intended to hurt or kill people.
2. Something that is violent happens suddenly and with great force: *A violent earthquake shook the city.*
>**violently** *adverb*
violet *adjective*
Something that is violet is a bluish-purple colour.
violet (violets) *noun*
A violet is a small plant with purple or white flowers.
violin (violins) *noun*
A violin is a musical instrument with four strings. It is held under the chin and played with a bow.
violinist (violinists) *noun*
A violinist is someone who plays the violin, especially as their job.
virus (viruses) *noun*
1. A virus is a very tiny germ, which you cannot see without a microscope. Viruses can cause diseases.
2. A disease caused by a virus can also be called a virus.
visible *adjective*
1. Something that is visible is large enough to be seen, and in a position where it can be seen.
2. You can use the word visible to describe an effect that can be seen by other people.
>**visibly** *adverb*
visit (visits, visiting, visited) *verb*
If you visit a person or a place, you go to see them.
visitor (visitors) *noun*
A visitor is someone who is visiting a person or a place.
visor (visors) *noun*
A visor is a movable part of a helmet, which can be pulled down to protect a person's eyes or face.
vital *adjective*
If something is vital when you are doing something, you will not succeed without it: *It is vital to get the measurements exactly right.*
>**vitally** *adverb*

vitamin (vitamins) *noun*
A vitamin is something which people need to stay healthy. There are vitamins in many kinds of food.
vivid *adjective*
1. Something that is vivid is very bright in colour.
2. Memories or descriptions that are vivid are very clear and remain firmly fixed in your mind.
>**vividly** *adverb*
vocabulary (vocabularies) *noun*
Someone's vocabulary is the total number of words in a language that they know.
voice (voices) *noun*
Someone's voice is the sound they make when they speak or sing.
>**at the top of your voice** *phrase*
If you say something at the top of your voice, you say it as loudly as you can.
volcano (volcanoes) *noun*
A volcano is a mountain with a hole called a crater in the top. Sometimes hot, melted rock, gas, steam and ash burst from the crater.
volume (volumes) *noun*
1. A volume is a book.
2. The volume of an object is the amount of space that it takes up.
3. The volume of something such as a radio or television is the amount of sound that it is making: *She played her radio at full volume.*
volunteer (volunteers, volunteering, volunteered) *verb*
If you volunteer to do something, you offer to do it without expecting any reward.
vote (votes, voting, voted) *verb*
1. If you vote, you make a choice, usually by raising your hand or writing on a piece of paper: *We had to choose a group leader and we all voted for Tim.*
2. If you vote that a particular thing should happen, that is what you suggest: *I vote we all go swimming.*
voucher (vouchers) *noun*
A voucher is a ticket or piece of paper that can be used instead of money for a particular purchase.
vowel (vowels) *noun*
In the English language, the letters a, e, i, o and u are vowels.
voyage (voyages) *noun*
A voyage is a long journey on a ship or in a spaceship.
vulture (vultures) *noun*
A vulture is a large bird which feeds on dead animals. Vultures live in hot countries.

W

waddle (waddles, waddling, waddled) *verb*
If a person or animal waddles, they walk with short, quick steps, swaying slightly from side to side: *A family of ducks waddled past.*
wade (wades, wading, waded) *verb*
To wade means to walk through fairly shallow water.
wafer (wafers) *noun*
A wafer is a very thin, crisp biscuit.
wag (wags, wagging, wagged) *verb*
When a dog wags its tail, it keeps waving its tail from side to side because it is happy.
wagon (wagons) *noun*
1. A wagon is a strong cart for carrying heavy loads. Wagons are usually pulled by horses or oxen.
2. A wagon is also a railway truck.
wail (wails, wailing, wailed) *verb*
If someone wails, they make a long, sad, crying noise.
waist (waists) *noun*
Your waist is the narrow middle part of your body, just below your chest.
wait (waits, waiting, waited) *verb*
If you wait, you spend some time before something happens.
waiter (waiters) *noun*
A waiter is a man who works in a restaurant, serving people with food and drink.
waitress (waitresses) *noun*
A waitress is a woman who works in a restaurant, serving people with food and and drink.

wake (wakes, waking, woke, woken) *verb*
When you wake, you stop sleeping.
walk (walks, walking, walked) *verb*
When you walk, you move along by putting one foot in front of the other.
wall (walls) *noun*
1. A wall is one of the vertical sides of a building or room.
2. A wall can also be used to divide or go round an area of land. This kind of wall is long and narrow, and is made of stone or brick.
wallet (wallets) *noun*
A wallet is a small, flat, folded case that fits in a pocket. It is used to hold things such as paper money and library tickets.
wallpaper *noun*
Wallpaper is thick, coloured or patterned paper that is used for covering and decorating the walls of a room.
walnut (walnuts) *noun*
A walnut is a nut that you can eat. It has a wrinkled shape and a very hard, round shell that is light brown in colour.
walrus (walruses) *noun*
A walrus is an animal that lives in the sea and looks like a large seal. It has coarse whiskers and two long tusks. Walruses are found mainly in the Arctic region.
wand (wands) *noun*
A wand is a long, thin rod that magicians and fairies wave when they are performing tricks and magic.
wander (wanders, wandering, wandered) *verb*
When you wander, you walk about without planning to go in any particular direction.
want (wants, wanting, wanted) *verb*
When you want something, you wish for it or need it.
war (wars) *noun*
A war is a period of fighting between countries. Weapons are used and lots of people get killed and injured.
wardrobe (wardrobes) *noun*
A wardrobe is a tall cupboard where you can hang your clothes.
warehouse (warehouses) *noun*
A warehouse is a large building which is used to store things in.
warm (warmer, warmest) *adjective*
1. Something that is warm has some heat but not enough to be hot.
2. Clothes and blankets that are warm are made of material, such as wool, which stops you feeling cold.
>**warmly** *adverb*
warm (warms, warming, warmed) *verb*
If you warm part of your body, you put it near something hot so that it stops feeling cold.
warmth *noun*
1. Warmth is enough heat to make you feel comfortable.
2. The warmth of clothes or blankets is the ability that they have to protect you from the cold.
warn (warns, warning, warned) *verb*
If you warn someone, you tell them about a danger or problem that they might meet.
warning (warnings) *noun*
1. A warning is something which is said or written to tell people of possible danger or problems.
2. A warning is also advice which is given to someone not to do something.
3. A warning can also be notice in advance of something that will happen, often something unpleasant or dangerous: *If the river floods, we shall only get a few hours' warning.*
warren (warrens) *noun*
A warren is a group of holes in the ground which rabbits live in. The holes are connected by tunnels.
warrior (warriors) *noun*
A warrior is a brave fighting man or soldier, especially one who fought in battles hundreds of years ago.
wary (warier, wariest) *adjective*
If you are wary about something, you are careful because you are not sure about it, for example because there may be dangers or problems.
>**warily** *adverb*
wash (washes, washing, washed) *verb*

If you wash something, you clean it with soap and water.

washer (washers) *noun*
A washer is a thin, flat ring of something, such as metal or rubber, with a hole in the middle. Washers are used to seal or fasten things.

washing machine (washing machines) *noun*
A washing machine is a machine for washing clothes in.

washing-up *noun*
If you do the washing-up, you wash the things, such as plates, cups and knives, which have been used in cooking and eating a meal.

wasp (wasps) *noun*
A wasp is an insect with wings and yellow and black stripes on its body. Wasps can sting.

waste *noun*
1. Waste is material that is no longer wanted. This is often because the useful part of it has been taken out.
2. Waste is also the careless use of things such as money or water.

waste (wastes, wasting, wasted) *verb*
If you waste something, such as time or money, you use too much of it on something that is not important.

watch (watches) *noun*
A watch is a small clock that you can wear on your wrist.

watch (watches, watching, watched) *verb*
If you watch something, you look at it carefully to see what happens.

>keep watch *phrase*
If someone keeps watch, they look out for danger. This is usually while other people are asleep or resting.

water *noun*
Water is a clear, thin liquid that all animals and people need to drink in order to live, and which has no colour or taste when it is pure.

water (waters, watering, watered) *verb*
If you water plants, you pour water over them in order to help them grow.

waterfall (waterfalls) *noun*
A waterfall is water that flows over the edge of a cliff to the ground below.

watering can (watering cans) *noun*
A watering can is a container shaped like a bucket, with a handle on one side and a spout on the other. A watering can is for watering plants.

waterproof *adjective*
Something that is waterproof does not let water pass through it.

wave (waves) *noun*
1. A wave is a raised line of water on the surface of the sea or a lake. It is caused by the wind, or by tides making the surface of the water rise and fall.
2. A wave is also a gentle, curving shape in someone's hair.

wave (waves, waving, waved) *verb*
1. If you wave, you move your hand in the air, to say hello or goodbye to someone.
2. If something waves, it moves gently up and down or from side to side. For example, flags wave in the wind.

wax *noun*
1. Wax is a solid, slightly shiny material made of fat or oil. It is used to make things such as candles and polish. Wax goes soft and melts when it is heated.
2. A special kind of wax is made by bees.
3. Wax is also the yellow, sticky material that is found in people's ears.

way (ways) *noun*
1. A way of doing something is how it can be done.
2. If you say someone is doing something in a particular way, you mean that is how they are doing it: *I don't like the nasty way you said that.*
3. The way to a particular place is the direction you have to go to get there.
4. If someone or something is in your way, they are blocking your path.
5. Way is used to say how far something is: *It's a long way to the shops from here.*

>have your own way *phrase*
If you have your own way, everything happens as you want.

weak (weaker, weakest) *adjective*
1. People or animals that are weak do not have much strength or energy.
2. If an object or part of an object is weak, it could break easily.
3. Sounds and lights that are weak are very faint.
4. Drinks, such as tea or coffee, that are weak do not have a strong taste.
>**weakly** *adverb*
wealthy (wealthier, wealthiest) *adjective*
Someone who is wealthy has a large amount of money, property or valuable possessions.
weapon (weapons) *noun*
A weapon is an object, such as a gun or missile, which is used to hurt or kill people in a fight or war.
wear (wears, wearing, wore, worn) *verb*
1. When you wear things, such as clothes, you have them on your body.
2. When something wears out, it cannot be used any more.
weary (wearier, weariest) *adjective*
If you are weary, you are tired.
>**wearily** *adverb*
weather *noun*
The weather is what it is like outside; for example, raining, sunny or windy.
weave (weaves, weaving, wove, woven) *verb*
1. When someone weaves cloth, they make it by crossing threads over and under each other, using a machine called a loom.
2. If you weave something such as a basket, you make it by twisting twigs or cane together.
web (webs) *noun*
1. A web is a fine net made by a spider to catch flies.
2. A web is also a piece of skin between the toes of water birds. The web helps them to swim well.
wedding (weddings) *noun*
A wedding is when a man and woman become husband and wife.
wedge (wedges) *noun*
A wedge is a piece of something like wood or plastic which has one pointed edge and one thick edge. The pointed edge can be pushed into a gap, for example under a door, and the thick edge then prevents any movement.
wedge (wedges, wedging, wedged) *verb*
1. If you wedge something, you force it to stay in a particular position by using a wedge or something that acts like a wedge.
2. If you are wedged somewhere, you are squeezed into a narrow space.
Wednesday *noun*
Wednesday is one of the seven days of the week. It is the day after Tuesday and before Thursday.
weed (weeds) *noun*
A weed is any wild plant that grows where it is not wanted. Weeds grow very strongly and stop the other plants growing properly.
week (weeks) *noun*
A week is a period of seven days.
weekend (weekends) *noun*
A weekend is Saturday and Sunday.
weep (weeps, weeping, wept) *verb*
If someone weeps, they cry.
weigh (weighs, weighing, weighed) *verb*
1. If something weighs a particular amount, that is how heavy it is.
2. If you weigh something, you use scales to measure how heavy it is.
weight *noun*
The weight of something is its heaviness. This can be measured in units such as pounds or kilos.
weird (weirder, weirdest) *adjective*
Something that is weird seems strange and peculiar.
>**weirdly** *adverb*
welcome (welcomes, welcoming, welcomed) *verb*
If you welcome someone, you speak to them in a friendly way when they arrive.
well (better) *adjective*
If you are well, you are healthy.
well (better, best) *adverb*
If you do something well, you do it to a high standard.
well (wells) *noun*

A well is a deep hole in the ground that has been dug to reach water or oil.
wellington (wellingtons) *noun*
Wellingtons are long, rubber boots that you wear to keep your feet dry.
west *noun*
West is one of the four main points of the compass. If you face the point where the sun sets, you are looking west.
wet (wetter, wettest) *adjective*
1. If something is wet, it is covered in water or some other liquid.
2. If the weather is wet, it is raining.
3. If something such as ink or cement is wet, it has not yet dried.
whale (whales) *noun*
A whale is a very large mammal that lives in the sea and looks like a huge fish. Whales breathe through an opening in the top of their head.
wharf (wharves) *noun*
A wharf is a platform built of stone or wood along the side of a river or the sea. Ships can be tied up there while goods are loaded or unloaded, or while people get on or off.
wheat *noun*
Wheat is a plant whose seeds are used to make flour. The seeds are called grains.
wheel (wheels) *noun*
A wheel is a circular object which turns round on a rod fixed to its centre. Wheels are fitted under things such as cars, bicycles and prams so that they can move along.
wheelbarrow (wheelbarrows) *noun*
A wheelbarrow is a cart shaped like an open box. Wheelbarrows usually have one wheel in the front, and two legs and two handles at the back. People such as gardeners and builders use wheelbarrows.
whimper (whimpers, whimpering, whimpered) *verb*
If people or animals whimper, they make little, low, unhappy sounds.
whine (whines, whining, whined) *verb*
1. To whine means to make a long, high noise, especially one that sounds sad or unpleasant.
2. If someone whines, they talk about something that does not matter very much in a miserable and annoying way.
whinny (whinnies, whinnying, whinnied) *verb*
When a horse whinnies, it neighs softly.
whip (whips) *noun*
A whip is a thin piece of leather or string fastened to a stiff handle. It is used for hitting people or animals.
whip (whips, whipping, whipped) *verb*
When someone whips cream or egg white, they stir it very fast until it becomes frothy or stiff.
whirl (whirls, whirling, whirled) *verb*
When someone or something whirls, it moves round very fast.
whirlpool (whirlpools) *noun*
A whirlpool is a small area in a river or the sea where the water is moving quickly round and round. Objects floating near a whirlpool are pulled into its centre.
whirlwind (whirlwinds) *noun*
A whirlwind is a wind which spins round and round very fast, and moves across the land or sea.
whisk (whisks, whisking, whisked) *verb*
1. If you whisk something away, you move it away very quickly.
2. If you whisk something like eggs or cream, you stir air into it very fast.
whisker (whiskers) *noun*
The whiskers of an animal such as a cat are the long, stiff hairs that grow near its mouth.
whisper (whispers, whispering, whispered) *verb*
When you whisper, you speak very quietly using only your breath.
whistle (whistles) *noun*
A whistle is a small metal tube which you blow in order to make a loud noise.
whistle (whistles, whistling, whistled) *verb*
1. When you whistle, you make a loud, high noise. You can do this by using a whistle, or you can do it by forcing your breath out between your lips.
2. If something whistles, it makes a loud, high sound as it moves quickly through

the air: *The arrow whistled past his ear and thudded into the tree trunk.*

white (whiter, whitest) *adjective*
Something that is white is the colour of snow or milk.

whole *noun*
The whole of something is all of it.

whole *adverb*
If you swallow something whole, you do not chew it.

wholesome *adjective*
Wholesome food is good for your health.

wicked *adjective*
Someone or something that is wicked is very bad.
>wickedly *adverb*

wicker *noun*
A wicker basket or chair is one that is made from woven twigs, canes or reeds.

wide (wider, widest) *adjective*
1. Something that is wide measures a large distance from one side to the other.
2. You use wide when you are talking about how much something measures from one side to the other: *How wide is this doorway?*

wide (wider) *adverb*
If you open something wide, you open it a long way.

widespread *adjective*
If something is widespread, it exists or happens a lot or over a large area.

widow (widows) *noun*
A widow is a woman whose husband has died and who has not married again.

widower (widowers) *noun*
A widower is a man whose wife has died and who has not married again.

width (widths) *noun*
1. The width of something is the distance that it measures from one side to the other.
2. If you swim a width in a swimming pool, you swim from one side to the other.

wife (wives) *noun*
A man's wife is the woman he is married to.

wig (wigs) *noun*
A wig is a head covering made of hair. People wear wigs because they are bald, or because they want to cover their own hair.

wild (wilder, wildest) *adjective*
1. Animals and birds that are wild live naturally. They are not kept by people as pets or farm animals.
2. Wild plants grow naturally and are not specially grown by people as crops.
3. Wild is used to describe something like a movement or a blow which has a lot of force but is not controlled at all.
>wildly *adverb*

wildlife *noun*
Wildlife is animals and other things that live in the wild.

willing *adjective*
1. If someone is willing to do something, they do not mind doing it.
2. A willing person is someone who does things cheerfully.
>willingly *adverb*

willow (willows) *noun*
A willow is a tree which likes to grow in damp places.

win (wins, winning, won) *verb*
1. If you win when you are taking part in something, such as a race or a game, you do better than the others taking part.
2. If you win something, such as a prize or a medal, it is given to you because you have done something very well.

winch (winches) *noun*
A winch is a drum with a rope or chain wound around it, which is used to lift heavy objects or people who need to be rescued.

wind (winds) *noun*
A wind is a current of air that moves across the earth's surface.

wind (winds, winding, wound) *verb*
1. If something such as a road or river winds, it has lots of bends in it.
2. When you wind something round something else, you wrap it round several times.
3. When you wind something such as a clock, you turn a knob, key or handle round and round to make it work.

windmill (windmills) *noun*
A windmill is a building with large sails on the outside, which turn as the wind blows.

This works a machine which crushes corn or wheat to make flour.
window (windows) *noun*
A window is a space in a wall or vehicle. It has glass in it so that light can come in and you can see through.
window sill (window sills) *noun*
A window sill is a ledge along the bottom of a window, either inside or outside a building.
windscreen (windscreens) *noun*
The windscreen of a car or other vehicle is the glass window at the front.
windy (windier, windiest) *adjective*
If it is windy, the wind is blowing a lot.
wine *noun*
Wine is a strong drink made from the juice of grapes or other fruit.
wing (wings) *noun*
1. The wings of a bird or insect are the two limbs on its body that it uses for flying.
2. The wings of an aeroplane are the long, flat parts sticking out of its sides, which keep the aeroplane in the air.
wink (winks, winking, winked) *verb*
When you wink, you close one eye for a moment. This is usually a signal to someone that something is a joke or a secret.
winner (winners) *noun*
The winner of a prize, race or competition is the person, animal or thing that wins it.
winter *noun*
Winter is the season between autumn and spring. In the winter, the weather is usually colder than during the other seasons, and many trees and plants have lost their leaves.
wipe (wipes, wiping, wiped) *verb*
If you wipe something, you rub its surface lightly with something, such as a cloth. This is usually to remove dirt or liquid.
wire *noun*
Wire is long, thin metal which is used for fastening things and for making things such as bird cages or baskets. Wire can also carry electric current.
wisdom *noun*
Wisdom is a person's ability to use their experience and knowledge to think and act sensibly.
wise (wiser, wisest) *adjective*
Someone who is wise is sensible.
>**wisely** *adverb*
wish (wishes, wishing, wished) *verb*
If you wish that something would happen, you would very much like it to happen.
wit (wits) *noun*
1. Wit is the ability to use words or ideas in a clever and amusing way.
2. Your wits are your ability to think quickly and cleverly in a difficult situation.
witch (witches) *noun*
In fairy stories, a witch is a woman who has evil magic powers.
withdraw (withdraws, withdrawing, withdrew, withdrawn) *verb*
1. If you withdraw, you leave the place where you are and go to another place.
2. If you withdraw something from a place, you remove it.
wither (withers, withering, withered) *verb*
If a plant withers, it shrinks and dries up and dies, usually because it does not get enough water.
wizard (wizards) *noun*
In fairy stories, a wizard is a man who has magic powers.
wizened *adjective*
A wizened person, fruit or vegetable is old and shrunken, with wrinkled skin.
wobble (wobbles, wobbling, wobbled) *verb*
If someone or something wobbles, they make small movements from side to side.
wolf (wolves) *noun*
A wolf is a wild animal that looks like a large dog. Wolves live in a group called a pack. They usually live in forests.
woman (women) *noun*
A woman is an adult female human being.
wonder *noun*
Wonder is a feeling of great surprise, usually at something marvellous.
wonder (wonders, wondering, wondered) *verb*
1. If you wonder about something, you think about it and wish you knew more about it.
2. If you wonder what to do about something, you are not sure what to do about it.

wonderful *adjective*
If you say something is wonderful, you mean it makes you feel very happy.
>**wonderfully** *adverb*
wood (woods) *noun*
1. Wood is material from the trunks of trees which can be used to make things, such as furniture.
2. A wood is a large area of trees growing near each other.
wooden *adjective*
An object that is wooden is made of wood.
woodpecker (woodpeckers) *noun*
A woodpecker is a bird with a long, sharp beak. It makes holes in the trunks of trees so that it can eat the insects which live there.
woodwork *noun*
1. The woodwork in a house or room is all the parts that are made of wood, such as the doors and window frames.
2. Woodwork is making things out of wood.
wool *noun*
Wool is the hair that grows on sheep and on some other animals. Wool can be knitted or woven into material that is used to make things, such as clothes.
woollen *adjective*
Woollen clothes or materials are made from wool, or from wool mixed with other fibres.
word (words) *noun*
A word is a single unit of language that can be written or spoken. In English, a word has a space on either side of it when it is written.
word processor (word processors) *noun*
A word processor is an electronic machine with a keyboard and a screen. You can use a word processor to store and organize information and to produce printed documents.
work (works, working, worked) *verb*
1. People who work have a job which they are paid to do.
2. When you work, you spend time and energy doing something which is useful.
3. If something works, it does what it is supposed to do.
world *noun*
The world is the planet we live on.
worm (worms) *noun*
A worm is a small animal with a long, thin, hairless body. Worms have no bones and no legs. They live in the soil.
worn *adjective*
1. Something that is worn is damaged or thin because it is old and has been used a lot.
2. Someone who is worn looks old and tired, for example because of hard work or illness.
worry (worries, worrying, worried) *verb*
If you worry, you keep thinking about problems or about unpleasant things that might happen.
worth *preposition*
1. If something is worth a particular amount of money, it could be sold for that amount.
2. If someone says that something is worth doing, they mean it is enjoyable or useful.
wound (wounds) *noun*
A wound is a cut or a hole in someone's flesh, usually caused by a weapon.
wrap (wraps, wrapping, wrapped) *verb*
When you wrap something, you cover it tightly with something, like paper or plastic.
wrapper (wrappers) *noun*
A wrapper is something, like paper or plastic, that covers and protects something that you buy.
wrapping (wrappings) *noun*
A wrapping is a piece of something, like paper or plastic, that is used to cover and protect something.
wrapping paper *noun*
Wrapping paper is special pretty paper which is used for wrapping presents.
wreck (wrecks) *noun*
1. A wreck is an aircraft, car or other vehicle which has been very badly damaged in an accident.
2. A wreck is also a ship which has sunk or been destroyed at sea.
wreck (wrecks, wrecking, wrecked) *verb*
If someone or something wrecks something, they destroy it completely.
wren (wrens) *noun*
A wren is a very small, brown bird. It is one of the smallest birds in Britain.

wrestle (wrestles, wrestling, wrestled) *verb*
When people wrestle, they fight, using special holds to try to force each other to the ground.
wriggle (wriggles, wriggling, wriggled) *verb*
When a person or animal wriggles, they twist and turn their body with quick movements.
wring (wrings, wringing, wrung) *verb*
1. If you wring a wet cloth or piece of clothing, you squeeze the water out of it by twisting it strongly.
2. When someone wrings their hands, they hold them together and twist and turn them, usually because they are very worried or upset about something.
wrinkle (wrinkles) *noun*
1. A wrinkle is a line in someone's skin, especially on their face, that forms as they grow old.
2. A wrinkle is also a raised fold in something like cloth or thin paper.
wrinkled *adjective*
1. A person who is wrinkled has wrinkles as a result of old age.
2. If something is wrinkled, it has raised folds or lines in it.
wrist (wrists) *noun*
Your wrist is the part of your body between your hand and your arm, which bends when you move your hand.
wristwatch (wristwatches) *noun*
A wristwatch is a watch with a strap or band that you wear round your wrist.
write (writes, writing, wrote, written) *verb*
When you write, you use something such as a pen or pencil to make words, letters or numbers.
writing *noun*
1. Writing is something that has been written or printed: *She could see some writing on the piece of paper.*
2. Your writing is the way that you write with a pen or pencil: *Julia has very nice writing.*
wrong *adjective*
1. Something that is wrong is not correct.
2. If a person does something wrong, they do something bad.
3. The wrong side of a piece of cloth or knitting is the side which faces inwards.
>**wrongly** *adverb*

X-ray (X-rays) *noun*
An X-ray is a ray that can pass through some solid materials. X-rays are used by doctors to examine bones or organs inside people's bodies.
xylophone (xylophones) *noun*
A xylophone is a musical instrument made of wooden bars of different lengths which are arranged in a row. You play a xylophone by hitting the bars with special hammers. Each bar makes a different sound.

yacht (yachts) *noun*
A yacht is a large boat with sails or a motor. Yachts are used for racing or for pleasure trips.
yard (yards) *noun*
1. A yard is a flat area of concrete or stone, usually next to a building. A yard often has a wall round it.
2. A yard is also a large area where a particular kind of work is done, or where vehicles deliver and collect things; for example, a builders' yard or a timber yard.
3. A yard is a measure of length. It is equal to 91.4 centimetres.
yarn *noun*
Yarn is thread made from something such as wool or cotton. It is used for knitting or making cloth.
yawn (yawns, yawning, yawned) *verb*
When you yawn, you open your mouth very wide and breathe in more air than usual. People usually yawn when they are tired or bored.

year (years) *noun*
A year is a period of time. It is equal to 12 months, or 52 weeks, or 365 days.
yell (yells, yelling, yelled) *verb*
If you yell, you shout loudly. People sometimes yell if they are excited, angry or in pain.
yellow (yellower, yellowest) *adjective*
Something that is yellow is the colour of lemons or egg yolks.
yelp (yelps, yelping, yelped) *verb*
If people or animals yelp, they give a sudden, short cry. This is often because they are frightened or in pain.
yesterday *adverb*
Yesterday means the day before today.
yet *adverb*
You say yet when you mean up till now: *She has not come yet.*
yew (yews) *noun*
A yew is a tree that has thin, dark green leaves on its branches all the year round. Female yew trees have red berries. Yew trees grow very slowly and can live to a great age.
yoghurt *noun*
Yoghurt is a slightly sour, thick liquid that is made from milk.
yolk (yolks) *noun*
A yolk is the yellow part in the middle of an egg.
young (younger, youngest) *adjective*
A young person, animal or plant has not been alive for very long.
yo-yo (yo-yos) *noun*
A yo-yo is a toy made of wood or plastic which moves up and down on a string.

Z

zebra (zebras) *noun*
A zebra is an African wild animal which looks rather like a horse with black and white stripes on its body. Zebras live in large herds.
zero (zeros/zeroes) *noun*
Zero is the number 0.
zigzag (zigzags) *noun*
A zigzag is a line which keeps changing direction sharply.
zip (zips) *noun*
A zip is a fastener used on clothes, bags and other things. It has two rows of teeth which are pulled together with a sliding catch.
zoo (zoos) *noun*
A zoo is a park where wild animals are kept so that people can look at them or study them.